TRIUMPH OF THE
RIGHT

THE RIGHT WING IN AMERICA

Glen Jeansonne, Series Editor

EXIT WITH HONOR
The Life and Presidency of Ronald Reagan
William E. Pemberton

TRIUMPH OF THE RIGHT
The Rise of the California Conservative Movement, 1945–1966
Kurt Schuparra

TRIUMPH OF THE
RIGHT

The Rise
of the
California
Conservative
Movement,
1945–1966

Kurt Schuparra

M.E. Sharpe
Armonk, New York
London, England

Library of Congress Cataloging-in-Publication Data

Schuparra, Kurt, 1956–
Triumph of the right: the rise of the California conservative movement,
1945–1966 / Kurt Schuparra.
p. cm.—(The right wing in America)
Includes bibliographical references and index.
ISBN 0-7656-0277-6 (hardcover : alk. paper)
1. California—Politics and government—1951–
2. Conservatism—California—History—20th century.
I. Title. II. Series.
F866.2.S39 1998
324.9794′93043—dc21   98-2897
CIP

Printed in the United States of America

The paper used in this publication meets the minimum requirements of the
American National Standard for Information Sciences—
Permanence of Paper for Printed Library Materials,
ANSI Z 39.48-1984.

∞

MV (c)   10   9   8   7   6   5   4   3   2   1

For Fred and Ruth Schuparra

Contents

Series Editor's Foreword

The Right has appalled and consumed historians, who have barely begun to describe and analyze it. Some of them have argued that the Right has no tradition in the United States, or that it is fueled by paranoia or a religious fervor inappropriate to politics. Others have seen it as linked closely to corporate capitalism, to a wealthy elite, to Western romantics longing for nineteenth-century rugged individualism. But the Right has always been a part of American society, whether in the mainstream, on the margins, or misunderstood. For good or ill, it has affected the course of history and warrants a rich historiography (although works on the Right sometimes are confined to obscure corners of academic bookshelves).

The M.E. Sharpe series The Right Wing in America is an attempt to resurrect the Right from the substratum of serious scholarship. By publishing biographies, studies of movements, institutions, and political, cultural, and religious developments from colonial times to the present, the series will present the Right in its variety and complexity and reveal its deep roots. Books in the series are reasonably succinct, thoroughly documented, analytical, and meant to appeal to a general audience as well as scholars and students.

Kurt Schuparra's *Triumph of the Right* is a major reevaluation of the conservative movement that arose in California in the 1950s and rolled East. This study of California has national implications because it shows the dynamic interaction of political leaders and grassroots activists. Fair and evenhanded, Schuparra considers the right-wing Republicans neither paranoid nor unflawed. Rather, he evaluates them realistically as major players in the era's political contests.

Schuparra examines four key elections from the Republican perspective: William Knowland versus Pat Brown for governor in 1958, Richard Nixon versus Brown for governor in 1962, Ronald Reagan versus Brown for governor in 1966, and Barry Goldwater versus Nelson Rockefeller in the 1964 presidential primary. The ineffectual Knowland and the red-baiting Nixon suffered defeats. Goldwater's campaign was the first to excite conservative Californians. A macho figure, his "rugged Americanism" was symbolic of the Western frontier of legend. Eastern politicians, he implied, were cowardly and incapable of defending America against communism. Liberals condemned Goldwaterites as simpletons: the Right returned the insult by labeling their opponents wishy-washy. Goldwater edged Rockefeller on the strength of his vote in southern California, yet was trounced by Lyndon Johnson nationally. Goldwater in defeat, however, was John the Baptist to Ronald Reagan.

Reagan rode out of the West to the rescue of the conservative movement. In Reagan, right-wing Republicans found the long-sought balance between right-wing ideology and electability. In 1966, for the first time, a candidate once identified with the radical right was elected governor. In part, this was because Reagan's congenial temperament and amiable personality disarmed critics of his views. In part, it was the result of a white middle-class backlash against anti-Vietnam demonstrators, the Great Society, and the urban riots. By 1966 the public mood had changed, and the center had shifted to the right. Reagan was both a cause and a beneficiary of this development. Schuparra shows how, beginning in the 1950s, the changes in the political environment occurred as an evolution, not as a sudden lurch. With a sure hand, Schuparra leads us through the era's tribulations with riveting personality portraits and perceptive analysis.

In the next century and the new millennium, conservatives face the prospect of revitalizing their ideology, replenishing their energy, striving to unite, and finding another charismatic torch bearer. This book is a primer and an admonition.

Glen Jeansonne

Acknowledgments

Though my name alone appears on the cover of this book, I could not have succeeded in producing this study without the help of many individuals. The special collections staff at UCLA helped me get my project under way and facilitated my effort over the long term. I was also ably assisted by the staff at the National Archives in Laguna Niguel, California and at the Freedom Center at California State University, Fullerton. Staff at the Richard Nixon Library made a diligent effort to provide me with copies of documents that they had not yet fully sorted or filed. In northern California, staff at the California State Archives, the Hoover Institute at Stanford University, and the Bancroft Library at the University of California proved very helpful as well. In particular, I wish to thank Jeff Rankin and Elliott Simon at UCLA, Laren Metzer at the California State Archives, and Gail Gutierrez at California State University, Fullerton.

I received thoughtful and constructive advice on my manuscript from Juan Garcia and Patrick Miller, and from Jack Putnam, whose knowledge of California politics proved invaluable. Many others, too numerous to mention, had an impact on the development of my study, but I am especially grateful for the help—as sounding boards and/or chapter critics—from Kent Anderson, Paul Carter, Matthew Dallek, Glen Jeansonne, Chris Jesperson, Kerwin Klein, and Michael Schaller. I also wish to thank the friends of mine who listened attentively and responded accordingly to my observations on American politics—probably to a far greater extent than they ever desired. Finally, I am thankful that my family encouraged me at every step in producing this manuscript, as moral support at times proved to be the most important support of all. As for the production of the book itself, Peter Coveney, Esther Clark, and Eileen Maass of M.E. Sharpe were proficient, patient, and considerate throughout the laborious process.

This book is a revised version of the manuscript I wrote to meet the dissertation requirement for my Ph.D. at the University of Arizona, Tucson. While there, I was fortunate enough to have the opportunity to venture into the Sonoran Desert—usually on a bicycle—whenever I needed the catharsis that the giant saguaros could provide. I am grateful for that as well, though, for scholarly purposes at least, I had to ward off romantic notions of the Old West.

I would like to thank the *Pacific Historical Review* and the *Southern California Quarterly* for allowing me to use revised versions of the following articles of mine in this book: " 'Freedom vs. Tyranny': The 1958 California Election and the Origins of the State's Conservative Movement," © 1994 by the American Historical Association, Pacific Coast Branch, published in *Pacific Historical Review* vol. 63, no. 4, November 1994; and "Barry Goldwater and Southern California Conservatism: Ideology, Image and Myth in the 1964 California Republican Presidential Primary," © 1992 by the Southern California Historical Society, published in *Southern California Quarterly* vol. 74, no. 3, Fall 1992.

Introduction

Scholarly studies of American conservatism since World War II have usually been undertaken by nonconservatives responding to upswings in right-wing activity. Until recently these studies have mostly cast conservatism in a negative light because its tenets and exponents purportedly went against the "liberal" American tradition. During the first two decades after the war, an influential group of liberal critics, predominantly in academia, found right-wing Americans to be in numerous ways as ideologically aberrant and threatening as communists who had pledged to overthrow capitalistic democracies.

In the wake of the anticommunist "witch hunts" by Senator Joseph McCarthy in the first half of the 1950s, these liberal intellectuals theorized that McCarthy's supporters suffered from "status anxiety." This angst particularly afflicted nouveau middle-class Americans, many of whom were resentful and fearful of government and the Eastern "establishment" and of the increased emphasis on social leveling in postwar society. In the early 1960s, sociologist Daniel Bell warned that this anxiety manifested as pathological political behavior on the part of an emergent "radical right," and that that behavior ultimately threatened the moderate pluralism and " 'fragile consensus' that underlies the American political system."[1] Culminating with the Republican nomination for president in 1964, the rise of Senator Barry Goldwater alarmed numerous liberals and other nonconservatives of the growing "danger on the right." Goldwater's ascent led the preeminent historian Richard Hofstadter to identify a certain "paranoid style" as a chief characteristic of the senator's "pseudo-conservative" backers. Hofstadter claimed that while not clinically paranoid, the exponents of the paranoid style saw a " 'vast' or 'gigantic' conspiracy as *the motive force* in history." Goldwater's failed presidential bid could be written off as an aberration born of the "animosities and passions of a small minority,"[2] but the election of Ronald Reagan as president in 1980 could not. The persistence and successes of the conservative movement after Goldwater's crushing defeat, and the concomitant decline of the GOP's liberal wing and liberalism itself, necessitated paradigms of new explanatory power.[3] Consequently, the status anxiety thesis and its corollaries have been reformulated or applied more precisely.[4] Moreover, virtually all the studies of the American Right undertaken since the mid-1960s have acknowledged at least some normative political beliefs and values among staid conservatives.

No one paradigm is currently widely employed by academics examining the American Right. Nevertheless, given the studies published in recent years, it seems fair to say that a growing number of scholars in this field would agree with historian Michael Kazin's statement that "conservative activists [need to be seen] as purposeful, flexible, and idealistic protagonists in the public dramas of their day."[5] This study of the California Right from 1945 through 1966 was undertaken with that idea in mind, to avoid the pitfalls of the a priori analytical frameworks that have categorized the vast lot of conservatives of the 1950s and 1960s as extremists or otherwise marginal figures.

This is not to say that there is no analytical value in these earlier paradigms. For example, Hofstadter's notion of a right-wing paranoid style, rooted in a pathological "history as conspiracy" world view, is still a valuable analytical construct for examining certain individuals and groups on the far right, especially during the Cold War; and these individuals and groups invariably harbored much anxiety, but there is little evidence that it was due primarily to status concerns. Theories of pathology notwithstanding, the "great fear" of communism, which seized a considerable number of Americans during the first two decades of the Cold War, sprang from largely legitimate apprehensions. But the paranoid language of that age, reflecting fears of conspiracy similar to those voiced during the American Revolution, inflated tensions to such an extent that the "politics of unreason" (e.g., McCarthyism) often prevailed, especially in the conservative decade following World War II.

In regard to this study, Hofstadter's paranoid style thesis can be applied effectively in examinations of conspiracy theorists such as members of the John Birch Society (JBS). A self-proclaimed anticommunist bulwark that flourished in southern California, the JBS and other radical right groups can be viewed through the lens of social pathology to a certain extent. To view the vast lot of California conservatives of the era in this way, however, blurs the distinct differences between the fire-eaters of the far right and the pragmatic conservatives, and sheds little light on the other members of the movement who fall within this ideological spectrum.

This study focuses mainly on pivotal elections from 1958 through 1966 and on southern California, specifically Los Angeles and Orange counties, because those two counties have long been strongholds of Republican conservatism, particularly during the period of interest here. Prior to the late 1950s there was no true conservative movement in southern California or elsewhere, but by 1957 a movement had begun to take distinct shape as GOP conservatives vociferously challenged the moderate "Modern Republicanism" of President Dwight Eisenhower. This created a split in the party that climaxed with the clash between the Goldwaterites and the Republican "establishment" in 1964.

As noted earlier, liberals (and those further to the left) for most of the 1960s—and beyond in numerous cases—equated Republican conservatism with "Goldwaterism" and extremism, with little or no differentiation. Therefore the conservative propensity of many southern California Republicans, who supported Goldwater en masse in his victory in the 1964 state presidential primary,[6] combined with the high-profile endeavors of the region's ultraconservative groups to bolster the popular image of the "Southland" as a bastion of extremist activity. To a fair extent, appearances reflected reality, for the JBS and other ultraconservative groups were firmly entrenched in Los Angeles and Orange counties.[7] Most of the region's conservatives, however, did not belong to any far-right organizations, but they usually shared these groups' "pro-American" views, which stood in adamant and uncompromising opposition to communism, and to the government activism (i.e., "statism") that grew out of President Franklin Roosevelt's New Deal of the 1930s. This unyielding animus toward communism and the "liberal welfare state" brought about fierce devotion to conservative candidates and causes.

The enthusiasm southern California conservatives displayed for their candidates and causes in political campaigns worked both for and against them. It worked for them when it came to organizing volunteers and raising money. The legions of right-wing activists that volunteered to campaign and raise funds for conservative candidates were driven by the exigencies revealed in the often apocalyptic admonitions of those political aspirants. Under the rubric of "freedom versus tyranny," these candidates, particularly from 1958 through 1966, ardently contended that voters had to choose whether to maintain the repressive liberal state or to save the free enterprise system, indeed, American freedom itself. In the effort to instill a sense of mission in their supporters, conservatives seeking public office usually took uncompromising and relatively extreme positions on prominent issues. These stands almost always led to electoral defeat, unless the race was for a local or representative office in a conservative district. Many conservatives, therefore, came to realize—or knew all along—that their candidates had to change their foreboding and uncompromising rhetoric in order to have realistic chances of winning major electoral offices such as the governorship and possibly the presidency. After Goldwater's defeat, a slow retreat from ideological purity ensued, at least on a rhetorical level, in an attempt to shed the extremist image. This led the California Right to back a like-minded but polished orator for governor in 1966, the handsome and congenial actor

Ronald Reagan. Aided further by a weak incumbent opponent and by a propitious shift to the right in public opinion, Reagan won because the extremist label that had been the bane of the California conservative movement since its inception in 1958, failed to adhere to his campaign.[8]

Though lacking a true movement until the late 1950s, conservative Republicans in California after World War II did not lack individual targets for their attacks on "socialistic" government policies. These attacks were usually aimed at Democrats, but, beginning in the latter half of the 1940s, a significant number of conservatives regarded Republican governor Earl Warren as an apostate due to his "liberal" views and policies. Warren's Republican adversaries, however, could not muster enough support for any right-wing candidate to oust the popular governor, nor could they persuade him to change his "nonpartisan" politics. Yet these conservatives did find a winning right-wing candidate in Richard Nixon in his 1950 Senate race against Democratic congresswoman Helen Gahagan Douglas. That electoral year proved favorable to fierce anticommunist candidates like Nixon, who, in good part, espoused the antistatist and isolationist views of the "Old Guard" conservatives of the East and Midwest.[9] Nixon's campaign and the efforts to oust Warren can be seen as portents of the actual conservative movement to come, but are not entirely reflective of the distinctly Western variety of populist antistatism that began to take shape in the late 1950s and became full-fledged in the 1960s.[10]

The right-wing movement in the Golden State began in earnest in 1958 with the gubernatorial campaign of William F. Knowland, the Republican minority leader in the U.S. Senate. Though he ostensibly entered the race with considerable stature due to his high-profile years in Washington, Knowland's candidacy alarmed liberal and moderate California Republicans due to his "extreme views," especially on labor issues. Further alienating party liberals and moderates, Knowland challenged and, in effect, ousted the incumbent, Republican Goodwin Knight. During the campaign, Knight caustically and publicly declared that the senator's political views were rooted in antiquated nineteenth-century ideas. Exploiting this Republican rift, Knowland's Democratic opponent, State Attorney General Edmund G. "Pat" Brown, effectively depicted the senator as the point man for the forces of Republican "reaction." Knowland's crushing loss to Brown clearly stemmed from his image as the insurgent torchbearer of a reactionary movement that militated against the pragmatic and progressive Republicanism that leaders of the party in California had long espoused.

Despite Knowland's thrashing at the polls, he did bring the state's Republican conservatives together for their first real postwar electoral crusade, and he established "freedom versus tyranny" as the operative metaphor of the right-wing movement that continued after his campaign.[11] Representative of the shift from the broadly unifying use of the word "freedom" during World War II and the early Cold War, the term as employed by California conservatives essentially became one of protest—an impending trend on both the right and the left in the often incendiary battle to define and defend personal rights and liberties.[12]

By the early 1960s the movement had gained considerable strength, and some avowed JBS members were elected to Congress. Nevertheless, for conservative candidates with higher electoral goals, the extremist label became an albatross that precluded the achievement of anything beyond the level of qualified successes.[13] Such was the case for State Assemblyman Joe Shell, who openly defended the JBS in the early 1960s but did not become a member. Garnering one-third of the vote against his famous opponent, former vice president Nixon, Shell scored a moral but not an electoral victory in the 1962 Republican gubernatorial primary. Bedeviled by Shell's opposition, even the antiextremist Nixon could not escape the vexations of the extremism dilemma. Nixon's primary victory proved pyrrhic, as his assaults on the far right alienated enough conservatives to significantly contribute to his loss in November.

On the other hand, despite his controversial refusal to denounce his extremist supporters, Barry Goldwater did triumph over New York governor Nelson Rockefeller in the pivotal California presidential primary. That victory was an ephemeral success, however; for en route to a landslide win in the general election, President Lyndon Johnson and his campaign strategists effectively portrayed Goldwater as a reactionary cowboy, especially in regard to foreign affairs—someone "who shot first and asked questions later."[14]

Out of the nadir of the Goldwater debacle, Ronald Reagan began to assume the leadership of the California Right. As the 1966 governor's race approached, he seemed to be the right candidate at the right time—a "goddamned electable person," as one "citizen advisor" put it.[15] In his campaign Reagan adroitly tapped the voters' growing disillusionment with "big government" and myriad welfare programs. (This message did not apply to the sacred cow of Social Security.) Reagan's argument had wide appeal in 1966 due in large part to the growing belief that Johnson's "War on Poverty" was a lost cause. Mounting crime and disorder in impoverished black inner city areas, which alarmed and angered many whites, provided evidence of this apparent failure, which Reagan ably exploited. He also capitalized on middle-class resentment of the nascent counterculture's "immorality" and the "un-American" protests on college campuses against the escalating Vietnam War. Given the rightward shift in public sentiment, to many Californians Reagan represented the voice of reason rather than the forces of reaction, despite his opponent's exhaustive efforts to depict him as a beacon of the latter.

Reagan's political success came not only from his well-timed message but from his actor-honed ability to deliver it. With a breezy and disarming charm, he chastised critics of the "American way of life" and stirred disaffection toward the "encroaching" welfare state, which increasingly threatened the self-reliant virtues that buttressed that way of life. Between the late 1950s and his gubernatorial candidacy, almost all of Reagan's political speeches were smooth variations on that theme.

The relative popularity of New Deal and other federal welfare programs notwithstanding, support for such programs had long been tenuous, and not just among conservatives. As historian James Patterson has stated, the predominant attitude of the middle class toward welfare has been "that many, if not most, of the destitute are undeserving; that large numbers of poor people exist in an intergenerational 'culture of poverty.' "[16] Perhaps nothing struck a more resonant chord in conservatives—indeed, in many Americans—than the belief in individual responsibility for one's place in society. Americans holding this view were not necessarily social Darwinists. Nevertheless, as Hofstadter asserted more than fifty years ago, "the very idea [of welfare] affronts the traditions of a great many men and women who were raised, if not on the specific tenets of social Darwinism, at least upon the moral imperatives it expressed."[17] Thus nineteenth-century notions of "rugged individualism" and the "self-made man" continued to shape the American ethos in the twentieth century. For southern California conservatives in particular, the faith in rugged individualism served as the supreme expression of freedom from the state, and that freedom, they believed, needed to be fervently defended by conservative politicians.

In claiming that he would champion freedom by following the "will of the people," Reagan created a powerful populist image. Steering clear of the sanctification of unbridled capitalism that in some ways had cast the "rugged" Goldwater as an economic royalist, Reagan also avoided the bludgeoning rhetorical style that had typified the attacks of McCarthy and to a lesser extent, Goldwater. Despite the fact that his campaign was financed by a "circle of millionaires," Reagan overcame this potential problem for his populist image by fulminating against "elite" liberal politicians, intellectuals and bureaucrats—the architects and advocates of Johnson's Great Society—who sought to aid an ungrateful and undeserving minority constituency. In so doing he defined elitism—that is, power—in cultural rather than economic terms and helped trigger the culture wars that have pervaded American politics since the late 1960s.

Lamenting the recent proliferation of groups and individuals who claim to represent "the people," historian T. J. Jackson Lears has described the conservative populist slant on elitism (that Reagan intoned so well) as "pseudo-populism." In the latter, hard-working "bankers and real estate developers [are identified] with the salt of the earth."[18] One can take issue with the applicability (and pejorative implications) of Lears's "pseudo" label given that the salt-of-the-earth populists of the late nineteenth century, like Reagan populists later, were grassroots groups against the Eastern politicians and other power brokers who controlled the political process in the nation's capital. His delineation of "populisms" is valid, however, to the extent that it characterizes the critical change in conservatism after Goldwater's defeat.

Leading the change toward a more effective conservative populism, Reagan all but dispensed with unabashed exhortations of the free market in favor of invidious societal distinctions; he implicitly praised the working class and entrepreneurs alike (property-owning "producers"), as well as law-abiding citizens, while inveighing against welfare recipients, privileged academics and bureaucrats (parasitic "non-producers") and those who violated the law and "moral decency."[19] Similar descriptions had been used by Alabama governor George Wallace, an avowed segregationist who proved especially popular in the South and with white blue collar voters in parts of the Midwest, but Wallace's raw rhetoric and support of working-class liberalism of the New Deal ilk offended many conservatives. Still, his assault on "pointy-headed intellectuals" resonated with the right, along with his strident attacks on the civil rights movement and urban unrest, in which he made "law and order" a legitimating phrase for racist positions.[20]

A crucial catalyst in America's right turn in the 1960s, the exploitation of the "white backlash" by Reagan and others played ·a critical role in the triumph of conservatism in California. Indeed, given that the race card played so well for Reagan on the hustings with numerous different, yet craftily intertwined, issues—crime and welfare, to name but two—the race factor became a driving force in the Reagan campaign. Bringing his campaign to full throttle, he linked the race factor with campus unrest and thereby nurtured the initial bloc of "Reagan Democrats." In doing so he helped place a cornerstone in the foundation of the conservative movement, because the social conservatism of these California Democrats and others like them around the country would prove instrumental in advancing the agenda and candidates of the American Right after 1966.

By the time of Goldwater's presidential campaign, if not before, the California Right had become the biggest cog in the national conservative movement. The latter's think-tank, however, was on the opposite coast, in the patrician and predominantly liberal environs of New York City. Urbane yet sardonic, the Yale-educated William F. Buckley Jr. had by the early 1960s become the movement's premier intellectual and mouthpiece. Buckley founded the New York-based conservative periodical *National Review* in 1955, with the intention of bringing conservatives of different stripes together to battle liberalism. Though the periodical served as a forum for different views, Buckley and most of his colleagues moved away from Old Guard isolationism due to the pervasive nature of the communist threat.[21] In his vitriolic attacks on liberalism, Buckley did not aim solely at Democrats, for he made clear at the time of his magazine's inception that "I intend . . . to read Dwight Eisenhower out of the conservative movement."[22] While many conservatives shared Buckley's displeasure with Eisenhower's policies, fiscal and otherwise, few chose to attack the popular president as explicitly and personally as he did. The California conservative movement was in part a reaction against Eisenhower's Modern Republicanism, but this opposition generally manifested itself in less strident forms, such as contrary stands on specific policies and issues.

Indicative of the shared opposition to certain Eisenhower policies, Eastern conservatives harbored the same fervent anticommunist and antistatist beliefs as their Western counterparts. Pulitzer Prize-winning journalist Haynes Johnson ignored this common bond when he claimed in a best-selling book that the Buckleyites and California conservatives did not prove to be "philosophical allies." Johnson went on to attribute contextually disparaging characteristics to the latter that applied essentially as much to the former.[23] The differences between the Buckleyites and Western conservatives were not on the rudimentary level of bedrock philosophy, but rather in disparate notions about electoral politics and Eastern patrician elitism.

Like Buckley, a fair number of the conservatives in the movement's Eastern intellectual vanguard came from well-to-do families and went to Ivy League schools or other elite institutions. (A few, such as Otto von Hapsburg, were even of European noble lineage.) With occasionally grating arrogance, the prevailing view among this cadre was that too much democracy, such as the populist and highly participatory variety practiced and celebrated in the West (e.g., the initiative and the referendum), would threaten the nation through the ascendancy of uneducated reason in the voting process.[24] In this vein, the Easterners saw themselves as an enlightened aristocracy destined to platonically lead and edify the hoi polloi.

Westerners had long possessed an anti-Eastern and antiintellectual strain that had grown primarily out of the resentment over the West's economic and bureaucratic dependence on the East. Increasingly salient in postwar Western conservatism, anti-Eastern sentiment became particularly pronounced during the Goldwater campaign, in no small part due to the senator's image as a "Man of the West." This image put into play the powerful myths of the rugged individualism of the Old West, which in turn fostered disdain not only for the Big Government of Eastern liberals—both Democratic and Republican—but for the East as a whole. In this contempt there could not help but be something less than affinity for the erudite posture of Buckley and his associates.

It is not coincidental or surprising that of the four major conservative presidential candidates of the 1960s, three hailed from the West, and one from the South.[25] The East above the Mason–Dixon Line could hardly match the emergent "Sun Belt" (the South and Southwest) as a strong conservative base.[26] And no locale could match the organized right-wing activism found in southern California in the 1960s. Numerous ideas have been put forth as to why the region became so hospitable to conservatism. An attempt to settle this debate will not be made in this study, for that is not its purpose. Nevertheless, it seems that a number of reasonable conclusions can be drawn from some of the theories and speculation on this matter.

Consideration of the conservative tilt of southern California politics must start with Carey McWilliams's classic work of 1946, *Southern California Country: An Island on the Land.* Though not focusing on politics, McWilliams, a leading liberal social critic, clearly saw the Southland's longstanding conservative outlook as deriving from the continuous immigration of "commonplace" people to the region from the American heartland (the Mideast and especially the Midwest). Coming in droves throughout the first half of the twentieth century, many of these largely Protestant and middle-class immigrants possessed in their westering impulse a "nostalgia . . . for an America that no longer exists."[27] McWilliams's observations clearly suggest that many of these immigrant southern Californians were predisposed to conservative perspectives and that the steady stream of immigration that continued from the heartland and the South after World War II nurtured a conservative political culture.

This explanation for the region's right-wing activism became part of a larger theoretical matrix on the effects of population growth. It coupled with the hypothesis that rapid postwar growth led to an atomistic and anxiety-ridden existence amid the urban sprawl of the Southland, which manifested in right-wing resistance to ideas and groups alien to the white middle class.[28] The rapid growth theory has been cogently challenged, however, in its application to California. In an extensive statistical study, political scientists Fred Greenstein and Raymond Wolfinger concluded that "conservatism [in California] does not appear to be associated with massive population growth." Yet they did suggest that the conservative politics of Southlanders, as well as the predominantly liberal inclinations of San Francisco Bay area inhabitants, "*may* be a result of the different backgrounds of residents of the two areas."[29] It appears, then, that McWilliams's observations provide at least a partial explanation for the differences in the state's regional voting behavior.

In the concluding essay of an important book on California politics, political scientist Michael Rogin offered another theory on the roots of southern California conservatism. He incorporated an anthropological angle in stating that right-wing Southlanders had been motivated by threatening "cultural symbols," such as "Communists, saloons, Negroes and pornography." For many southern Californians, Rogin deduced, the American dream became an exaggerated fixation. Consequently, "alien ideas [there] are peculiarly threatening . . . since they challenge the organizing principles of the symbolic [bourgeois] world and its very definition of reality." This produced a pattern of right-wing "hallucinatory politics."[30] While Rogin's psychohistorical analysis doubtless applied to certain Southland ultraconservatives, he made no differentiation between these individuals and those right-wingers with more pragmatic and reasonable politics. Rogin's hypothesis, therefore, suffers from the rather facile implication that the region's conservative demonology created a monolithic phalanx of right-wing extremists. He nonetheless made a valuable contribution toward the understanding that symbols did much to animate the conservative movement.

Of all the "alien ideas," nothing proved more harrowing or stirred more activism among Southland conservatives than the perceptions of the "communist peril." In her study of the grassroots right in postwar Orange County, historian Lisa McGirr found that "the discourse of anticommunism," buttressed by a "pro-defense" milieu, entrepreneurial individualism and conservative churches, "created a fertile climate for right-wing growth."[31] Surely a concern of many Americans, the acute fear of communism in the Southland was due in part to the economic dependence on the large defense contracts awarded to regional industries during World War II and on into the Cold War. To keep those contracts large and numerous the Cold War had to have a hot edge, at least rhetorically. Defense contractor alliances with the military helped in this regard. Formal organizations such as the Air Force Association and the Navy League became prominent in the Southland and had considerable influence in Congress. They warned of the need to "fight for, if necessary, the elimination of communism from the world scene." Culminating in anticommunist efforts like "Project Alert" in the early 1960s, these military-industrial organizations, along with increasingly conspicuous ultraconservative groups, used piercing admonitions in seeking support for "total mobilization for total war."[32]

Beginning in earnest during the early years of the Cold War, the greater Los Angeles area became the hub for that imminent massive mobilization. Though the defense industry provided an economic boon, many Angelenos early on saw potentially dire consequences as well. At the outset of the Korean War in 1950, for example, the mayor of Los Angeles warned that the city, "now a much more important industrial center and far more likely enemy target, is again facing the probability of being virtually on the front line."[33] Shortly thereafter the city council created a Civil Defense and Disaster Corps, which the council hoped would be largely funded by the federal government. The city's leaders, as Roger Lotchin has stated in *Fortress California,* possessed contradictory impulses in their actions regarding the city's status as a defense center.

> At the very time that the fragmented metropolis fought for more civil defense funds and for spacing out its industries to avoid total destruction in the event of an atomic attack, it also strove for more defense contracts. On the one hand, the metropolitan leaders moved to make the city less vulnerable, while on the other they steadily labored to make it more vulnerable.[34]

This paradox of vulnerability contributed significantly to the wave of alarmist rhetoric that brought a heightened element of insecurity to the Southland. Indeed, for many conservatives the region became the "front line."

To maintain southern California as the main armory of the "arsenal of democracy," of course, required huge expenditures by the federal government. It is ironic that in a region where the competitive free enterprise system stood as something sacred, defense contracts were mostly products of negotiation rather than competition.[35] The Southland's political representatives and business leaders displayed great sensitivity to canceled or diminished defense contracts and resultant layoffs, citing the detriment to the region's economy, as well as to the nation's preparedness for war. Apparently forgotten in the appeals for "help" in such situations was the fact that national defense was intended to protect Americans from enemies abroad, and not to uphold their middle-class way of life or to ensure the economic vitality of any given locale.[36] Nevertheless, the welfare aspects of this "metropolitan-military complex," as Lotchin has called it (in a variation on Eisenhower's "military-industrial complex" admonition), got buried beneath the patriotic fervor and effort to perpetuate "freedom" through "Americanism" and the latter's emblematic entrepreneurial society.

Of course, the strongest defenders of the metropolitan-military complex and the unencumbered entrepreneurial society—that is, the advocates of limited government (outside of myriad defense needs) and unrestrained capitalism—formed the backbone of the conservative movement in California's electoral politics. Though the ultraconservatives occasionally alienated the temperate right-wingers (and vice versa), they forged a formidable movement and eventually found the right candidates to achieve the significant electoral victories they had long sought. Led penultimately by Barry Goldwater and then by Ronald Reagan, this movement helped turn public opinion rightward in California and the rest of the nation, creating a conservative era that arguably still prevails.

TRIUMPH OF THE
RIGHT

One

"It's Not the Party—but the Man"

California became a state in 1850 on the heels of the great gold rush that filled the Sierra Nevada Mountains and foothills with prospectors determined to find the Mother Lode. Numerous others migrated to the state at mid-century and after in pursuit of the American Dream in the salubrious environs of the Golden State. Though California was blessed with a hospitable climate and an abundance of natural resources, federal aid would prove indispensable in making the state a thriving entity by providing many jobs and various subsidies for hydroelectric power and other water projects, timber harvesting, transportation, and ranching. State government facilitated this growth as well, but in a different fashion. After the Civil War, party politics in California came to be dominated by the "machine" politics of the railroad interests. Replete with the corruption and laissez-faire policies associated with the Gilded Age, California government would remain under the control of these powerful railroad companies (particularly the Southern Pacific) until reformers led by Republican governor Hiram Johnson broke their grip during the Progressive Era in the early twentieth century.[1]

In addition to greatly diminishing the influence of the railroads' political operatives in state government, the "nonpartisan" Johnson and his fellow reformers made changes of major importance in California's electoral process between 1911 and 1917. These changes included the authorization of the initiative and referendum, the recall and women's suffrage. Cross-filing in primary elections, in which candidates could run on all party ballots and win office with a majority of the overall vote, arguably proved to be the most significant of Johnson's reforms. Until its abolition in 1959, cross-filing played a significant role in keeping Republican governors in Sacramento but at the same time helped continue the state's nonpartisan political trend through the de-emphasis of party affiliation. The nonpartisanship of the cross filing era tended to be of the moderate yet progressive and pragmatic style that typified Johnson's governance.[2]

Progressive politics persisted in California in the 1920s despite the conservative inclinations of the state's Republican governors,[3] but the im-

3

poverished misery brought about by the Great Depression the following decade led to a serious challenge to this moderate political pattern. The most significant effort the far left would ever mount for a high state office, Upton Sinclair's campaign for governor in 1934, alarmed Republicans and Democrats alike. A onetime socialist, Sinclair stunned many Democrats in California and across the nation by winning the party's gubernatorial primary. Running on an "End Poverty in California" (EPIC) platform, Sinclair faced vicious Republican attacks and lacked strong support even from his own party due to his "radicalism." In addition to the backing generated by their invective, California Republicans garnered support by acquiescing to numerous New Deal public aid measures, thus stealing much of Sinclair's potential thunder and ensuring his defeat by Frank Merriam. Run by the "full-service" management team of Clem Whitaker and Leone Baxter, the Merriam campaign utilized innovative mass-media techniques and served as the prototype for later campaigns in California and the rest of the nation. That campaign also cemented a small but powerful right-wing coalition that supported conservative candidates into the 1950s.[4] Though Democrat Culbert Olson won the governorship in 1938, California politics maintained a bumpy but moderate course as the nation entered World War II and the California economy began its long-term boom with lucrative defense contracts.[5]

Seeking to recapture the governor's office for the GOP, the moderately conservative Republican Earl Warren challenged Olson's reelection bid in 1942.[6] While serving as the state attorney general during the Olson years, Warren had openly feuded with the governor on numerous issues, including wartime civil defense policy. Deciding finally to run for governor himself, Warren declared, "I just don't intend to run a nonpartisan campaign. I intend to conduct a nonpartisan administration." Still, Warren attacked Olson's "radicalism" mainly due to the governor's pardon of Thomas Mooney, a militant labor figure who served twenty-two years in prison after being convicted of murder on questionable evidence. Depicting Mooney as an "assassin," Warren maintained that the governor pardoned Mooney and other "communist radicals" to win union votes but that such transparent actions were "an insult to the intelligence of organized labor." Olson countered this assault by depicting Warren as a "reactionary" who represented the "aristocracy of wealth," but to no avail.[7] Warren won the election handily and then pledged, as he had during the campaign, to work diligently with the Roosevelt administration in the nation's war effort. California's role in that effort not only entrenched defense industries in the state's economy; it also provided the pragmatic Warren with an extraordinarily broad base of support.

He had proved adroit at winning broad backing during his years as district attorney of Alameda County, a position he held from 1925 to 1938, before becoming attorney general. Amassing strong support by taking on organized crime, Warren also won over many blue collar workers in the county's numerous labor union locals through his reputation for being firm but fair.[8] Moreover, he and his associate Ed Shattuck founded the California Republican Assembly (CRA) in 1934, after the party had lost many members and electoral contests to the Democrats. (The depression and the New Deal created a seismic shift in voter registration in California, giving roughly a 3-to-2 advantage to the Democrats, which the party held through the period of interest in this study.) The CRA became a powerful entity that helped organize effective Republican campaigns and shaped a new progressive image for the party despite the resistance of laissez-faire conservatives. Though the organization clearly provided a much needed boost to the party's electoral prospects, it also developed into Warren's political machine. Warren and the CRA formed a symbiotic relationship and charted a middle-of-the-road political course for the state GOP and California government.

That course was apparent in Warren's first term, especially in his effort to prepare the state for the potentially turbulent transition from the wartime economy to peacetime production. Addressing a nationwide radio audience in 1944 on the obligations owed to returning veterans, Warren maintained that families should be "assured the chance to make a decent income" and find adequate and "decent" housing. He also stressed the need for good schools, altruistic community organizations, and for "health services in the economic range for all."[9] To facilitate the latter, Warren aimed to establish a comprehensive health insurance system, financed equally by contributions from employers and employees, like Social Security. Probably the most controversial legislative proposal he ever made as governor, Warren's plan incurred the wrath of the powerful California Medical Association and the Republican right, as he repeatedly—and ultimately unsuccessfully—attempted to institute "socialized medicine" in California.

Shortly after the war's end Warren expressed his concerns about "Republican Party policy" to Herbert Brownell Jr., chairman of the Republican National Committee. In addition to a public health care initiative, Warren contended that the party should "have a definite program on Social Security . . . , [on] the conservation of our natural resources, and an anti-monopoly program." "Unfortunately," he lamented, "we are being held up to the public as the party that opposes legislation in all these fields." Believing that the GOP had taken its oppositional role to an ill-advised extreme, Warren declared, "[w]e must have an affirmative program which we offer to the public for the solution of our basic problems."[10] He clearly recognized what Republican conservatives did not: having endured the depression and the war with the considerable aid of government programs, the public by and large did not want another postwar "return to normalcy" with laissez-faire policies reminiscent of the 1920s; nor would voters long embrace a party seemingly intent on making the politics of negativity its most distinguishing characteristic.

In anticipation of Warren's reelection bid, disgruntled conservative naysayers in the legislature and in the state's Republican Party hierarchy in late 1945 coalesced behind Earl Lee Kelly for governor. A prominent San Francisco investment banker who had served as the state director of public works under governors James Rolph and Frank Merriam, Kelly attacked Warren for having policies "closely akin to those of the CIO [Congress of Industrial Organizations] Political Action Committee and all the radical riff raff elements in California. . . ." He insinuated that the governor was a "fellow traveler" abetting the communist effort to create a "regimented society" through the constrictive grip of a "master state." Warren's complicity in this iniquitous scheme could be seen in the "shameful spectacle" of his attempts to "out-deal the New Dealers in Washington. . . ." "We need men who will fight for the right," he declared, and "give the conservative people of this state the leadership they are demanding . . . [which] we have a sacred obligation to provide. . . ."[11] The religiosity of his commitment to the right reflected the crusading impulse that later sparked the conservative movement in California.

Kelly's fervid attempt to link Warren with the CIO-PAC and communist activities resembled the Republican assaults on Franklin Roosevelt in the 1944 presidential campaign. During that campaign the Republican presidential candidate, New York governor Thomas Dewey, charged that Roosevelt had pardoned the convicted "draft dodger" and "perjurer" Earl Browder, the leading communist in America, "in time to organize the campaign for his [Roosevelt's] fourth term." He claimed that Browder and the CIO-PAC chief Sidney Hillman had "taken over" the "great Democratic Party," paving the way for a full-fledged New Deal "corporate state."[12] Ironically, Warren had turned down Dewey's offer to be his running mate and subsequently refused to deliver the "canned" version of this Dewey diatribe against Roosevelt in his own speeches around the country in support of Dewey and other Republican candidates.[13] Similar to the negligible impact of Kelly's attack on Warren's "radicalism," Dewey's barbs barely dented Roosevelt's war-tested armor as FDR marched to his final commanding electoral victory.

Though Warren in 1946 had hardly attained the stature of the venerable (and now deceased) Roosevelt, the governor's opponents soon realized he would be about as hard to beat. Kelly apparently did not have problems raising funds for his campaign, but he had trouble finding much support within the party or from the state's prominent newspapers. In early 1946, officials at the *Los Angeles Times,* along with key Republican leaders, pressured Kelly to withdraw from the race. Even some prominent conservatives believed that winning the election with Warren was more important than persisting in the attempt to make a statement about "fundamental principles" with a sure loser such as the ultraconservative Kelly.[14] As a result, Kelly dropped out of the race and the party's factions came together behind the governor.

With the challenge from the Republican Old Guard behind him, Warren touted his tempered progressivism and especially his stewardship during the war when he formally announced his reelection bid in March 1946. He emphasized that he had assumed office "during the darkest days of the war" and noted "[t]here was no assurance that we ourselves would not be bombed and pressed for the defense of our homes." A portent of the "front line" mentality that later contributed to the proliferation of Southland anticommunist groups, Warren contended that "California's aircraft, ship-building and chemical industries, [and] its vital military installations . . . placed it in the most perilous position of all the States. . . ." Though Californians never had to "meet actual disaster" on the home front, he noted that they and the state were thoroughly prepared to do so.[15] In short, Warren reminded voters that he had guided the state through the treacherous waters of the "darkest days" and it had emerged not only unscathed but, due to his leadership and the emerging metropolitan-military complex, stronger economically than ever.

California Democrats therefore did not have an easy task in finding a candidate to challenge the formidable incumbent and to fit the rightward drift of postwar politics. Due to FDR's coattails, Democratic candidates had fared well in the 1944 election in California and elsewhere, but the palpable progressive spirit that had long pervaded the party and generated wide support withered in good part after Roosevelt's death in April 1945. Having reconciled their differences with capitalism by the war's end, most reform-minded liberals nevertheless believed that government could once again tackle challenges on the domestic front with an emphasis on creating a full-employment economy and on the maintenance of New Deal social welfare and insurance programs.[16]

The strongest backer of the "Roosevelt legacy" in California, organized labor joined with Democratic Party officials in persuading State Attorney General Robert Kenny to run for governor against the "unbeatable" Warren. A true New Deal liberal, the witty Kenny had been a Los Angeles judge well known for his devotion to the preservation of civil liberties—even for communist "radicals"—before being elected to the State Senate in 1938 and as attorney general in 1942. Drawing upon a friendship that started in the late 1920s, Warren had sought and received Kenny's endorsement for his attorney general candidacy in 1938, even though Kenny was serving as the treasurer for Culbert Olsen's gubernatorial campaign at the time. In turn, Warren did nothing to help Wallace Ware, Kenny's Republican opponent in the 1942 attorney general's race, and a number of Warren's deputies backed Kenny. Contrary to the feuding that had typified the relationship between Warren and Olson, Attorney General Kenny and Governor Warren worked well together, though Kenny opposed Warren's active role in maintaining wartime internment camps for Japanese Americans. Conservative Republican assemblyman Thomas Werdel, among others, believed that Kenny played an important role in turning Warren away from "traditional Republicanism."[17]

That Warren had indeed co-opted the general idea and practice of government activism into Republican politics in California did much to diminish Kenny's gubernatorial aspirations and the Democratic Party overall. Kenny had been the only Democrat to win statewide office in 1942, and as the party's "sole survivor" he came under intense pressure to run and ultimately felt obligated to do so. Though it was "hopeless," one party official recalled, "we had to have a candidate and we couldn't get anyone else as good."[18] To the limited extent that the California Democratic Party existed outside of its nearly three million registered voters, it was torn by intense factionalism. The party's pro-business conservatives, such as oilman Ed Pauley, battled against ultraliberals like Kenny and Congressman Ellis Patterson. This internal strife prevented the. Democrats from forming a strong party organization, despite FDR's success in carrying the state four times.[19] His wit and political savvy notwithstanding, Kenny faced the formidable challenge of trying to beat a popular incumbent without a united party, a solid campaign organization, or a compelling message.

Moving further to the left in the campaign's final months, Kenny made the rather untenable claim that Warren represented the "reactionary forces" opposed to "every ideal that Franklin D. Roosevelt ever stood for."[20] While this proclamation rallied members of the pro-Kenny CIO, the more conservative American Federation of Labor (AFL) endorsed Warren due to the strong influence of the Federation's Brotherhood of Teamsters. Publicly the Teamsters opposed Kenny because of his alleged communist affiliations, but several heated jurisdictional disputes between the AFL and the CIO may have been factors in the Federation's endorsement decision as well.[21] Not surprisingly, the Warren camp promoted perceptions that Kenny carried the banner of the radical left, claiming that he defended communist organizations on the pretext that "[o]ur main enemy today is still Fascism." Kyle Palmer of the *Los Angeles Times* leveled similar accusations, linking

Kenny and the Democratic Party to "leftists, pinkoes, and outright Communists," and later predicted that "Warren can polish off Kenny in the primaries if his advisors conduct their campaign wisely and aggressively."[22]

Proving Palmer correct, Warren defeated Kenny in the primary and in doing so foreshadowed the dim Democratic prospects in the general election in California and the rest of the country. In its effort to halt, if not turn back, liberal reforms, the Republican Party in 1946 asked American voters: "Had Enough?" The resulting repudiation of liberals such as Kenny proved resounding, as he lost to Warren by more than 60,000 votes among Democrats. Seeking his party's nomination for the U.S. Senate, Ellis Patterson lost to the moderate Democrat Will Rogers Jr. in a bitter primary fight that further split the party. In the general election, the Republicans claimed another liberal casualty when a young World War II veteran by the name of Richard Nixon defeated congressman Jerry Voorhis, a prominent and ardent New Dealer. The moderate Rogers fared no better, losing big to William Knowland, whom Warren had appointed to the Senate in 1945 upon the death of the venerable incumbent, Hiram Johnson. The publisher of the *Oakland Tribune* and a GOP heavyweight, Knowland's father Joseph had been instrumental in Warren's political success.[23] The governor chose to return the favor by granting William the political office that his father had run for, unsuccessfully, in 1914.

As an immensely popular two-term governor of one of the nation's largest and fastest growing states, Warren assumed a luminous position in the Republican firmament, which allowed him to seriously pursue the 1948 Republican presidential nomination. The speculation that he would run began immediately after he won his second term. He was, however, hampered by his image as a regional candidate, and his professed nonpartisanship raised doubts about his ability to win enough support among steadfast Republicans to garner the nomination. Though he began to downplay his nonpartisanship, party members were upset when he took on the state's oil industry in 1947 by pressing for a gas tax to generate much-needed highway and road construction funds.[24] In pushing legislation to institute the tax, he not only went against his party's aversion to taxes, but against a powerful industry that had generally aligned itself with GOP concerns and poured money into its campaigns, including Warren's. He eventually won the gas tax battle, but that did nothing to diminish his nonpartisan or liberal image among his Republican critics.

In an attempt to define his political philosophy, Warren published a brief article in the *New York Times Magazine* in April 1948. Perhaps reflecting his great interest in history, Warren defined liberalism in humanistic terms, evoking the European Enlightenment of the eighteenth century: "This [liberal] belief and movement, born of faith in mankind and in the dignity of the human soul . . . found their finest expression . . . in our Western civilization." Though he defended the institutions and rights "that are all part and parcel of the liberal tradition," he lamented that liberalism had become "the disguise of communists and communist sympathizers. . . ." He stated, however, that the term *conservative* "has also been distorted" because "[m]any people style themselves conservative when they are in fact reactionaries opposed to every effort . . . to solve the problems of the day." Warren expressed his preference for dividing "people into three groups—reactionary, progressive and radical," and noted, "I particularly like the term 'progressive,' not necessarily as a party label, but as a conception." Having identified his political label, he maintained that "[t]he progressive has faith in democracy" and "freedom . . . and to this end he is willing to subordinate his private interest to the common good."[25]

Warren's decision to so literally embrace the progressive image reflected his oft-touted honesty and, indeed, the essence of his ideology. But the way in which he described his politics may not have served him well with GOP loyalists. Even though he did not necessarily care for the "progressive" party label, his frequent and favorable use of the term ran the risk of bringing unwanted associations with the far-left Progressive Party presidential candidate of 1948, Henry Wallace. Vice president during Roosevelt's third term, Wallace alienated many liberals and outraged other Americans after the war with his sympathetic attitude toward the Soviet Union and his ideas on redistributing wealth by changing the "swollen profit structure."[26] Warren was hardly seeking a rapprochement with the Soviets or to challenge American capitalism, but his utilitarian willingness to "subordinate his private interest to the common good" was not likely to appeal to conservatives, whom he had essentially dismissed as obdurate obstacles to reform. Warren ultimately made an argument for the politics of the "vital center," much like that of postwar liberals dedicated to defending the progressive reforms of the New Deal from attacks by the reactionary right and the radical left.[27]

Warren's presidential candidacy received strong support from prominent Republicans in California,[28] but his politics and regional image made him a compromise candidate in the event of a deadlocked convention as opposed to a front-runner like Dewey, the eventual nominee. Dewey turned back a number of challengers, most notably the conservative senator from Ohio known as "Mr. Republican," Robert Taft. Numerous conservatives at the convention ended up supporting Dewey because he was perceived as a winner who supported the conservative party platform.[29] Moreover, despite his centrist leanings, Dewey had ingratiated himself to Republican right-wingers by vehemently attacking Roosevelt's "communist" connections in the 1944 campaign—something Warren had refused to do. Warren had also refused Dewey's offer to be his running mate that year, but when the same request came in 1948, he reluctantly agreed to join the ticket.[30]

Warren later told journalist I.F. Stone that he had accepted Dewey's offer mainly to use his position to champion "all the things I fought for all my life" and to counter the "influence [that] would be exerted from Wall Street" in a Dewey administration.[31] On the hustings, however, Warren could not veer from the restrictive, Dewey-directed script. He was advised to refrain from voicing his views on "socialized medicine" and to present his political career on a "business basis."[32] Never a dynamic speaker, Warren plodded through the campaign, bereft of the forthright manner and independence that had been his greatest political assets.

Dewey and Warren headed into the general election campaign as overwhelming favorites to beat President Harry Truman and running mate Alben Barkley. But Truman's now-legendary "give-'em-hell" campaign in the last weeks of a whistle-stop whirlwind, combined with Dewey's smug overconfidence, led to the greatest political upset in American history. The Republican ticket lost even in California, where Dewey's callousness toward critical water issues proved especially unpopular. Two days after the election, Warren, more relieved than humiliated, declared, "[i]t feels as if a hundred-pound sack had been taken off my back."[33]

As Warren eased back into his gubernatorial duties in early 1949, State Senator Jack Tenney began preparing for another term of hearings for the joint fact-finding committee on un-American activities, which he chaired. Formed in 1941, the committee grew out of an investigation headed by Tenney in the previous year that looked into allegations of communist influence in the Olson administration's state relief program. From 1941 through 1948 (with a lull during the war) the committee queried and "exposed" many Californians suspected of being communists or fellow-travelers. By 1947, if not before, the committee operated from the assumption that a worldwide communist conspiracy, targeting California due to its strategic industries and location, sought ultimately to establish a Soviet dictatorship in America.[34] As the Cold War escalated, this belief did not in and of itself necessarily prove highly controversial, but the committee's inquisitional methods did. The standard procedure of Tenney and his cohorts, the *San Francisco Chronicle* maintained, "is to call a witness, ask him questions calculated to produce evidence that he is a Communist or fellow-traveler . . . and then chop him off from further answers." Adamantly defending the committee's purpose and methods, Tenney later stated that he had gauged "the committee's effectiveness in exposing the Kremlin's stooges by the amount of profane and lying abuse heaped upon it by the Communist press."[35]

By 1949 Tenney and his committee faced mounting opposition from prominent and respectable groups outside of organized labor, one of Tenney's favorite targets.[36] Opposed to the committee's methods and to its legislative proposals for a series of loyalty oaths, the senator's critics in the legislature and elsewhere became incensed when the ultraconservative Ed Gibbons, whom Tenney had hired to write the committee's 1949 report, impugned a number of well-known state Democrats in his anticommunist newsletter, *Alert*. Seeking to topple Tenney from his position as chief inquisitor, Assemblyman Sam Yorty, a more tempered red-baiter who had served with Tenney in the investigation of the state relief program, led the successful effort to kill Tenney's surviving antisubversive bills in June. Shortly thereafter the Senate Rules Committee in effect forced Tenney to resign as chair of the Un-American Activities Committee, bringing his tenure to an end. Writing for the *Nation,* Carey McWilliams contended that Tenney's repudiation came about "because the powers that be have discovered that red-baiting caters to a constantly shrinking political market."[37] Joe McCarthy, the quintessential red-baiter, would of course soon disprove this assertion.

Though Tenney faded as a force in the legislature, the issue of loyalty oaths, which he had strongly backed, became increasingly contentious, particularly with regard to oaths for faculty at University of California (UC) campuses.[38] The Tenney Committee in January 1949 had introduced a bill allowing the legislature, instead of the university's board of regents, to evaluate the loyalty of UC employees. The regents had instituted a noncommunist employment policy in 1940 and reconfirmed it in 1949, but this policy did not involve oaths. Subsequently, UC president Robert Sproul instructed the university's comptroller to draft a loyalty oath to head off Tenney's stricter stipulations and to avoid potential problems with the legislature's approval of the university's budget.[39] The proposal ran into staunch opposition from faculty, and Sproul soon withdrew his support for the oath. This led to a battle between Sproul and several conservative regents, in which Warren sided with the UC president.

A Berkeley graduate and friend of Sproul, Warren entered the fray in early 1950 at the behest of a UC economics professor and oath opponent who had been an advisor to Warren in his 1948 presidential campaign.[40] Regent John Francis Neylan, a San Francisco attorney and one-time Republican liberal reappointed to the board by Warren in 1944, led the fight for the oath in February 1950. He engineered the passage of a resolution requiring a signed oath from all university employees. Voicing his opposition to the resolution shortly after its passage, Warren made a formal statement in late March, declaring, "I don't believe that the faculty at the University of California is Communist; I don't believe that it is soft on Communism, and neither am I."[41] After much debate, the regents, with the governor's approval, eventually passed a compromise resolution that made the oath requirement less exacting and allowed nonsigners a full hearing to make their case for not signing. Nevertheless, in August the board voted, with Warren dissenting, to dismiss thirty-one individuals who had refused to sign the compromise pledge, disregarding the favorable reports on these individuals from the university committee that had reviewed their cases.

Seeking to resolve the loyalty oath dispute, Warren requested in September that the legislature require all state employees to sign an oath pledging that they did not support or belong to "any party or organization . . . that now advocates the overthrow of the Government of the United States or the State of California." Five days later the legislature passed the Levering Act, which established the oath requirement, and Warren signed the bill in early October.[42] Running for an unprecedented third term as governor in 1950, Warren no doubt dropped his opposition to loyalty oaths because McCarthy and heightened Cold War tensions had made attacks on communism more strident and politically vital than ever. His dislike of the Levering Act, however, became clear when, as chief justice of the Supreme Court, he assented in the decision to invalidate state loyalty oaths in 1967. Recalling the loyalty oath matter in his memoirs, Warren was particularly critical of Neylan and fellow regent Mario Giannini, the president of the Bank of America. The two men "carried their [anticommunist] hysteria to such an extent that they deprived the university of badly needed dormitories . . . on the ground that the concept of dormitories was socialistic." "They let McCarthyism dominate their lives," he maintained, "and endeavored to impose it on others."[43]

In July 1950, a *Life* magazine headline proclaimed, "A Trend Is Running Toward an Enlightened Conservatism,"[44] but in reality the trend was heading in the opposite direction due primarily to the rise of McCarthy. World and domestic events set the stage for McCarthy and others seeking to exploit the growing anxiety over the "red menace." In 1949 the Soviet Union detonated an atom bomb, Nationalist China fell to communist forces led by Mao Zedong, and postwar spy scandals at home and abroad created a "contagion of fear" in America. In this apprehensive political climate, Republican conservatives prevailed over the party's Dewey wing in adopting "Liberty against Socialism" as the GOP slogan for the 1950 congressional campaign.[45] That campaign targeted the "socialistic" policies of the Truman administration and drew upon McCarthy's repeated charge that communists occupied critical positions in the federal government. McCarthy's fusillades made red-baiting an effective tactic for Republicans—and some Democrats—on the hustings, a tactic well suited to politicians like Richard Nixon.

Running for Congress in southern California's twelfth district, Nixon began his political career as a red-baiter in 1946 when he declared that his opponent, Congressman Jerry Voorhis, was controlled by the "communist-dominated" CIO-PAC and had received the group's endorsement. In fact, the CIO-PAC did not endorse Voorhis in 1946. Furthermore, among New Dealers, he was the least favored liberal in California's congressional delegation due largely to his service on the House Un-American Activities Committee (HUAC, but known as the Dies Committee when Voorhis served), his sponsorship of anticommunist legislation and criticism of Soviet expansionism in Eastern Europe.[46] But every attempt by Voorhis to counter Nixon's incessant charges fell flat due to a combination of Nixon's craftiness and underhanded tactics, Voorhis's mistakes on the campaign trail, and the salience of the anticommunist and PAC issues.

Nixon handily defeated Voorhis and went on to become a national figure when he led the effort to prove that Alger Hiss, the liberal head of the prestigious Carnegie Endowment for International Peace, had been a spy for the Soviet Union in the 1930s. A State Department official and Roosevelt associate during the New Deal, Hiss adamantly denied the allegations. The charges initially came from the repentant ex-communist Whittaker Chambers in testimony before the HUAC. Hiss subsequently sued Chambers for libel, but Hiss's denial did not convince Nixon, a HUAC member, who offered his services to Chambers as an attorney and became committed to proving Hiss guilty in court. In a case that took many twists and turns, in January 1950, after an earlier hung jury, a second jury found Hiss guilty of perjury after reviewing evidence that appeared to substantiate Chambers's allegations. The highly publicized case divided conservatives and liberals as much, if not more, than the debate over government policy. Gloating immediately after the Hiss conviction, Nixon maintained that there had been a "determined and deliberate effort on the part of certain high officials in two administrations to keep the public from knowing the facts" of the case. Several days later he reiterated his determination to thwart the red "Master Plot" that the Hiss case had exposed.[47]

His next target in this battle would be Democratic congresswoman Helen Gahagan Douglas, a former actress who challenged Nixon in 1950 for the Senate seat being vacated by Democrat Sheridan Downey. Like Voorhis, Douglas had a liberal image at which Nixon, with the help of strategist Murray Chotiner, took sharp aim. Casting Douglas in a new role as the "pink lady" ("pink right down to her underpants"), the Nixon camp circulated a "Pink Sheet" that linked her congressional voting record to that of "the notorious Communist party-liner, Congressman Vito Marcantonio of New York." (Marcantonio was a member of the left-wing American Labor Party.) Distorting the voting records of both Douglas and Nixon, the Pink Sheet proclaimed that Nixon "has voted *exactly opposite* to the Douglas-Marcantonio Axis."[48] Harnessing invaluable support from newspaper baron William Randolph Hearst and from the *Los Angeles Times* and Kyle Palmer, Nixon rode roughshod over Douglas, who ill-advisedly chose not to respond directly to the Nixon smear. As a result, the Pink Sheet would be widely accepted as fact.[49]

The message in the Pink Sheet was a variation on a recurrent foreboding theme in postwar conservatism: the impending collapse of American freedom could only be turned back by virtuous voters in the ballot booth. In this vein, the chairman of the Republican Central Committee of Los Angeles County advised members that the "County may well be a proving ground to determine whether or not all of America will be able to stem the 'statist' tide which varies in color from misguided pink to Marxist red." Even the most conservative of the state's Democratic candidates, he contended, "are committed to Truman's socialistic policies." Writing in *Alert,* Ed Gibbons declared that the major Democratic candidates in the state "have records of collaboration with and appeasement of the Communists and their noisy fellow-travelers." Still smarting from the Tenney Committee's abrupt demise, he maintained that Warren was the "key factor in this entire election," but "[h]e must be kicked, shoved or led off the mugwump position he has taken on the issue of Communism . . . and Communist treason at home."[50]

Mired in the loyalty oath matter and jostled by dissension within the state GOP, Warren faced potential opposition to his quest for a third term from Lieutenant Governor Goodwin Knight, who favored the regents' oath proposal. In early 1949, 125 prominent Southland conservatives, shocked by the defeat of the Dewey–Warren ticket, formed a dissident group called "Partisan Republicans," and derided the governor as "wishy-washy and namby-pamby."[51] The Knight for Governor Committee grew out of this disenchantment. Soliciting support for Knight from fellow Republicans, the committee's chairman, without directly naming Warren, claimed that "liberal socialistic candidates have been losing popularity throughout the world." Given the decline of the left and the "return to popularity of Herbert Hoover," Knight provided "the only possibility of a Republican victory in 1950. . . ."[52]

Knight, who had the backing of the Hearst newspapers, clearly wanted to be governor and appealed to conservatives by noting that he never had supported Warren's "compulsory health insurance." Increasingly annoyed by Knight's challenge, Warren confounded the lieutenant governor's efforts by insisting that "he [personally] has always . . . expressed his loyalty to my administration."[53] But Warren in fact viewed Knight as a conservative stalwart opposed to progressivism, as revealed in his memoirs: "I might not have run for a third term had it not been for the intransigence of the lieutenant governor." Knight's criticism of Warren's administrative skills and programs led the governor to believe that Knight would not carry out his postwar plans for the state. The slim chance that Knight had of toppling Warren essentially vanished when the governor turned back an effort by Artie Samish, a notorious Sacramento lobbyist, to dismantle the state Crime Commission in fall 1949. In defeating the imperious and powerful Samish, Warren showed he was still the most formidable political figure in the state.[54]

Seeking to pose a serious challenge to Warren this time around, the California Democratic Party pinned its hopes on James ("Jimmy") Roosevelt, FDR's eldest son, who had moved to California in 1938. After serving as an officer in the Marines during the war, he became the chairman of the state party in 1946 and a national party committeeman in 1948, when he led an unsuccessful effort to draft General Dwight Eisenhower for the Democratic presidential nomination. Party conservatives in particular viewed Roosevelt as a liberal Eastern "carpetbagger" who had used his name and FDR-like voice to take over the party and position himself for the gubernatorial nomination. Dismissing such criticism, Robert Brownell, a writer for *Frontier,* a liberal periodical based in Los Angeles, noted, "the [Democratic] old liners who have called the turns for years . . . are out and the new official Party potentates are the band of liberal leaders who have been aiming at control for years."[55]

The electoral prospects of these new potentates, however, did not prove promising, especially for Roosevelt, who narrowly defeated Warren among Democratic voters in the June primary. Warren, on the other hand, received almost all of the Republican votes. Though the Republican right had become increasingly alienated by Warren's "liberalism," they "had no place to go but Warren," one prominent Democrat recalled. "They might swear at him and damn him," but they could never vote for anyone named Roosevelt. Indeed, as Gibbons declared, "we will not agree with those who will refuse to support Warren against James Roosevelt," who was backed by a "motley crew of opportunists, flaming liberals, [and] Kremlin Kutups. . . ."[56] Warren's re-election to an unprecedented third term seemed assured.

Nevertheless, the road to the general election in November did have some bumps, mainly due to the governor's differences with organized labor. He declined to veto a "Hot Cargo" bill—which denied unions the right to refuse to handle goods produced by strikebreakers—and opposed jurisdictional strikes. Warren tried to mollify labor leaders by voicing objections to a number of provisions in the controversial 1947 Taft–Hartley Act, particularly the requirement that union members take a loyalty oath, and the elimination of federal protection of the "closed shop." Taft–Hartley allowed individual states to decide whether union membership would be mandatory in a unionized, closed shop workplace, or optional (in an "open shop") by virtue of a "right-to-work" law. Warren's opposition to the idea of right-to-work laws did not prove sufficient to win the formal backing of organized labor, which instead endorsed Roosevelt and provided him with campaign funds and a plane for touring the state. Though Roosevelt won the formal support of labor's political campaign committees, he did not command the labor vote. In addition to their generally favorable opinion of Warren, many union members resented Roosevelt's role in the effort to oust Truman in 1948, which worked to Warren's reelection benefit. Truman, who had a rocky relationship with labor early in his presidency, vetoed the Taft–Hartley Act in 1947. Ultimately overridden, his veto still won him widespread union support.[57]

Despite the tensions of the red scare and the attendant tactical chicanery of Nixon and others, Warren did not engage in red-baiting during his campaign. Moreover, he publicly criticized the "blanket accusations against groups and individuals" made by McCarthy without proper evidence. Warren's staff did possess information from HUAC's "Rankin Report" on Roosevelt supporters with "Communist connections," but Warren himself never used this information to assail his opponent.[58] He did not have to, of course, given the frequent attacks on Roosevelt's "connections" and "socialistic" views from conservative Republicans. Always strident and often shrill, these attacks nonetheless appeared tame alongside those of the notorious racist and superpatriot Gerald L.K. Smith, who came to Los Angeles in early November to lead several "Stop Roosevelt" rallies. Schooling his followers on the "treacherous and treasonable background of the Roosevelt dynasty," Smith exposed "their Jewish family tree" and discussed "[w]hat . . . the departure of large numbers of Jews indicate[s] concerning the safety of this city." The *Los Angeles Times* deplored Smith's history of "intolerance and hate," and Warren made clear he did not welcome Smith's visit or support.[59]

Throughout his campaign Roosevelt made the usual Democratic charge that Warren was actually a conservative posing as a liberal who played into the hands of greedy and selfish interests in California and on Wall Street.[60] In so doing Roosevelt followed in the campaign footsteps of Kenny and, ultimately, suffered the same electoral fate as well. In what proved to be a strong Republican year nationwide, Warren defeated Roosevelt by more than a million votes. In the state's other major race, Nixon beat Douglas by almost 700,000 votes, but during the campaign Douglas tagged Nixon with a name that would stick: "Tricky Dick." Though ill-inclined toward name-calling, Warren resented Nixon's attacks on Douglas and the fact that so many anti-Warren Republicans found a haven in the Nixon camp.[61] Indeed, Nixon's victory as a champion of conservative Republicanism made him Warren's chief rival in the battle for the control of the state GOP.

Similar to the aftermath of his reelection in 1946, Warren was once again considered a force in the race for his party's 1952 presidential nomination, but not necessarily a truly viable candidate. Dewey informed his inner circle in 1951 that he would not seek a third nomination. Joining a growing number of influential Republicans, he got behind the incipient yet unofficial presidential campaign of World War II hero Dwight ("Ike") Eisenhower, a political neophyte who began to reveal his Republican inclinations with a relatively centrist sensibility and appeal.[62] Warren again appeared to be a compromise candidate if delegates at the Republican Convention became deadlocked—this time, over the choice between Eisenhower and Taft. Warren would at the very least be a major powerbroker if he controlled the large California delegation, which appeared all but certain given the likelihood that neither Taft nor Eisenhower would challenge him in the California primary.

In the midst of the Korean War in 1951, Warren informed the legislature that he would not propose any new taxes given the demands of the legislative "war session," and for the first time since 1944 he did not propose a health insurance program.[63] Warren's earlier health insurance initiatives had been defeated through public relations efforts led by the firm of Whitaker and Baxter, which had run Warren's 1942 campaign, and by powerful lobbyists for the California Medical Association. Whitaker and Baxter's success in undermining the governor's health plans led the American Medical Association (AMA) to enlist the firm's services in 1949 in its $3.5 million fight against the Truman administration's proposal for a national health insurance system. Claiming that the "real objective" of the advocates of "socialized medicine . . . is to gain control over all fields of human endeavor," the AMA sank the Truman plan with red-baiting attacks.[64]

Despite such powerful opposition, Warren's efforts to promote "compulsory health insurance" did not abate. After the AMA invited Taft to speak in California in late 1951, Warren wrote the senator and complained that "the [AMA] wants you to speak in California for, among other reasons, the purpose of discrediting me on the health question." Warren called the AMA's attacks on him "vicious" and declared that his plan for "prepaid medical care . . . is in no sense socialized medicine. . . ." In May 1952, he explained "Why I'm Fighting for My Health Plan" in an article with that title in *Look* magazine. Warren, whose daughter Nina had contracted polio in 1950, declared that he was seeking "safeguards" to protect "decent, hard-working families" from the potential financial ruin brought about by cata-strophic illness. Perhaps with Taft in mind, one month earlier, in the conservative periodical the *American Mercury,* he had responded to Repub-lican assaults on his "socialized medicine" program by bemoaning those in his party "who would like to turn the clock back if they could." On a broader note, Warren chastised the federal government for not giving more responsibilities to state and local governments; yet, "I don't know of any essential program that has been initiated by the Federal Government in recent years that I would repeal" as president.[65]

Spurred by Warren's longstanding "heretical" views, organized opposi-tion to his prospective presidential bid began in November 1951. Gathering in Los Angeles for a dinner meeting, 400 conservative Republicans dis-cussed strategy to block Warren's control of the state's Republican National Convention delegation in 1952. Jack Tenney delivered the keynote speech, during which he hailed McCarthy as "a modern Paul Revere," praised Gen-eral Douglas MacArthur and promoted the general's presidential candidacy. Extremely conservative in his political beliefs, the maverick MacArthur had been dismissed from his command of American forces in Korea by Truman in April, an unpopular decision that made the defiant general the toast of every town upon his return to the states. Though MacArthur's campaign prospects and active pursuit of the presidency proved marginal at best, his devoted followers urged fellow Republicans to help them forge a draft movement. A MacArthur victory, a "Draft MacArthur" flyer proclaimed, would be "so convincing and so clean and so dynamic that every true American will know the redemption of our nation is at hand."[66]

The anti-Warren faction backed Bakersfield congressman Thomas Werdel in the California presidential primary. Touted as the candidate of the "Free Republican Delegation," Werdel was the governor's only opponent. The congressman's supporters had tried to persuade a number of prominent conservatives—including MacArthur—to challenge Warren in the primary, but to no avail. Werdel promised to "release the members of this delegation after the June 3 primary . . . to vote for any legitimate candidate, capable of supporting a real Republican Platform." Reflecting the opinion of his sup-porters, Werdel charged that Warren was not a legitimate presidential candi-date, but rather sought to control California's seventy convention votes "in a deal for personal gain—an appointment to the Supreme Court or a Cabinet post." Countering Werdel's allegations, Warren maintained he had made no deals with any other candidates and would release his delegates if it appeared he could not win the nomination.[67]

Among the prominent Werdel backers were Tenney, John Francis Neylan, actor Adolphe Menjou, San Diego banker C. Arnholt Smith, and independent oilman William Keck.[68] Responding to a reporter's inquiry, Warren stated that he believed that independent oil interests "are pouring a lot of money" into the Werdel campaign: "I mean Bill Keck and his messenger boy, Jack Smith" (C. Arnholt's brother). Enraged by the governor's statement, Smith, in an open letter, gave a biting retort: "My associates and I ceased to support you when you . . . sought to gouge the California taxpayers . . . by your attempt to raise the state gasoline tax by an additional three cents per gallon in 1947." Vilifying Warren for everything from his opposition to the regents' loyalty oath proposal to his "socialized medicine" initiatives, Smith thundered, "I will resist your effort to force . . . Republican voters to accept the Hitler-Stalin choice you offer them of voting 'ja' or not at all in the coming primary."[69]

The freedom-versus-tyranny rhetoric of the Werdel camp in a sense presaged the theme of later conservative campaigns in California, but it was used primarily against Warren and his "dictatorial" campaign tactics, not against the "tyranny" of "big government." Werdel campaign literature encouraged Republicans to "Free Your GOP" and assured voters that his delegation was "NO MAN'S Captive!" The "real issue," of course, "is real Republicanism versus Warren's Trumanism," but Werdel brochures emphatically proclaimed: "VOTE WERDEL JUNE THREE, AND FREE THE REAL G.O.P.!"[70] Of significant note, the principal Werdel backers were not, at least early on, among the major supporters of Goldwater's 1964 presidential campaign or Reagan's subsequent gubernatorial bid. Of Werdel's seventy delegates and a handful of other noteworthy backers, only C. Arnholt Smith held a prominent position in the 1964 California Goldwater Campaign; and no one in the Werdel camp could be found among the initial forty-two fundraising "Friends of Ronald Reagan" in 1965 or the dozen-or-so members of his gubernatorial "Kitchen Cabinet."[71] It is reasonable to assume, however, that most, if not all, of the surviving Werdel backers supported Goldwater and Reagan.

Touting Taft and cool to Eisenhower, Werdel's troops created a rather ugly spectacle for Warren and the Republican Party in the primary. Even though Warren won by almost a two-to-one margin, the results indicated a decline in his popularity. Werdel won in Orange County and did well throughout southern California where he focused his amply financed campaign. Though the primary results did not bode well for Warren, Werdel also suffered, as he would have the dubious distinction of being the only Republican congressional incumbent in California to lose his seat in the November election. Not finished with politics, Werdel ran in 1956 as the vice presidential candidate for the segregationist States' Rights Party.[72] Jack Tenney, a vociferous Werdel delegate and Warren critic, went on to accept the 1952 vice presidential nomination of Gerald L.K. Smith's Christian Nationalist Party.[73]

In July, Warren and his state delegation headed by private train to the Republican Convention in Chicago with palpable exuberance given the indications that Taft and Eisenhower could well be deadlocked after the first ballot. By the time the train arrived in Chicago, however, Nixon, in what has been dubbed the "great train robbery," had managed to swing the California delegation, in effect, behind Eisenhower. Boarding the train in Denver, the senator met surreptitiously with many of the delegates. He convinced most of them to cast critical votes for a "fair-play" amendment on the convention floor which would eliminate Taft's control of disputed Southern delegates and assure Ike's nomination on the first ballot. Enraged but unable to effectively counter Nixon's machinations, Warren saw his last chance to win the presidency evaporate with Eisenhower's subsequent nomination. Along with stunned Taft supporters, Warren then had to witness the selection of Nixon as Eisenhower's running mate, given that Ike and his inner circle deemed the senator the best man to balance the ticket, both geographically and ideologically. His own vice-presidential aspirations dashed, Bill Knowland had remained a loyal Warren delegate throughout the fair-play maneuvers. When he received a request from Murray Chotiner and Nixon to formally nominate Nixon from the convention podium— which he later dutifully did—he replied, "I have to nominate that dirty son of a bitch?"[74]

The ill will among Republicans notwithstanding, the Democrats faced a daunting task in taking on Eisenhower. Truman, burdened by the Korean War and scandal in his administration, did not choose to seek reelection. The Democrats eventually pinned their hopes on the liberal reformer Adlai Stevenson, governor of Illinois. The Stevenson campaign depicted Eisenhower as a political newcomer whose actions as president would be orchestrated by "reactionaries" like McCarthy, Taft, and Nixon. Too many Americans, however, could not resist the combination of Eisenhower's easygoing charm—reflected in the ubiquity of "I Like Ike" buttons and stickers—and his heroic military background as the architect of the D-Day invasion and victory in Europe. In addition, Republicans targeted Democrats through an effective campaign "formula" for victory: K_1 (one part Korea), C_2 (Communism and Corruption). The only significant problem for the Eisenhower–Nixon ticket came in September when the press reported the existence of a "secret fund," established by California businessmen, that Nixon used to live in a style "far beyond his salary."[75] Nixon responded to this charge in a nationally televised speech in which he provided conflicting information about the fund, but generated a groundswell of support with an account of his humble life-style and the acquisition of his family's cocker spaniel, Checkers. Though Nixon survived the ordeal through the "Checkers" speech, his relationship with Eisenhower suffered.[76]

Defeating Stevenson in a landslide in November, Eisenhower ushered in a new era for the country and for the resurgent Republican Party. In accordance with his campaign pledge of "peace with honor," the president brought the Korean War to a tolerable negotiated end in July 1953. On the home front, the avuncular Ike presided over rapid industrial and suburban growth, particularly in California. In this increasingly affluent yet rather conformist American society, nonconformists, with few exceptions, were relegated to the margins of popular culture and public discourse. Frequently photographed on a golf course, Eisenhower appeared to be more of a caretaker than a leader, which clearly fit the public mood.[77] In keeping with the centrist "consensus" of postwar politics, he chose to stay in the "middle of the road" politically, much to the chagrin of conservative Republican stalwarts.

Eisenhower in fact despised the Old Guard conservatives, which was one of the reasons he admired Earl Warren. After meeting with Warren at the Republican Convention, Eisenhower had told reporters that he and the governor were "not going to get dragged back by a lot of old reactionaries. . . ." Impressed by Warren's professional competence and integrity, Eisenhower soon decided that he would make an excellent Supreme Court justice. The president got the opportunity to place Warren on the Court after Chief Justice Fred M. Vinson died in September 1953. Shortly before Vinson's death Warren had announced he would not seek a fourth gubernatorial term, with the expectation that he would be appointed to the Court upon the first vacancy. Commenting on the governor's philosophy and qualifications, Eisenhower told his brother Milton that as a "liberal-conservative," Warren "represents the kind of political, economic, and social thinking that I believe we need on the Supreme Court." In January 1954, Eisenhower nominated Warren to replace Vinson as chief justice. Though the nomination met resistance from conservatives, the senate confirmed Warren in March, thus bringing one California era to a close, and beginning another for the High Court.[78]

Warren had resigned as governor on October 4, which allowed the gregarious Goodwin Knight to rise to the governorship after his long and anxious wait in the wings. Knight first entered the Republican spotlight in 1934 when he delivered a fiery denunciation of Upton Sinclair at the GOP state convention. Rewarding Knight for his invective, Frank Merriam appointed him to the superior court bench in Los Angeles in 1935, where he served for eleven years and received much publicity as the "mender of broken hearts" due to the number of Hollywood stars who came before him with their marital woes. Deciding to run for lieutenant governor in 1946, Knight won in a landslide and soon became a Warren antagonist, once dismissing the governor as "nothing but a New Dealer." At the height of the debate over loyalty oaths at UC, Knight, in addition to opposing Warren on the oath issue, attacked Truman's secretary of state, Dean Acheson, as an appeaser who "kowtowed to communism and plotted the dismissal of General MacArthur."[79] With Knight's ascent to the governorship, the California Right appeared to have secured power in Sacramento.

The new governor, however, faced an election in 1954 and did not want to alienate the liberal and moderate factions of Warren's diverse voting coalition. Hoping to win a cross-filing victory in the June primary, he made clear that he did "not believe in repressive legislation against either management or labor," declared his opposition to a right-to-work law, and raised the minimum unemployment insurance payment rate. Consequently, Knight won the endorsement of the AFL. Among other factors, the AFL's leaders noted that as a judge, he had never issued an injunction against unions, "despite the fact that employer powers in southern California were . . . constantly getting injunctions to deny our unions their basic rights. . . ."[80]

Mindful of the need to hold his conservative support, the governor also appealed to management, fervent anticommunists, and voters in the expanding metropolitan-military complex. He maintained that "[w]e should be eternally grateful" for free enterprise, which "has enabled us to create the sinews of defense which have halted all who would have trespassed upon our shores." He excoriated the most dreaded of these potential trespassers, the "brutal bureaucrats" of communist regimes, "who would dictate our every move." Urging unity, Knight declared, "let those of us here in California, a western bastion in the path of this terrible threat, do our part to turn back this doctrine of a godless group of tyrants."[81]

Struggling to find a candidate to take on Knight, a natural campaigner, the Democrats settled on Richard Graves, the executive director of the League of California Cities. Not only had Graves never held political office, he had been a registered Republican until late 1953. More prominent Democrats, such as Attorney General Pat Brown, who would win reelection in 1954, did not believe the time was right to challenge the incumbent governor. Hobbled by his seemingly eleventh-hour party switch and his political inexperience, Graves nonetheless won the support of the CIO and a small dissident group within the AFL, but generally did not excite Democrats.[82]

Indeed, some "progressive" Democrats backed Knight through campaign groups and billboard ads. Facilitating such efforts, the governor followed in Warren's nonpartisan footsteps with a widely run campaign ad shortly before the primary, which maintained: "The cornerstone of Democratic Government is not the Party—but the Man."[83]

Though Graves narrowly beat Knight among Democratic voters in the primary, the governor commanded the Republican vote by a ten-to-one margin, which all but assured a Knight victory in November. Thus, the ensuing campaign proved lackluster, with Graves during one stretch directing his campaign from a hospital bed due to an illness. The biggest question was whether Knight, after winning in November, could move out of Warren's imposing shadow.[84] Winning 55 percent of the vote in the general election, Knight got his chance to chart his own course for California politics and the state Republican Party. He would, however, essentially seek to maintain the centrist policies of predecessor, while claiming them as his own.

Though Knight won his electoral contest handily, 1954 did not prove to be a good year for the Republicans, who were running without Eisenhower's coattails. Contributing to the shift in the party's electoral fortunes, McCarthy's anticommunist inquisition came, appropriately enough, to an ignominious end after the increasingly reckless senator charged that communists had infiltrated the Army. Even conservatives who had generally supported McCarthy understood that he had gone too far and could not prevent him from being censured by the Senate in December 1954. McCarthy's downfall and repudiation were victories for Republican moderates and liberals, but his long reign had tainted the party and torn it asunder. "We have the spectacle of cannibalism holding forth," McCarthy supporter Barry Goldwater declared. "We find the Republican Party busily chewing on itself."[85]

With the Republican right in disarray, Eisenhower in 1955 made a major effort to reshape the GOP in his own image and at the same time mend factional fences. Speaking to the forty-eight state Republican Party chairmen at a breakfast meeting in September, the president addressed the question of GOP philosophy and party labels: "I, myself, have sometimes used such phrases as moderate progressive and dynamic conservative, because we want to be known . . . [as] the party of progress." He concluded, however, "I don't believe you can sloganize the kind of honest philosophy that the Republican Party is trying to promote. . . ." Nevertheless, two months later the Republican National Committee (RNC) circulated a description of "The Eisenhower Conservative," who sought to conserve, by government action if necessary, the forces "to which this country owes its phenomenal material growth," including the "market mechanism."[86]

Intent on relentlessly antagonizing Eisenhower and his brand of conservatism through the new periodical, *National Review,* chief editor William F. Buckley Jr. convinced Bill Knowland to contribute an article for the magazine's first issue, which came out in November 1955. In the article, the senator lambasted the administration for negotiating with the Soviet Union. Buckley and fellow editors Willi Schlamm and James Burnham also urged Knowland to pursue the presidency in 1956, as it appeared that the president would not seek reelection due a heart attack he had suffered in September. Despite this encouragement, the *National Review* never endorsed Knowland for the presidency because Eisenhower eventually decided to run again, which ruled out the senator's candidacy, and because there was skepticism about Knowland's intellect and electability. Describing middle-of-the-road politics as "intellectually ... and morally repugnant,"[87] Buckley did relent somewhat in his criticism of Eisenhower by the time of the 1956 election. Indeed, compared to the program of the Democrats, he proclaimed that "the program of the Republicans, which is essentially one of measured socialism, looks wonderfully appealing to the conservative." Yet he stopped well short of a solid endorsement of the president. Instead of "I Like Ike," he maintained, "I prefer Ike."[88]

While there were concerns about the president's fitness for another term in office, once he made the decision to run again, his reelection was almost a foregone conclusion. Amid the celebration of Ike and "the spirit of Bob Taft" (who had died in 1953), Knight declared at the Republican National Convention in San Francisco that Republicans would leave the city "marching arm in arm." Knowland, Nixon, and Knight, however, elbowed for opportune meetings and glad-handing at the convention to help bolster their future political prospects. Just prior to the convention, Nixon had survived a weak effort to oust him from the ticket, as conservatives rallied to his support.[89] The conservatives also unified behind Eisenhower at the convention, hoping to capitalize once again on his coattails. Furthermore, though they understood the GOP was no longer the party of Taft, Eisenhower was hardly a government activist like Truman or Roosevelt; and his uncomfortable attitude toward the nascent civil rights movement—a movement many conservatives castigated as "radical" in the course of defending the segregated South—placated the right-wing ranks. Yet, as one reporter noted, "[t]he stillness [among conservatives] at San Francisco was less that of an enemy vanquished or even cowed than of one patiently biding its time."[90]

In a repeat of the 1952 presidential campaign, Stevenson challenged Eisenhower and went down to defeat in another landslide. The president's margin of victory proved even greater than in the previous election, but the Republicans did not fare well overall, particularly in congressional contests.

In addition, the unity that had prevailed at the Republican Convention dissipated during the succeeding months as conservatives became increasingly marginalized by the president's "Modern Republicanism." Drawing upon descriptions of the "Eisenhower conservative," and from a 1956 book by an assistant secretary of labor, Arthur Larson, Modern Republicanism became the centrist slogan for the GOP "establishment" in the latter half of the Age of Eisenhower.[91] Though intended as a big-tent party philosophy, Modern Republicanism ultimately led to a revolt within the ranks, with the conservatives fighting to regain control of the party's image and agenda. California soon became the main arena for this battle.

Two

"Freedom versus Tyranny"

As 1957 came to a close, the country was saddled with a mild recession, which led to the highest unemployment rate in almost twenty years, but Eisenhower remained highly popular. The overall trend during the Eisenhower years was one of prosperity and peace, the latter marked by a thaw in the Cold War by the late 1950s. Ike continued to blend an affable grandfather image with that of a dignified elder statesman, which made him comforting and congenial, yet serious and resolute. Despite the president's popularity, Republican conservatives turned decidedly against him early in his second term, due mainly to his refusal to roll back the big-spending and regulatory liberal state. Longing to return to the largely laissez-faire policies of earlier eras, Barry Goldwater brazenly promoted the opinion of his conservative brethren in 1957 by charging that the Eisenhower administration had been lured by "the siren song of socialism."[1] The prevalence of such views further fractured the Republican ranks as the 1958 elections approached, thus opening the door to disaster for the Grand Old Party.[2]

While the Republican fissure did not prove a factor in electoral contests in every state, it had profound consequences in California. In 1957 a bitter battle between Republican conservatives and moderates erupted over who the party's gubernatorial candidate would be in the election the following year. In what one state Republican official called "the greatest political blunder of the generation,"[3] party heavyweights pressured the popular Goodwin Knight not to seek reelection in order to make way for the candidacy of William Knowland. Among those putting the squeeze on Knight were *Los Angeles Times* columnist Kyle Palmer, who informed Knight that his campaign funds would disappear if he did not bow out of the race, and Vice President Richard Nixon, who saw an opportunity to undercut the presidential aspirations of both Knight and Knowland in favor of his own. Without strong support from the party or from the *Times,* the embittered Knight had little choice but to decline to run for a second term. Not wishing to drop out of politics, however, Knight declared his candidacy for Knowland's Senate seat with the blessing of the same party figures who had bulldogged him out of the governor's race.[4]

The intraparty acrimony created by the "Big Switch" between Knowland and Knight sowed the seeds for the defeat of both candidates. This episode and the Republican rout in general have been examined by a number of authors.[5] Most of the significant details and assessments in these works have been corroborated by subsequent oral histories provided by members of Knowland's family, Knowland and Knight associates, and other knowledgeable and prominent figures.[6] There is, therefore, no need here to reconsider those Republican woes in the gubernatorial contest. What needs to be emphasized instead is the importance of Knowland's campaign in marshaling the state's conservatives into a movement that eventually had great political influence. Previous works have clearly acknowledged the strong impact California conservatives had on Goldwater's successful quest for the Republican presidential nomination in 1964 and on Reagan's landslide victory in the 1966 governor's race. These studies, however, have not adequately recognized, if at all, that despite Knowland's loss, his campaign gave many conservatives their initial sense of unity and mission, thus providing the spark for ensuing political activism and electoral successes.[7]

The conservative movement that impelled the Knowland crusade has been overlooked due to the failure of its principal cause and candidate and because it lacked the vast legions of support that later made it so formidable. The movement of course gained strength as an opposition force in the early and mid-1960s in California and elsewhere, as conservative Republicans rallied against the liberal Democratic administrations of Presidents Kennedy and Johnson. During this time conservatives also fired salvos at the man who defeated Knowland, the liberal Democrat Pat Brown, whose "leftish" leanings they had long assailed.[8] The "dictatorial" and "socialistic" governance of these liberals provided far better targets for right-wing wrath than had the moderate Eisenhower administration. Nevertheless, the origins of the conservative movement in California can be traced to the jousting between Republican factions in 1957 and 1958, when Knowland directly challenged the Modern Republicanism of President Eisenhower by choosing to run for governor on a right-to-work platform.

Right-wing California Republicans in 1958 coalesced around "Big Bill" Knowland the man and his staunch antilabor conservatism. Of paramount importance was his adamant advocacy of a right-to-work law for the state, to make union membership there voluntary. Proclaiming that "as a free people we must always be on guard against the concentration of excessive power," Knowland contended that labor unions had become the tyrannical bastions of corrupt bosses. To break this oppression he believed that "free men and women" should have the "basic civil right" of choosing whether they wished to join a union or not.[9] In framing this issue in terms of "freedom versus tyranny," the senator established the clarion call that would rally California conservatives, especially in Los Angeles and Orange counties, for years to come.

Under the tutelage of his conservative father, "Billy" displayed a predilection for right-wing causes at the age of twelve by giving speeches for Republican presidential candidate Warren Harding. As a young man he served as a state legislator, and at the age of thirty he became the youngest member of the Republican National Committee. After Earl Warren selected Big Bill to serve out the remainder of Johnson's term, Knowland went on to win his Senate seat by a healthy margin in 1946. Following the "fall" of China, Knowland became the most vociferous congressional critic of Truman's Far Eastern policy, and became widely known as the "Senator from Formosa." He scored an impressive reelection victory in the 1952 primary by cross-filing and receiving the majority of the Democratic vote.

While in the Senate, Knowland became an admirer of fellow conservative Robert Taft. The most prominent Republican in the Senate, Taft had won reelection in 1950 despite intense opposition from organized labor, which he drew on account of his sponsorship of the Taft–Hartley Act. Knowland succeeded Taft as Senate majority leader upon the latter's death from cancer in 1953 and became one of the leading Senate opponents of "Big Labor" and the closed shop. When Knowland made clear he would run for governor, he used Taft's own words in describing the challenge to rout "the labor bosses who have marked me for political extinction."[10] Therefore, while many moderate and liberal Republicans were further disappointed when the senator declared he would campaign for governor on a right-to-work plank, few could have been surprised.

Republicans of the moderate Eisenhower ilk considered the right-to-work matter to be moribund. Moreover, they viewed the senator's parsimonious approach to fiscal concerns and his opposition to the president's "ultra-internationalism" in foreign affairs as passé.[11] Eisenhower himself believed that in addition to being ideologically primitive, Knowland was a dolt. In the senator's case, the president noted in his diary, "there seems to be no final answer to the question 'How stupid can you get?' "[12] Differences and disdain notwithstanding, shortly before the senator's departure from Washington to begin his gubernatorial campaign, Eisenhower praised him in an open letter for his "tireless efforts . . . and devotion in the service of the nation." Knowland returned the compliment in an open letter to the president, and, as if priming himself for the hustings, added: "I know how deeply you believe that human freedom is a greater force than totalitarian tyranny. We shall not stand idly by," he concluded, "while freedom is being nibbled away bit by bit."[13]

When Knowland arrived in California in late August of 1958 to officially launch his campaign, he trailed badly in the polls. His poor standing stemmed in part from the resentment among the many Republicans who would not forgive him for forcing Knight out of seeking a second full term. This problem, however, was compounded by Knowland's determination to base his campaign on the right-to-work issue, which took the form of a ballot initiative known as Proposition 18. This decision further alienated liberal and moderate Republicans, and even some conservatives, because it portended a break from the generally progressive and pragmatic policies that had, with one exception, kept the governorship in Republican hands since 1910.[14] Knowland's attack on unions also assured that he would get few Democratic votes, which in turn assured his defeat, because registered Democrats outnumbered Republicans by roughly a three-to-two margin. The senator's only victory would be a moral one, in that he held fast to his convictions.

Knowland might have escaped this fate if a group of prominent California businessmen had followed through on their desire to have a right-to-work initiative on the state ballot in 1956. Led by Charles Jones, head of the Richfield Oil Company and an Eisenhower crony, these businessmen did begin an effort to get the initiative on the ballot. Jones, however, soon reported to his associates that the president had personally told him he would rather not have to take a position on the issue during his reelection campaign. Yielding to Eisenhower's wish, this group decided to hold off on the initiative until the 1958 election.[15]

In late 1957, polls revealed that Californians favored a right-to-work measure by almost a two-to-one margin.[16] On that evidence it appeared to be a propitious time for Knowland's gubernatorial candidacy. Using polls and other calculations, some state Republican officials predicted that Knowland would defeat his likely Democratic opponent, state Attorney General Pat Brown, by more than 400,000 votes.[17] Nevertheless, at virtually the same time leaders of the Republican State Central Committee presciently warned that "as an extreme conservative with views increasingly repugnant to labor," Knowland would be hard-pressed to "muster the broad popular support" needed to win the governorship.[18] An eleventh-hour attempt to head off Knowland's candidacy in favor of Knight, this admonition, and others echoing it, failed to dissuade the senator from his gubernatorial ambition.[19]

Knowland declared his intention to run for governor in early October of 1957, and Brown followed suit shortly thereafter. Knowland's announcement speech was replete with old Republican platitudes, and the liberal Brown wasted no time in attacking the senator as a "modern McKinley . . . who has evidenced in all his acts and statements a reactionism [sic] that even the Republican Party has long since passed." Conservatives, however, dismissed Brown's words as a familiar liberal tirade against a pillar of true Republicanism. Reflecting this view, the *Los Angeles Times* praised Knowland for his "integrity in his convictions, his courage in action, and his intelligence," which made him "one of the nation's outstanding men."[20]

Knowland's thinly concealed presidential aspirations indicate he indeed thought he was one of the country's "outstanding men." He did not, then, conceive of losing the governor's race, even though he had been away from state politics—and the state itself—for over twelve years. In calculating his chances of winning the governorship, Knowland overestimated his own popularity and underestimated that of the gregarious and amiable Brown. As one journalist noted, the senator suffered from "Potomac myopia—the notion that years of prestigious activity in Washington can be translated into voting strength back in California."[21] This "affliction" doubtless contributed to Knowland's decision that he could afford to conduct his campaign largely in absentia until two months before the election. While Brown tirelessly glad-handed his way around the state and picked up labor-union and other important backing, Knowland was confident that his image, cause, and faithful followers would create a ground swell of support that he could secure in the waning weeks of his gubernatorial quest.

Symbolized by a bus tour led by Knowland's wife and two daughters, the "Rollin' for Knowland" campaign skidded into a steady decline in early 1958. Problems arose for the senator on two fronts. First, Knowland and his staff did not anticipate that organized labor would make the greatest political effort in its history (up to that time) to defeat Proposition 18 and elect Brown. As Brown later recalled, "[w]e didn't have to worry about fundraising drives"; the money flowed "in buckets." Led by the AFL-CIO (the two groups had merged in 1955) and its Committee on Political Education (COPE), the movement against the right-to-work initiative began to slowly sway voter sentiment to its position, taking support from Knowland in the process.[22] Second, the lingering animosity of important Knight backers, who were generally against Proposition 18, hurt the Knowland campaign's ability to raise funds. Appeals to Republican businessmen for "generous financial assistance" to help in the senator's "crusade" against organized labor often went unanswered, especially in northern California, where pro-union sentiments prevailed.[23] While support from conservative businessmen in southern California proved strong, a "considerable number" of their moderate counterparts in the San Francisco Bay region—Brown's home territory—were accused of being "lazy and indifferent," and of "muffing their job."[24] Reflective of the general ideological division between Republicans in the state's two distinct regions, the breach between northern and southern Republican businessmen, and the intense opposition from labor, did not bode well for prospects of a Knowland victory in November.

Confirmation of Knowland's electoral problems came in the June primary. This contest served as a reliable indicator of the candidates' chances of winning in the general election due to California's cross-filing system. Since Brown and Knowland faced no other serious contenders, the primary would clearly signify which of the two held the early advantage. Brown out-polled Knowland by an eyebrow-raising 662,050 votes, which included 22 percent of the Republican vote. (Knowland won support from 14 percent of the Democrats.)[25] The senator, who had appeared to be a solid favorite in the fall of 1957, now faced the fight of his political life. Knowland's poor showing so alarmed his zealous supporters that the rhetoric of his campaign and that for Proposition 18 would in the ensuing months escalate to a fire-eating pitch, redolent of a messianic crusade.

The *Los Angeles Times* sought to raise voter concern two days after the primary with the alacritous declaration that "we do not propose to stand like a vegetable" while California knuckles under to union domination.[26] The *Times* had long led the considerable opposition to organized labor in Los Angeles, especially since 1910, when labor radicals blew up the newspaper's main building. Having thrown his weight behind an unsuccessful right-to-work effort in 1944, the *Times*'s influential political columnist, Kyle Palmer, promoted both Proposition 18 and Knowland. Echoing the senator's "freedom versus tyranny" theme, the *Times* declared in September of 1957 that "voluntary unionism . . . is as fundamental a right as is the right to worship God without forced affiliation with a religious group." Editorialized litanies of this sort, along with apocalyptic warnings about the consequences of a Brown victory, became frequent as the general election approached. Describing Brown as an "obsequious yes-man of union political bosses" bent on controlling California, a front-page editorial shortly before the election touted Knowland as "the only man with the nerves and staying power to prevent the catastrophe."[27]

In conservative Orange County, the Santa Ana *Register* went beyond editorial promotion of Knowland and Proposition 18. Owned by the ardent libertarian Raymond Cyrus Hoiles, the *Register* covered the Brown campaign scantily, and then only through the comments of his critics, while Knowland and other supporters of the right-to-work initiative received exclusively favorable reportage almost daily.[28] Though less shrill in tone than the *Times,* the *Register*'s editorial praise of Proposition 18 proved more relentless. Due to his belief that even representative government constituted a form of tyranny, Hoiles had less enthusiasm for Knowland. The senator's thematic emphasis on the sanctity of individual freedom, however, made him and other like-minded politicos useful agents in Hoiles's reactionary and libertarian cause.

Some conservative religious figures contended that the question of freedom and the right to work in a certain sense transcended politics. The Reverend Edward W. Greenfield of San Jacinto argued that "when the right of the individual to determine whether or not he wishes to join a union is taken from him, he ceases to be a free soul and becomes a puppet."[29] Reflecting Greenfield's concern over the supposed spiritual detriment of compulsory unionism, the Reverend James W. Fifield of Los Angeles thundered that "the sovereignty of the individual soul ... is in the right of freedom, under God, through voluntary unionism." Fifield concluded his jeremiad, however, with an invocation of the sacred in the secular realm of American political culture. To deny an individual the freedom of choosing whether or not to join a union, he asserted, "is to renounce the idea of democracy and prove ourselves unworthy of the faith of the founding fathers."[30]

Seeing themselves as devout followers of "constitutionalism" (i.e., limited government), California conservatives often cited the maxims of the founders to legitimate their causes. In support of his right-to-work campaign Knowland was particularly fond of quoting Thomas Jefferson's opposition to "every form of tyranny." Though this aphorism could apply to the "excessive" power of big business as easily as it could to labor unions, the senator did not choose to question the imperious motives that regimented most corporate managers behind the drive for the open shop. This oversight stemmed from the conservatives' preoccupation with sacrosanct "free market" capitalism, in which restrictions of almost any sort violated the Constitution by infringing on prescribed individual and corporate rights and liberties. A vulgarization of the founders' intent,[31] the impetuous defense of unrestrained capitalism as a defining principle of "Americanism" took on new urgency for California conservatives in 1958 due to their heightened sense of peril from "socialist" labor leaders.

Among the labor "dictators" for whom Brown was a "willing captive," United Auto Workers (UAW) president Walter Reuther loomed as the greatest threat to "free industry."[32] Shortly before a major investigation of corruption in labor unions in 1957 by a Senate committee chaired by John D. McClellan of Arkansas, Barry Goldwater declared that "Reuther and the UAW are a more dangerous menace than *Sputnik* or anything Soviet Russia might do to America."[33] The Senate investigation, however, found nothing to substantiate Goldwater's charges against Reuther, but did expose corruption in certain unions, including the UAW. Corrupt or not, Reuther's great success in the effort to secure the union shop and empower labor leadership during and since the New Deal made him the chief architect of the "New

Slavery" targeted by the emancipatory Proposition 18. Full-page newspaper ads suggesting that mandatory membership in unions constituted bondage were intended in part to evoke an image of Knowland engaged in a Lincoln-like mission, fighting for "the priceless gifts of freedom and opportunity, won and bequeathed by our forefathers. . . ."[34]

In keeping with the invocations of the founders and the Constitution, Knowland had introduced a "bill of rights for labor" in the Senate in January of 1958 during the McClellan Committee investigation. Overwhelmingly rejected in a Senate vote, Knowland's "bill of rights," like his "voluntary unionism" crusade, ultimately aimed to undercut labor leadership and union bargaining power. Depicted by his political enemies as the candidate of "wealthy, behind-the-scenes special interests,"[35] Knowland seemingly added veracity to that assertion with his Senate proposal. Though occasionally overstated, the case against Knowland and the right-to-work initiative was effectively made through numerous newspaper and billboard ads, and labor newsletters and political speeches. The senator, therefore, had a nearly impossible task when it came to winning over rank-and-file union members in sufficient numbers for victory.

Though Knowland faced a daunting challenge in wooing labor votes, the Brown camp feared that the McClellan Committee might come to California to hold hearings before the election. In a letter to Democrat John F. Kennedy, chair of the Senate Labor and Public Welfare Committee, Brown aide Roger Kent asked the senator to do what ever he could to make sure the McClellan Committee steered clear of California. "The only thing that could heat up the somewhat dormant labor issue," Kent declared, "would be a circus by the McClellan Committee which would be vastly overplayed by the Republican press." The committee did not make a preelection appearance in the state. In August, Republicans and a coterie of conservative Democrats narrowly defeated a labor reform bill sponsored by Kennedy, which Knowland had opposed in favor of his bill of rights. Kennedy then circulated one of his speeches on the "labor issue" to prominent California Democrats to help them show the "unreasonableness of those who opposed a basically strong bill." Intended to quell Republican attempts to associate Democrats with union corruption, the speech also gave the Brown campaign another pointed issue with which to needle Knowland.[36]

Acknowledging that Knowland faced an uphill battle against Brown and organized labor, Raymond Moley, a onetime New Deal reformer turned conservative journalist, compared the senator's predicament to that of Robert Taft in 1950. While in California in October on a "fact-finding trip," Moley contended that Taft's success in his fight against labor eight years earlier showed that Knowland could still win. "The issues are very much the same," he stated.[37] Moley, however, ignored the many differences between the two campaigns: Taft had solid support from his party, whereas Knowland's candidacy had split California Republicans; and Taft's opponent was not as popular with labor and other middle-class voters in Ohio as the avuncular Brown proved to be in his state. Furthermore, Taft's campaign organization carried out its tasks like a well-oiled machine while Knowland's sputtered due to party disunity. Finally, 1950, in stark contrast to 1958, was a Republican year.[38]

Painfully aware of his party's division and grim electoral prospects in 1958, President Eisenhower nonetheless had to attempt to foster unity and optimism by campaigning for his fellow Republicans. Though most of the party's right-wingers had attacked him for retreating from "true Republicanism," many of them looked forward to an appearance with the president on the campaign trail, hoping to gain political mileage from his radiant smile and great popularity. Still, the ripples of disagreement among the party factions early in the Eisenhower years had now grown to swells, producing a schism that could not be ameliorated in an election year by a facade of smiles and rhetorical back-patting. The president would find no better example of the problems besetting the party than in California, where the conservative periodical *Human Events* had declared Eisenhower Republicanism "dead" with the advent of the Knowland campaign.[39]

Eisenhower arrived in Los Angeles on October 20 and received a tumultuous welcome from a huge crowd that lined downtown streets as his motorcade drove by. As he made his way through the city he passed two billboard ads, one erected by the pro-Knowland and the other by the pro-Knight forces, which linked them to contradictory positions on Proposition 18. After a brief conference with the two candidates the president attempted to alleviate the divisiveness of the Knight–Knowland feud by appealing to Republicans for an end to the "family bickering—fancied or real."[40] The two men responded by giving the appearance that their differences had been resolved as they cordially hovered around the president for photo opportunities during his Los Angeles visit.

In a major speech to a large cheering and stamping crowd of GOP faithful, Eisenhower delivered an unusually scathing partisan assault on "self-styled liberal" Democrats and their "radical" agenda. "Either we choose left-wing government," he declared, "or sensible forward-looking government." The president's charge that the Democratic Party "is hopelessly split—right down the middle," however, applied as much, if not more, to the Republicans in 1958, especially in California. In addition, while his repeated emphasis on "forward-looking" government served as an explicit attack on the Democratic "extremists," it implicitly assailed the reactionary right, with which Knowland had become associated. Eisenhower's oration, though strongly partisan, was largely a plea for the politics of moderation.[41]

The president did in part reflect Knowland's concern about labor in a speech in San Francisco the next day by calling for a law to "fumigate" dishonest unions.[42] While he desired to purge unions of corrupt influences, Eisenhower maintained his expedient election-year position that the right-to-work matter should be left to the states to decide. (Vice President Nixon maintained the same position.) The president remained above the fray while other moderate Republicans challenged the need for right-to-work laws. RNC Chairman Meade Alcorn had told a National Press Club Luncheon in September that "aggressive advocacy of that kind of legislation is doing something bad for labor and the country." A few days after the President's California visit, Labor Secretary James P. Mitchell not only questioned the wisdom of such laws but stated that Reuther, while too active politically, "has been a pretty good labor leader."[43] For conservatives, Mitchell's assessment of Reuther doubtless attested further to the apostasy of Modern Republicanism.

In spite of Mitchell's lukewarm compliment to Reuther, the RNC had decided to make the labor leader an issue in 1958 by depicting him as the dominant force in the "ultraliberal wing" of the Democratic Party. In making this effort the RNC hoped to divert the electorate's attention from the lingering recession and other economic problems.[44] Like Goldwater, however, California conservatives viewed the UAW president as a real danger to democracy, not as a convenient distraction. Believing the California Right's opposition to Reuther to be reactionary, Knight described to a reporter an early August meeting with "two hundred of the richest men in the state, grilling me on why I'm not supporting Bill Knowland and the right-to-work." The governor stated that these men expressed a deluded fear that "if Pat Brown is elected, Walter Reuther will be running the state." This "ultra-conservative palaver" reinforced Knight's belief that many California Republicans "are living in the nineteenth century," out of touch with modern realities.[45]

While perhaps not dreadfully worried about Reuther himself, several major national corporations joined in the attack on him in California by actively backing Proposition 18.[46] The first and largest company to take such a stand, General Electric (GE) announced in mid-September that it would back the right-to-work initiative with a series of newspaper ads. A vice president at GE's regional headquarters in San Francisco declared that the consensus among the company's managers throughout the state was that open-shop laws had helped rather than hurt unions.[47] In a more urgent and foreboding tone, GE president and Eisenhower consultant Ralph Cordiner exhorted businessmen to become more active politically in an effort to thwart union ideologies, which resulted in "damage to progress and a withering of freedom."[48]

His ardent defense of capitalism and individual freedom notwithstanding, actor Ronald Reagan, then GE's most well known employee, opposed Proposition 18. Host of *General Electric Theater* and unabashed promoter of the company's corporate image, Reagan lent his name to a statement circulated by the Screen Actors Guild (SAG) in early 1958 imploring its members not to sign petitions seeking to place the right-to-work initiative on the ballot.[49] Reagan never actually spoke out against Proposition 18 during the 1958 campaign, as that would have glaringly conflicted with GE's position. Not wholly supportive of unions, Reagan did express some reservations about "big" labor unions during his time with GE, but was far more concerned about the threat from "big government."[50] Therefore, during his eight years as GE's television host and roving ambassador (1954–1962), Reagan adroitly honed and polished his attack on the "totalitarian" liberal state. This diatribe, which became known as "The Speech," would later endear him to the legions of the California Right during the height of liberal activism in the mid-1960s.[51]

A significant number of Reagan's key supporters in his 1966 gubernatorial campaign, including those who convinced him to run, had worked hard in the Knowland crusade eight years earlier. In addition, 30 of the initial 42 members of Reagan's southern California finance committee were contributors to the Proposition 18 effort.[52] Integrally involved in Goldwater's presidential campaign in California as well—along with numerous other former Knowland backers—Los Angeles businessmen A.C. (Cy) Rubel, Henry Salvatori, Holmes Tuttle, and Edward Mills formed the "Friends of Ronald Reagan" in 1965 and personally persuaded him to challenge Pat Brown. These men also handled the finances for this effort. In 1958 they all served as Republican fund raisers for Knowland and the right-to-work initiative.[53] Mills also chaired a committee offering $10,000 to anyone who could prove that Proposition 18 would be detrimental to union members.[54] Strong support for the right-to-work measure could still be found in southern California in 1966. George Christopher, Reagan's opponent in the Republican primary, recalled that "you'd be surprised at how many people [there] still wanted to discuss that [issue] and make that a part of the campaign. . . ." Recognizing the right-to-work matter as a political albatross, Reagan made clear during the campaign that "I have been and remain unalterably opposed to right-to-work laws. I think we have a right as free men to join a union. . . ."[55]

In Orange County, one of the few counties in which Proposition 18 passed, many moderate Republicans were so alienated by the Knowland–Knight feud that they abandoned their active roles in the party. Zealous arch-conservatives came to fill the power vacuum over the next few years.[56] Becoming a major player in Republican politics as of 1958, Western theme park owner Walter Knott headed the "Yes On 18" office in Orange County and avidly backed Knowland (and later Goldwater and Reagan). Shortly after the election, Knott and a few other conservative Orange County businessmen formed the "California Free-Enterprise Association" (CFEA), which extolled the virtues of unimpeded capitalism and attacked big government through the mass circulation of pamphlets.[57] Using buzzwords such as "the great free enterprise system" and "states' rights," the CFEA and similar organizations in Orange and Los Angeles counties helped make the conservatives the dominant wing in the California Republican Party by the mid-1960s.

A number of Republican women active in later conservative campaigns also held important positions in the Knowland organization and/or the right-to-work effort. Among this group were Cecil Kenyon, president of the California Federation of Republican Women, Lucile Hosmer, head of the Federation's northern division, and Gladys O'Donnell, the Federation's leader in southern California and cochairperson of Knowland's campaign in that region. Hosmer, who along with O'Donnell traveled around the state as part of the "Rollin' for Knowland" tour, later stated that she and other members of the Women's Federation "fought like tigers" to keep Proposition 18 out of the senator's campaign. Marjorie Benedict, another prominent player in the Federation's northern division and an ardent Knowland backer, recalled that some of the southern California women "were very strong for the right-to-work [initiative]," and did not realize the negative consequences of their zealous support. Kenyon, whose husband was on the executive board of the Southern California Edison Company, which actively backed Proposition 18, "was like a steamroller" in dealing with dissenters and effectively marshaled these women behind Knowland and the initiative. As it would in subsequent campaigns, the Women's Federation, the largest Republican volunteer group in the state, played a major role in getting out the conservative vote in the 1958 election.[58]

Helen Knowland, the candidate's wife, who had led the "Rollin' for Knowland" campaign in the months leading up to the primary, maintained her efforts to convince voters to support the senator as the race wound down. Despite her best intentions she caused problems for her husband in September when she distributed about 500 pamphlets that viciously attacked Reuther. Written by Joseph Kamp, an arch-conservative fire-eater from Connecticut, the pamphlet labeled the UAW president a Marxist and further savaged his character by charging that "he is a ruthless, reckless, lawless labor goon." The circulation of the anti-Reuther tract embarrassed the senator, for Kamp had been jailed for contempt of Congress and widely condemned by prominent Republicans, including the late Robert Taft.[59] In mid-October Helen Knowland made another tactical blunder by sending a letter to a number of influential state Republicans that vilified Knight by calling him a spineless "tool of the labor bosses." Made public ten days before the election, the letter further alienated party liberals and moderates from conservatives. In the wake of this disclosure, the senator emphatically reaffirmed his support for "the whole [Republican] ticket, including Governor Knight," and claimed the letter did not reflect his own opinions.[60]

When it came to his electoral chances the senator's own conservative beliefs proved lethal enough in themselves, for the primary results and the polls that followed showed him well behind Pat Brown long before his wife's indiscretions. Few would dispute Knowland's contention that his campaign positions stemmed from conviction, not expediency.[61] His refusal to abandon his right-to-work stance—even when it became baldly evident that it was a losing cause—attested to this. His certainty that the cherished American principle of freedom was in peril compelled him to stay the course on the right-to-work issue. The senator, therefore, viewed his task as a patriotic mission and himself as a duty-bound crusader. Elevating her husband to the status of earthly savior, Helen Knowland proclaimed in a campaign circular that "we should get down on our knees and pray with thankfulness that there is such a man . . . to awaken the people to the danger [from labor bosses] around us."[62] Despite this and other efforts to frame the election of the senator as a matter of the utmost civic urgency, he and his devotees could not rally the necessary electoral forces to win this battle of Armageddon, as both he and Proposition 18 went down to crushing defeats in November. Brown received 59.8 percent of the vote to Knowland's 40.2 percent; voters rejected the right-to-work initiative in almost exact proportion to the vote for Brown. Knight fared only slightly better than Knowland, garnering 43 percent of the vote in his loss to Democrat Claire Engle.

In the aftermath of the Republican disaster in California, the animosity between the two party factions became more evident and the geographical division more pronounced. For example, the *San Francisco Chronicle,* in a defense of Eisenhower Republicanism, declared in an editorial assailing the Knowland campaign that an "extreme" Republican group, "largely Southern Californian . . . decided over a year ago to take California back into the 19th Century, away from the 'modern Republicanism' that the members of that group so heartily loathe."[63] As opposed to seeing themselves as reactionaries, the Knowland conservatives believed they held dear the timeless and tested principles of limited government and individual liberty as espoused by the founders. In this light, William F. Buckley Jr. denounced Eisenhower Republicanism as "fundamentally . . . a retreat from an explicit expression of the meaning of American society."[64]

While the GOP suffered huge losses in congressional races across the country in 1958, Barry Goldwater emerged victorious and emboldened, intent on leading his party back to its "true conservative" roots. The senator won a landslide victory over his Democratic opponent, Governor Ernest McFarland, by running as the candidate who would not "surrender Arizona to Reuther." In a campaign laden with Western-frontier hyperbole (not unlike Knowland's), the *Phoenix Gazette* warned that if "Big labor . . . can tear apart Goldwater, it can frighten all lesser figures into bondage."[65] After winning the *High Noon* showdown against the supposed candidate of the labor bosses, the senator became the leading spokesperson for conservative Republicans and began to fill the void created by Knowland's fall in California. More charismatic than Knowland, the Arizonan made numerous speeches in California in 1959 and 1960, particularly in the Southland, and was a leading party fund raiser.[66] In addition, in January of 1960 he began writing a syndicated political column for the *Los Angeles Times*. After the defeat of the erstwhile conservative Richard Nixon in the 1960 presidential race, support for a 1964 Goldwater presidential bid swelled in southern California.

Concurrent with the rise of Goldwater, the John Birch Society (JBS) began to attract a significant number of southern Californians soon after it was established in December of 1958. Dedicated primarily to fighting an alleged threat from communist subversives in America who operated under the guise of liberalism, the society's founder, Robert Welch, aimed to mobilize "more manpower and more resources than . . . Reuther's COPE," to assist conservative Republicans in future elections.[67] Numerous other right-wing organizations flourished in southern California, including Dr. Frederick C. Schwarz's Christian Anti-Communism Crusade, which began to receive large financial contributions for its efforts in 1958.[68] By the early 1960s, Orange and Los Angeles counties were major urban strongholds for the JBS in particular and right-wing groups in general. The more outlandish and extreme contentions of these organizations angered and put off some California conservatives, but the Republican right evinced steadfast ideological unity in its fierce and uncompromising anticommunism and great antipathy toward the liberal state and its "encroachments" on individual freedom.

Conservatives had long believed that modern liberalism fostered a coercive authoritarian state and circumscribed personal liberty; but this notion gained greater salience in California in 1958, for Knowland and his adamant backers perceived a rising threat from "dictatorial" labor leaders who had been and continued to be empowered by the liberal state. In stressing that the right-to-work issue came down to a matter of "tyranny versus freedom," Knowland framed the central figurative concern for the state's conservatives in 1958 and for succeeding years. Of particular note, this theme could be found on billboards and in literature in the Proposition 14 crusade to repeal the Rumford Fair Housing Act in 1964. The "freedom from forced housing" campaign rallied opposition to the Rumford Act, which was depicted as "a giant step toward socialism."[69] A conservative cause célèbre equal to that of the right-to-work campaign, Proposition 14 passed by a two-to-one margin, with widespread support among voters of both parties. The success of this initiative revealed the incipient wave of resentment in the electorate toward the alleged intrusions and excesses of liberalism, a mounting disaffection that candidate Ronald Reagan deftly tapped two years later.

After his reelection, Goldwater broadened the application of Knowland's motif, which helped solidify his image as the leading conservative spokesman. He attacked authoritarian power in general, but particularly the liberal state, and, like Knowland, extolled the "ancient and tested truths that guided our Republic through its earliest days. . . ." Freedom, he declared, "depends on effective restraints against the accumulation of power in a single authority."[70] Sober yet "ruggedly" dynamic, Goldwater and his message created a juggernaut of support in southern California that eventually secured the 1964 Republican presidential nomination for him. Similarly, Reagan, a smoother and more reassuring orator than Goldwater, reaped political capital for his gubernatorial run by dwelling on a single theme in his speeches from 1960 to 1965. In assailing liberalism he invariably averred: "The issue of our times is totalitarianism versus freedom."[71] Beginning with Knowland, then, and later assiduously intoned by Goldwater and Reagan, "freedom versus tyranny" became the shibboleth of the California conservative movement.

Though a Republican calamity, the 1958 election proved far from a total loss for California conservatives. Knowland did fail to slay the dragon of "Big Labor" and its "captive" candidate, but his attempt to do so provided a strong sense of unity and patriotic purpose for conservatives and vivified their demonology. In addition, the senator's candidacy, combined with the campaign for Proposition 18, made for the first true conservative crusade in California of the post–World War II era. The fact that this crusade failed electorally and split the state's Republicans should not obscure its importance in coalescing the nascent core of the movement that later brought success to Goldwater and Reagan, as well as to other candidates and causes.

Three

"A Little Piece of America"

While Knowland took a pummeling at the polls in 1958, he garnered 54 percent of the vote in Orange County, where Proposition 18 passed as well. Those results reflected the county's longstanding conservative tradition. Achieving its independence from Los Angeles County in 1889, Orange County did not vote for a Democrat for president until 1932, but even then Franklin Roosevelt won by only 1,200 votes. Though he triumphed again in 1936, no other Democratic presidential candidate has won there since. With the exception of the brief Democratic ascendancy during the Roosevelt years, the Republican Party has dominated the county's politics. Orange County Republicans, however, were not uniformly conservative. In fact, during World War II and the decade after, county Republicans did not stand out as being conspicuously right-wing when compared to county party members in the 1960s. Sparked by the revolt against Modern Republicanism, the shift to an overwhelmingly conservative trend began in the latter half of the 1950s, as the county changed rapidly from a rural orange grove and farming region to an urban industrial center.[1]

The rapid population growth in Los Angeles during and after World War II eventually spilled over into Orange County, as both home buyers and industries sought cheaper land. In addition, as Los Angeles became more congested, people were drawn to the county by the utopian images of a trouble-free, healthy and wholesome life, which attracted mostly white middle-class families to the largely suburban communities that took shape during the 1950s.[2] The completion of the Santa Ana Freeway in 1955 (the same year Disneyland opened) further spurred the population boom, helping to make Orange the fastest growing county in the United States during the 1950s and 1960s. By the mid-1960s, nearly one-third of the 400,000 employees in the county worked in the manufacturing sector, and more than half of these individuals worked for aerospace and defense contractors. This reality, as one observer noted, made the county's communities an aggregate " 'federal city,' whose economic destiny hangs on [government] decisions about contracts and programs."[3] The emergence of Orange

County as an important aerospace and defense industry locale added to the Southland's metropolitan-military complex, which ran from Los Angeles down to San Diego.

Despite the county's rapid industrial and population growth during the first two decades of the postwar era, its pervasive suburbanization amid pastoral open space provided an environment that helped sustain provincial attitudes among its citizenry. An architect and planner responsible for the "garden style" development of Irvine and other Orange County communities, William Pereira believed that county homeowners of the 1950s and 1960s were "staking out" a claim, much like earlier pioneers. He declared that if "a man can own his own home on his own land he thinks he can control his destiny. It amounts to his holding an agrarian outlook in an urban environment." Echoing Pereira on the importance of property in the Orange County homeowner's worldview, Walter Knott observed that "[p]eople get out here and associate with people who understand this conservative philosophy. They become homeowners ... [acquiring] a little piece of America."[4]

Largely detached from the increasing urban problems and clutter of Los Angeles, Orange County's golden hills and splendid beaches appeared to be tailor-made for those seeking the American dream on the secure edge of a vibrant urban frontier, and whose aspirations culminated in land and home ownership. The latter—the suburban symbol of having "made it"—provided some semblance of personal dominion in an increasingly impersonal world dominated by bureaucratic government and powerful corporations.[5] Attendant to the sanctity of property, its acquisition and development proved paramount and elemental to the entrepreneurial spirit of the county's residents. In this latter-day frontier boom, federal and state government largesse contributed greatly to Orange County's economic vitality. When it came, however, to the other side of the coin of governance (i.e., taxes and government authority), protests reverberated throughout the county's valleys.

With the exception of certain ultraconservative pamphlets and books, the sharpest diatribes against the alleged evils of "The State" came from the Santa Ana *Register* and its arch-libertarian publisher, Raymond Cyrus Hoiles, a self-described "radical for freedom." Looking as though he had stepped out of Grant Wood's painting, "American Gothic," "RC" purchased the *Register* in 1935 and proceeded to create controversy in and outside the county with his firm opposition to virtually every facet of government. Evident in his adolescence during the laissez-faire 1890s, Hoiles's strong entrepreneurial drive probably accounted in part for his ardent libertarianism, but certain authors influenced him as well. Referring to the wellspring of his strident views, he once remarked, "I have in my library the masters of the ages who are always with me."[6] Just who these "masters" were, however, is unclear, because he usually did not cite literary works in his columns except for tracts by contemporary libertarian authors; but few if any of these could be categorized as classic.[7] Hoiles appears to have been influenced by prominent libertarians of the 1920s and 1930s such as Albert Jay Nock, whose views of the state as criminal and totalitarian abound in his anti–New Deal polemic, *Our Enemy, the State.*[8]

Whatever the case, Hoiles's observations on the state certainly jibed with Nock's, for Hoiles believed that taxation amounted to robbery committed under the guise of legitimacy by "tyrannical" government. He once said of the chief architect of this "tyranny," Franklin Roosevelt, that the world would have been better off if he had never learned to read or write.[9] In addition to his opposition to, among other things, Social Security, the United Nations, and the minimum wage, Hoiles fulminated against public schools and child labor laws. Of the latter he once proclaimed: "Give him a pick and shovel and let him get started."[10] While a smattering of readers doubtless subscribed wholeheartedly to Hoiles's antiquated libertarianism, it is likely that far more harbored the "queer, ghostly feeling" of the reader who declared that "Hoiles is [often] not arguing with me but with my great grandparents."[11]

During the 1960s, the increasingly moderate *Los Angeles Times*—a moderation directed by Otis Chandler after he replaced his more conservative father, Norman, as publisher in 1960—gained more readers percentage-wise in Orange County, but the *Register*'s circulation increased greatly with the county's population boom.[12] Hoiles's invective notwithstanding, most residents, new and old, understood and accepted that growth created the need for more streets, sewer systems, and other public works projects, and that taxes were required to pay for and maintain them. Nevertheless, as one prominent county politician stated, for many middle-class homeowners, who had "too many debts already," the *Register* helped inculcate anti-government views by incessantly labeling government officials as "dictators" whose main purpose was to add to one's indebtedness.[13]

The *Register*'s libertarian fusillades likely had the strongest impact on opinions about social spending by the federal government, particularly on the urban social problems targeted by Lyndon Johnson's Great Society programs. At least up to the mid-1960s, the many problems of big cities were for the most part as removed from Orange County as the neon lights of Hollywood and the impoverished streets of Watts and certain other minority areas of Los Angeles. Mexican Americans, the county's largest minority group, made up only 5.8 percent of its population, while blacks accounted for an almost-invisible six-tenths of 1 percent.[14]

Minorities, especially blacks, had never been welcome in Los Angeles's suburbs or Orange County. In addition to the discriminating practices of white homeowners' associations, the Ku Klux Klan in the 1920s terrorized blacks throughout the region, and in 1924 briefly ran Anaheim, Orange County's largest city. The county grew rapidly during the Second World War, as conservative Midwestern Republicans, along with Democrats from the segregated South, flooded into the booming region. White neighborhoods throughout the Southland, with the help of realtors and developers—and with the countenance of judges and the Federal Housing Authority—maintained restrictive race covenants to keep minorities out. In 1948 the Supreme Court ruled against restrictive covenants. Nevertheless, as urban theorist Mike Davis has stated, white homeowner activists continued to collaborate with realtors and developers "to plan postwar racial and class segregation in the *Leave it to Beaver* suburbs."[15]

Consequently, for Orange County's white middle class, minorities were essentially out of sight and out of mind, but, due to federal and state policies, not out of their wallets. This perception contributed to the resentment behind the white backlash, which played a major role in the conservative ascendancy in California and in Reagan's gubernatorial victory. Though widespread, the politics of resentment that grew out of the white backlash played especially well in Orange County, due in part to the relative absence of urban maladies, though this did not preclude a pronounced fear of their encroachment. In addition, the attacks on big government by Goldwater and Reagan, and their emphasis on the virtues of self-made success, could not help but spread antistatist views and increase their legitimacy in the fertile conservative milieu that the *Register* helped create and maintain.

Equally important in maintaining the county's rightward political tilt, Walter Knott became a significant force in the California Republican Party during the 1960s. An election endorsement from Knott, who founded and ran a popular Western theme park that still bears his name, could generate campaign contributions from many individuals and groups that valued his judgment.[16] That judgment was rooted in the gospel of "rugged individualism" to which he devoutly subscribed. Possessing a sobriety that friends said rendered him "almost totally humorless," the humble Knott had within his theme park a ghost town and silver-mining camp to remind people of the "pioneer spirit that had developed the West."[17] Knott also established a "Freedom Center" in the 1950s, complete with a research library, and later constructed a replica of Independence Hall.[18] Knott's Berry Farm thus sought to offer its visitors the quintessential patriotic tour, which they could experience between amusement rides. "Only Washington and Lincoln," one of his reverent employees declared, "have done as much for America as Mr.

Knott." A Knott administrative aide echoed that opinion: "Mr. Knott is second only to Jesus Christ among men who have walked this earth."[19]

Known as "Mr. Republican" in Orange County, Knott shared many of Hoiles's libertarian beliefs. The Founders, he stated, knew "that government in time would, if permitted, enslave the people. . . ." Having "screamed and cried" when he had to start paying Social Security taxes, Knott opposed virtually every aspect of government intervention on the grounds that it undermined the self-reliant perseverance that had accounted for his success (as a farmer), and that of countless others.[20] The popular view of his life as a Horatio Alger story resulted in a laudatory biography titled *Walter Knott: Twentieth Century Pioneer.*[21] Steadfastly touting the pioneer spirit through pamphlets and speeches, by the early 1960s Knott and Goldwater became southern California's celebrity patriots, as both espoused the rudimentary aphorisms that Reagan would later use in a more polished form to win over legions of voters who had been leery of Goldwater.

Unlike Hoiles, who considered politics to be the devil's work, Knott became active in the California Republican Party during the Knowland campaign due to his staunch opposition to labor unions. Involved in the affairs of the Republican State Central Committee (RSCC) as a fund raiser, Knott also engaged in letter-writing efforts to encourage local precinct workers as well as other conservatives throughout the country "[who] were helping to make a better America." Knott supported virtually all Republican candidates in general elections, though not necessarily enthusiastically, conservative or not.[22] Richard Nixon, for example, whose conservative credentials were at the very least questionable by 1960, received strong support from Knott throughout his career. Knott's attachment to Nixon probably stemmed from the latter's anticommunist credentials, particularly from his relentless efforts in the Hiss case. Knott apparently had no compunctions about backing Eisenhower either, even though he later embraced the John Birch Society, the organization that had excommunicated both Eisenhower and Nixon from the ranks of "true Americans."[23]

Knott's most enthusiastic support for a candidate in terms of generating money came in 1964 when, with the help of aides, he raised $4 million for Barry Goldwater through his office alone.[24] Knott's views were in near-perfect harmony with Goldwater's antistatism, at least until the senator had to move away from some of his more uncompromising positions during his presidential campaign. In 1966 Knott avidly backed Reagan, but maintained a lower profile in that campaign, perhaps due to the effort of Reagan's advisors to limit his association with reminders of the creaky conservatism that had often locked the Goldwater crusade in the politics of nostalgia.[25] In southern California, however, support from Knott was always an asset for

Republican candidates. He proved to be a major player in California Republican politics from 1958 on into the Reagan gubernatorial years, before he became incapacitated by Parkinson's disease.

The statements of Knott and Hoiles notwithstanding, perhaps no one did more to create Orange County's "kooky" image than the often outrageous Republican, James Utt. Elected to Congress in 1952, Utt gained national notoriety in 1959 by reintroducing the so-called Liberty Amendment, which entailed the elimination of the income tax.[26] In addition to tirelessly promoting the amendment throughout the 1960s, Utt likened government welfare programs to a "child molester who offers candy before his evil act."[27] Utt created his biggest stir in 1963 when he issued a newsletter describing pending military exercises in Georgia in which "barefooted African hordes" might be involved.[28] His letter caused widespread alarm in Georgia over what turned out to be NATO training maneuvers. A CBS television documentary detailed Utt's role in this matter and disparaged right-wing zealotry in Orange County.[29] Despite his outrageous statements and quixotically conservative propositions, Utt easily won reelection to Congress up to his death in 1970.

The ultraconservative triumvirate of Hoiles, Knott and Utt, which later became a formidable foursome with the emergence of State Senator John Schmitz, largely defined the county's political image during the 1960s. In addition to these individuals, entities such as Knott's Free Enterprise Association and the Orange County Industrial Committee helped mobilize right-wing activists. Prominent companies in the county that supported this effort included the Fluor Corporation, Quick-set Lock, John B. Kilroy Construction, Anaheim Truck & Transfer and Carl's Jr. Burgers. These companies were joined by Los Angeles–based firms such as Eversharp-Schick Razor, Technicolor Corporation and Coast Federal Savings.[30]

As elsewhere in southern California, the conservative mobilization in Orange County began in the latter half of the 1950s in a political battle of attrition, pitting the Republican right wing against the party's moderates and liberals. The Knowland campaign proved to be the initial big battle that began to turn the tide in the conservatives' favor. For Gordon X. Richmond, the congenial party activist known in Orange County as "Mr. Republican" before Knott assumed that moniker, the Knowland–Knight feud was the final factor in his decision to withdraw from partisan politics. A moderate in the Warren mold, Richmond chose not to serve as an arbiter amid the factional rancor of 1958 "because I would have gone down with the ship in my own party, fighting my own people."[31]

The ship may have begun to sink for moderate (or "responsibly conservative") Republicanism in Orange County and the rest of California in

1958, but the county was well represented by a diverse coalition of state legislators until 1962. In tandem with Democratic assemblyman Richard Hanna, Republican senator John Murdy and GOP assemblyman Bruce Sumner accomplished much for their constituents over the course of the six years they worked together. Circumventing ideological differences in achieving their goals for the county, Sumner would handle fellow moderate Republicans while Hanna dealt with the Democrats and Murdy negotiated with fellow conservatives.[32] Sumner recalled that Murdy, "though conservative in his fiscal policies, really was involved in [numerous] . . . 'liberal' problem-solving programs." Sumner believed that Murdy subscribed to the "true" conservatism that characterized the views of many county Republicans during the 1950s, those who "recognized the role of the government in doing the things that people can't do for themselves."[33]

Sumner himself would eventually fall victim to the Republicans who opposed active government, and who likely believed that Murdy was about as conservative as that alleged neo–New Dealer, Dwight Eisenhower. In 1961, Sumner angered the strident conservatives in the county by coauthoring a fair employment practices bill and supporting a fair housing act. Under fire from groups such as the Conservative Coordinating Council, a prominent Republican volunteer group, and desiring to earn more money than his duties as a state assemblyman would allow, Sumner decided not to seek reelection in 1962.[34] He did agree, however, to head U.S. senator Thomas Kuchel's successful 1962 reelection campaign in southern California. Deciding to seek political office once again in 1964, Sumner chose to run for the State Senate seat being vacated by Murdy but ran into strong and unexpected opposition from a political unknown by the name of John Schmitz.

An avowed member of the JBS, Schmitz taught classes on philosophy and American government at Santa Ana College. As he entered the Republican primary, his only formal backing came from the California Republican Assembly (CRA), which had been taken over by Goldwaterites at the organization's convention earlier in the year. Almost all Republican leaders endorsed Sumner, who received support from local newspapers as well. (Due to Hoiles's disdain for government, the *Register* did not formally endorse candidates.) Despite his prominent support and reputation as an effective politician and upstanding citizen, Sumner lost to Schmitz in a close election in the primary, which exacerbated the tensions between GOP factions in the county.[35]

Two factors weighed heavily against Sumner: Goldwater had emerged victorious from his California presidential primary with Nelson Rockefeller, and nowhere was his support stronger than in Orange County, where indefatigable Goldwater precinct workers touted Schmitz as well. Sumner also suffered from his opposition to Proposition 14 (the initiative to repeal the Rumford Fair Housing Act), which "wildly" rallied the county's realtors against him, sending them in droves to Schmitz, who then used their money in an effective ad campaign.[36] Riding the crest of this wave of support, Schmitz managed to edge out Sumner and had no trouble beating his Democratic opponent, Robert Battin, in the general election. Upon defeating Battin, Schmitz declared, "I hope we here in Orange County, in Southern California, can furnish a beachhead to win back the country from socialistic advance."[37]

Numerous Southlanders, of course, shared Schmitz's fear that liberal Democratic programs had put American freedom in its greatest jeopardy. For many of these individuals the JBS provided an outlet for their anxieties over the encroachment of communism and an opportunity to do their patriotic part in thwarting it. Highly visible rather than secretive, Birch chapters in Orange County and Los Angeles suburbs served as important community groups.[38] For example, chapters participated in public celebrations by displaying allegiant parade banners emblazoned with "The John Birch Society." Several studies indicate that by the mid-1960s Californians accounted for 25 to 34 percent of the society's membership and that most of these individuals lived in the state's southern coastal region, where support among nonmembers proved to be relatively strong as well.[39]

Confident of their relative good standing in southern California in the early 1960s, the JBS ran a full-page ad in the *Los Angeles Herald-Examiner* in April 1962 which welcomed the California Senate Committee on Un-American Activities to Los Angeles for its investigation of the Society. The ad contained a list of 192 greater Los Angeles chapters (including Orange County), and many members freely offered statements on the organization's operations. Headed by conservative Democrat Hugh M. Burns, the Committee found that although "there have been instances of imprudent activity and indefensible statements" by Birchers, the "great majority" of the group's California members were not mentally unstable or hysterical about the threat of communist subversion. The Committee concluded that the Society attracted so many members in southern California because it appeared to offer an organization through which one could "learn the truth about the Communist menace and then take some action to prevent its spread."[40] The JBS, which had requested the investigation in the hope of quelling critics and luring new members, had been vindicated.

Considering the Society to be a "peril to conservatives" from the beginning, the *Los Angeles Times* maintained a cautiously critical position after the Committee's report. Other Southland newspapers, however, hailed the report. For example, the *Pasadena Star-News* stated that "the committee's

finding that the Birchers are not subversive is both reassuring and credible."
The *Los Angeles Herald-Examiner* declared that "[n]o other group of
Americans has been more unjustly vilified in modern times than the John
Birch Society." Moreover, criticism of the JBS apparently was not always
detrimental to recruitment. In a letter circulated to his affluent Rolling Hills
neighbors, one member stated that the Society received an "unprecedented
flood" of applications after the *Los Angeles Times* ran a series of tempered
but disparaging articles on the JBS in March 1961.[41]

Receiving a further boost in both popularity and notoriety from
Goldwater's presidential candidacy, the JBS in Orange County had about
5,000 members at its mid-1960s peak.[42] The Society emerged as a disrup-
tive force in county politics in 1962, coinciding with the bitter campaign
debate between Nixon and Joe Shell over the organization's literature and
activities. Nixon's condemnation of the JBS provoked Shell's ire and became emblematic of the split between the moderates and the conservatives
that year. The meetings of the county's Republican Central Committee
often became fierce shouting matches that accomplished little or nothing.
Amid the tumult, Dennis Carpenter won a seat on the Central Committee
and, apparently as the least objectionable committeeman, was quickly
"given" the group's chairmanship in an attempt to ameliorate such fractious
disputes. Appeasing the moderates as a former Democrat without Bircher
credentials, Carpenter, who had been recruited by Knott, recalled being
somewhat befuddled and amused by the chair selection process, during
which "conservatives supported me because I had just gotten out of the FBI
and wasn't a communist." Neither Carpenter nor anyone else, however,
could settle matters between the hostile Republican factions in the county or
the rest of the state, for the disagreements went well beyond local and state
politics and the usual palliative of compromise.[43]

In particular, the anticommunist issue—which had not abated much in
southern California after the McCarthy hearings—became even more
heated after the Cuban missile crisis of October 1962.[44] An angst-laden
reminder of the perils of living in the nuclear age, the discovery of secret
missile installations in Cuba provided further proof for numerous Americans that the Soviet Union aimed to gain control of the world through the
threat of nuclear attack and a pervasive yet covert communist conspiracy.
Several months after the crisis, Goldwater strongly encouraged aggressive
action against Cuba: "Do anything that has to be done to get rid of that
cancer. If it means war, let it mean war." For fervid anticommunists in
particular, the missile crisis compounded the anxiety created by previous
Soviet actions and the notion that perfidious agents within the U.S. had long
endangered the country's security. (A year later the Kennedy assassination

made conspiracy theories seem all the more plausible). Adding to the rising right-wing anticommunist din after the missile crisis, Goldwater's popular book *Why Not Victory?* warned that Americans seemed largely oblivious to the "enormity of the conspiracy created to destroy us."[45]

While Goldwater did believe that communist agents operated "conspiratorially in the heart of our defenses," his descriptions of this infiltration—unlike McCarthy's—never went much beyond such generalities. Furthermore, he stated that the Kremlin's effort to win American converts "is almost a complete failure."[46] On this significant level, at least, Goldwater and JBS founder Robert Welch disagreed. Infamous for his attacks on Eisenhower's "communist" connections, Welch declared Goldwater to be "absolutely sound in his Americanism" and the best man to counter the conspirators in the "political field." He cautioned, however, that "I think he is still not aware of the nature and totality of the [subversive] forces at work."[47] In the eyes of Welch, these forces had weaved an entangling web of "collectivism" in which the fate of Western civilization appeared trapped.

Welch believed that the drift of the United States toward collectivism could best be understood through the theory offered in 1918 by German social critic Oswald Spengler in *The Decline of the West.* Spengler's theory, Welch contended, cogently showed that the Western world, including America, was in decline in accordance with Spengler's idea of a cyclic rise and fall of civilizations throughout history. Once possessing the "strength and vigor and promise of a healthy young man in his late teens," the United States, Welch declared, had in the twentieth century grown older and weaker and thus could no longer resist the "cancerous disease of collectivism" and the duplicity of its domestic agents.[48] Echoing Welch's Spenglerian anxiety, upon his election to the State Senate John Schmitz stated, "I was hoping that America would be different than other nations of the past." He warned that "unless this country begins to change its course, I am afraid we are in for perilous times."[49]

Welch and Schmitz, among other far right-wingers, reflected the worldview Richard Hofstadter called the "paranoid style"—the belief in an immense conspiracy as the "motive force" in history.[50] Schmitz may have fit this description even better than Welch, for as a graduate student Schmitz did much research on the "conspiracy view of history," and concluded that secret societies and front groups had long subverted established governments and their loyal citizenry. He therefore likened the New York–based Council on Foreign Relations (CFR), an influential internationalist organization, to the diabolical Bavarian Illuminati, which, according to Schmitz, had covertly fomented the French Revolution.[51] Like the Illuminati, the CFR and other "liberal" Eastern groups and individuals operated as "conspiratorial agents," which had by the mid-1960s undermined the "American way of life" to the brink of its collapse. Schmitz believed that in this eleventh hour only educational programs of the sort offered by the JBS could save America.[52]

In contrast to Schmitz, fellow Orange County Bircher James Toft did not find JBS literature immediately appealing. Ironically, he had worked for Nelson Rockefeller's campaign in the challenge to Goldwater in the California primary. Upon Goldwater's triumph in that contest, Toft decided to read *Why Not Victory?* and *The Conscience of a Conservative,* and subsequently attended a few JBS meetings. Some of the assertions in the *Blue Book* initially "insulted my intelligence," but Toft eventually joined the Society after finding corroborating evidence for many of these statements. He then went through a period of vacillation, "where I was watching [NBC TV newscasters] Huntley and Brinkley, and reading some [JBS] material, and wondering where the real world was."[53] Recalling that his JBS compatriots knew he would "wake up . . . sooner or later," Toft indeed decided to commit himself to the Society and its goals.

Having completed the transformation from a moderate Rockefeller Republican to a JBS anticommunist, Toft came to see "international" communism as the "battering ram" in the destruction of freedom. Paradoxically, behind the communists were the "international money interests" who had in common with the Soviets a desire to maintain "capitalistic monopolies," but for themselves and not the state.[54] In addition to the money interests, Toft cited the usual litany of JBS villains: the activist chief justice of the Supreme Court, Earl Warren (the Society led an "Impeach Warren" movement in the early 1960s); the CFR and other advocates of "World Government"; and the "communist-led" civil rights movement.[55] To Birchers, then, McCarthy's warning of "a conspiracy of infamy so black [and] . . . so immense" proved as true in the 1960s, if not more so, as during the senator's inquisition. Having established their own "beachhead" in Cuba under Castro, the communists, as the missile crisis had shown, had established a position for a potential quick strike from nearby shores. Domestic infiltration, however, loomed as a larger concern for the JBS, an overwhelming trepidation perhaps best expressed by a bold-lettered admonition in one member's Los Angeles home that exclaimed: "They're Not Just 90 Miles Away. They're Here."[56]

While many southern Californians shared the JBS's concern over communism and the increasing role of the state, it is likely that a large percentage of these individuals found the Society's conspiracy theories to be convoluted and overly apprehensive. For instance, Sam Campbell, a reporter for the *Register,* joined the JBS for a short time in the early 1960s but could not "live in a continual state of distress." He had considered himself a "liberal" until the "turning point" in 1961, when he attended a seminar at the Disneyland Hotel conducted by Dr. Fred Schwarz, head of the popular Christian Anti-Communist Crusade.[57] Deciding to become a member of the JBS shortly after this pivotal experience, Campbell believed that the Society offered good educational programs, but surmised, "the conspiratorial aspect [of communism and big government] was mostly in our own minds," because their actions had been so "open." Fellow *Register* reporter Marvin Olsen, a strident libertarian like Hoiles, thought the alleged subversion of the CFR and the international money interests appeared "far-fetched." Conceding that conspiratorial groups might exist, Olsen declared that "unless I can see some proof in this, I'm not a believer." Of the true believers, though, some became so paranoid about conspiracy theories that they apparently dropped out of the political process altogether.[58]

Like Campbell and Olsen, the Reverend Claude Bunzel, head of the Colonial Research Library at Knott's Berry Farm, had "mixed feelings" about conspiracy theories. A better explanation for the threat from "collectivism," he contended, "is the natural evil that resides in man's heart . . . as a result of the Fall."[59] Ironically, Bunzel's belief in original sin conflicted with Knott's simple faith in the essential goodness of man, according to which "[n]o one really wants to hurt or exploit anyone." Knott used this belief to justify his opposition to labor unions, contending that corporate managers would not truly exploit their workers, so unions were unnecessary. He apparently did not see the paradox this view created when he spoke of the "international communist conspiracy" and the need for such groups as the JBS to combat it. Possessing "nothing but respect and affection" for the Society members he knew, Knott declined to join the JBS due to the controversy generated by the "unfortunate propensity" of Robert Welch to arrive at "doubtful conclusions" about the conspiratorial network.[60]

Welch, of course, was not alone in his "doubtful conclusions." Orange County native Thomas Kuchel, the Republican whip in the U.S. Senate, reported in a speech in 1963 that about 10 percent of the letters he received each month from his California constituents qualified as "fright mail," informing him of "the latest plot to overthrow America." He described the "fright peddler" as "the self-appointed savior of our land who finds conspiracy, treason and 'sell-out' in almost every act or pronouncement of government." Kuchel's salvos against the far right brought vitriolic responses from James Utt and the Western states' director of the JBS, John Rousselot. Utt charged that Kuchel had made "an hysterical defense of his position" and "smear[ed] millions of patriotic Americans," while Rousselot stated that Kuchel showed "a complete lack of knowledge about the Birch Society."[61]

Kuchel's speech and the right-wing response provided more fuel for the epithetical fire that had already consumed most of the comity between the two principal factions of the California Republican Party. This feud would only get worse, in California and the rest of the nation, as legions of Goldwater supporters began serious preparations for what seemed certain: the senator's 1964 presidential bid and the strong opposition from the party's establishment.

Viewed by historian Richard Hofstadter as the culmination of the "pseudo-conservative revolt," the Goldwater movement, during the campaign and well after, was seen by most nonconservative pundits largely as an aberration. That did not, however, preclude the movement from also being viewed by these individuals as an authoritarian threat to democracy, cloaked in populist rhetoric. Of particular importance to such perceptions, Hofstadter's influential "Paranoid Style" essay appeared in 1965, along with a revision of his treatise on pseudo-conservatism, which in 1955 had elaborately introduced his concept of "status politics." In "Pseudo-Conservatism Revisited," Hofstadter admitted that in his earlier essay he had given "disproportionate weight" to status, but that he needed only to subject the concept to "some refinements" and place it in a broader context. The Goldwater movement furnished an "almost ideal test case" for his refined paradigm, which, when coupled with his paranoid style thesis, bolstered the interpretations of "pathological" right-wing politics.[62]

While explicitly describing the "extreme right wing" of Goldwater's supporters as "exponents" of the paranoid style, Hofstadter implicitly placed *all* ardent Goldwater backers in that category. He contended that

> Goldwater's zealots were moved more by the desire to dominate the party than to win the country, concerned more to express resentments and punish "traitors," to justify a set of values and assert grandiose, militant visions, than to solve actual problems of state.

As Michael Kazin has noted, Hofstadter and like-minded critics "beheld the modern right as a looming 'populist' danger to civility and intellectual freedom rather than as a full-fledged alternative, at least potentially, to the reigning New Deal order."[63]

Hofstadter focused his attack on the contemporary right but identified similar aberrant movements in American politics—including the populist movement of the 1890s—dating back to the years immediately after the Revolution.[64] Inspired by Hofstadter and by Bernard Bailyn's *Ideological Origins of the American Revolution,* which detailed the fears of American colonists regarding conspiracies against liberty, a number of historians of early American political culture came to ascribe paranoia and related social neuroses to the political behavior of the Founders themselves. Even though Bailyn saw the colonists' fear of conspiracy as largely rational, later scholars, in effect, synthesized Bailyn's argument on the motive force of conspiracy theories with the paranoid impulse described by Hofstadter, and thus found an irrational basis for the anxieties of the revolutionaries.[65]

It is, perhaps, somewhat odd that southern California conservatism and the postwar American Right in general can be better understood after considering a cogent argument against assertions that the American Revolution was born out of irrationalities stemming from political paranoia. The essay of interest here is historian Gordon Wood's perspicacious examination of conspiracy and the paranoid style in the eighteenth century. Wood argued that due to McCarthyism in particular, most historians recognize "that there may be rational explanations for fears of conspiracy, [but] cannot help assuming that such fears are mainly rooted in nonrational sources." This tendency, Wood claimed, made historians overlook the fact that during the eighteenth century "[e]verywhere people sensed designs within designs, cabals within cabals . . . [and] conspiracies [of all kinds] that cut across national boundaries and spanned the Atlantic." The prevalence of conspiratorial views, therefore, should be seen as essentially rational; for the paranoid style, Wood concluded, "was a mode of expression common to that age."[66]

After this convincing argument Wood went on to say that "due to modern social science, in our own time . . . conspiratorial interpretations have become so out of place . . . that they can only be accounted for as mental aberrations, as a paranoid style symptomatic of psychological disturbance."[67] This assertion, however, does not pan out, for if the paranoid style was a "mode of expression common to the age" of the American Revolution, and thereby rational, the same could be said for the rhetoric of the early Cold War, modern social science notwithstanding. Moreover, to accept Wood's view of those who harbored conspiratorial beliefs in recent times as categorically disturbed is to assume the implausible: that a majority of Americans at some point in the decade after World War II suffered from mental instability.

While it appears that no polls were taken on the public's belief in conspiracy theories, 50 percent of Americans had a favorable opinion of the chief conspiracy theorist, McCarthy, in late 1953. (Twenty-nine percent were unfavorable.) Furthermore, throughout the early 1950s, at least two-thirds of all Americans believed that communists posed a serious threat to domestic government and society at large. It is, therefore, reasonable to assume that a majority of Americans believed that a communist conspiracy was operating on one level or another during the early 1950s.[68]

While not rooted in some sort of mass neurosis, notions of a "Great

Conspiracy," as historian Eric Goldman described it, did grip the American psyche during the early Cold War. This proved particularly true during and after 1949, the year the world witnessed the "fall" of China to the communists, and learned of the detonation of an atomic bomb by the Soviet Union. "The shock of 1949," Goldman stated, "loosed not only a sweeping anticommunism but a tendency to denounce anything associated with the different or disturbing as part of a communist conspiracy."[69] This tendency, of course, along with McCarthy's ambition and brutish guile, accounted for his rise. That many Americans supported him, however, should not be seen as evidence of an aberrant national psychology but of generally legitimate concerns that were manifested in paranoid language and sometimes dreadful excesses, as exemplified by the ascent of McCarthy, the pathological careerist.[70] As historian Stephen Whitfield has asserted, the assaults on civil liberties, tolerance, and "fair play" during the red scare were a "disgrace," but not a "collective tragedy."[71]

In the latter half of the 1950s, after the Wisconsin senator's demise, the fervent trepidation over communism abroad began to wane along with fears about communists in domestic government. Events as harrowing as those in 1949 would not so completely seize the American public again, nor would any government investigation with the distressing aspersions of the McCarthy hearings (though the House Un-American Activities Committee lived on). Despite the ebbing of the red scare, apprehensions of a communist conspiracy remained strong, especially among Americans of a conservative ilk, who had believed in McCarthy's investigation, but not necessarily in its scope or his tactics. The worries of these individuals and others were maintained mainly by international occurrences, such as the brutal Soviet repression of the Hungarian Revolution, the initial Soviet edge in the space race and, most worrisome, Fidel Castro's rise to power in Cuba.

The establishment of a communist regime in Cuba in 1960 triggered the second big chill of the Cold War. The anxieties of 1949 were rekindled, if not stoked to full flame, during and immediately after the Cuban missile crisis. The predominant centrist political culture of the early 1960s relegated the superpatriotic warnings of the communist peril to the realm of the right wing, but most everyone shared at least some of the angst that spurred the right's rhetoric. As historian Allen Matusow has noted, only after the Soviet-American détente of 1963 did the "international tension that for so long had sustained the Cold War mentality . . . [begin] to dissipate" (though not for staunch conservatives) and yield to other concerns.[72] Up to that point, Americans tended to divide the postwar world into spheres of absolute good and absolute evil, and envisioned, to one extent or another, a conspiracy against freedom by the forces of communist tyranny. Thus, during this era of the "great fear," the shrill locutions and tracts of the right had largely understandable causes. Some of the manifestations of this anxiety, however, took irrational forms, as exhibited by extremist groups like the JBS.

Anticommunists on the extreme right, who saw world politics and liberal domestic reforms as Kremlin-directed, were exponents of a distorted worldview, consumed by a "conspiratorial fantasy," as Hofstadter described.[73] Nevertheless, to interpret the conservative movement that culminated in the Goldwater campaign as extremist, rather than seeing extremism as a component in the sum of the movement's parts, is in itself distorted and myopic. While conservative anticommunism proved more virulent than that of liberals, the difference could be measured in degrees of the same latitude as opposed to polar distinctions; and though the antistatism of the Goldwaterites may have been more than a generation out of date, their beliefs grew out of a deeply rooted American tradition of rugged individualism—however mythical that might have been—that had long spurned government activism. The conservative movement that began inauspiciously in the late 1950s in California and elsewhere often proved both reactionary and simplistic in its positions. But the movement was animated mainly by a set of ideals and principles, and not by the pressures of status and other "abnormal" anxieties.

Therefore when Ronald Reagan told the Orange County Press Club in 1961 that "[w]e now have a permanent structure of government . . . [that] is the very essence of totalitarianism," he was alarmingly reactionary in his use of powerful Cold War imagery.[74] Nevertheless, the gist of his attack on big government was narrowly within the normative parameters of conservative, laissez-faire Republicanism; but because that sort of Republicanism had been largely discredited in the preceding thirty years, such views posed a threat to the pluralistic "consensus" of the centrist politics of the age. Relegated to the periphery of acceptable political debate, the conservative movement was effectively defined by its liberal detractors—especially in 1964—as being controlled by zealots on the far right, which it was in some cases. Ironically, in the late 1960s, when conservatism acquired a more mainstream appeal, many liberals, in a quandary over seemingly failed policies at home and in Vietnam, struggled to differentiate their beliefs from those of the "un-American" far left.

It is not surprising that the extremist label stuck to the conservative crusade in the early 1960s given the salience of the radical right issue, especially in southern California. In addition to the JBS, a veritable constellation of right-wing extremist groups, some of them paramilitary, could be found in the region. The only two avowed Birchers in Congress, Republicans Edgar Heistand and John Rousselot, won their seats in 1960 and represented districts in metropolitan Los Angeles. Both were defeated in reelection bids in 1962. The region's political milieu also provided receptive audiences for racist agitators such as General Edwin Walker and the Reverend Billy James Hargis and his Christian Crusade.[75] While none of these organizations were directly affiliated with the Republican Party, many of their members supported Republicans—even if only through the vilification of "socialistic" Democrats—and some actively sought to influence the party's official positions on the state level.

GOP conservatives viewed these incursions with mixed emotions given that they generally agreed with the unyielding anticommunism and antistatism of the extremists but were often put off by their more bizarre ideas and militancy. Party moderates and liberals, on the other hand, unequivocally saw the far right as a pariah that could only split the party and deliver the death knell to many of its candidates. Amid the rising acrimony between the party's two broad factions, an unenthused Richard Nixon chose to seek the Republican nomination for governor in 1962. Nixon's book *Six Crises,* published that same year, detailed what he described as the six greatest challenges of his political career. Had he released the book a year later he might have added a seventh crisis, for his gubernatorial campaign proved to be the most bruising electoral battle of his life.

Four

"The 'Old Nixon' Is the Real Nixon"

It seemed logical to assume in late 1961 that Richard Nixon, who came so close to winning the presidency a year earlier, would have little problem being elected governor in his native state in 1962; but logic ran up against the vagaries of politics. While most polls in 1961 indicated that Nixon could beat Pat Brown by a comfortable margin, the pollsters could not then calculate the effects of a divisive Republican primary battle. In addition, California Democrats had found new life after Brown's triumph over Knowland and would have the rare advantage of incumbency in taking on the Republican challenger. Perhaps Nixon's biggest problem, as he recalled, "was that I had no great desire to be governor of California."[1] Sensing this lack of commitment, Californians had no great desire to elect him, for he failed to generate the requisite widespread enthusiastic support for his candidacy, even within his own party, and therefore lost to Brown.[2]

Dating back to the early 1950s, Nixon's problems with fellow Republicans grew out of his career aspirations. Strained from the start, his relationship with Earl Warren and the governor's backers got worse when he worked rather deviously to swing Warren's California delegates behind Eisenhower at the 1952 Republican Convention. "Honorable men," Kyle Palmer wrote afterward, "don't stab their friends—or enemies—in the back."[3] Upsetting the state's Taft supporters through his convention maneuvers as well, Nixon both served and semi-redeemed himself by garnering the vice-presidential nomination, which enhanced the prospects for a California Republican to reside in the White House after the Eisenhower years. Successfully defending his integrity as Ike's running mate in the now-famous "Checkers" speech, Nixon also proved adroit at handling his critics within the party four years later by warding off an effort to replace him on Eisenhower's reelection ticket. In 1958 Nixon helped engineer the "musical chairs" between Knowland and Knight, which cleared the way for him to control the California delegation at the 1960 Republican Convention. Nevertheless, Nixon's political past plagued him, for he entered the presidential race with the "Tricky Dick" image that had hung with him since his senate race against

Helen Gahagan Douglas. This problem likely contributed to the significant fluctuations in Nixon's popularity in California and elsewhere in the months leading up to the 1960 presidential election.[4]

By the time of that race, Nixon found himself in a particular bind with some of his state's conservative Republicans, especially in southern California. Among these individuals were members of the burgeoning JBS, who wanted to get Nixon "back into the fold" of true Republicanism, and away from the party's liberal Eastern wing. Reflecting the disappointment in the vice president, many conservatives already preferred Goldwater's leadership to Nixon's,[5] an indication of the persistence of conservatism after Knowland's defeat, and a portent of the impending Goldwater boom. Conservatives, however, likely agreed with Robert Welch's description of Jack Kennedy as Walter Reuther's "stooge," and with Goldwater's assault on the Democratic platform as a "blueprint for socialism. . . ." As unpalatable as Nixon might have been to certain right-wing Republicans in California, he stood as the only hope against Kennedy and "a new type of New Deal," as Goldwater forewarned, "far more menacing than anything we have seen in the past."[6]

Before facing Kennedy in the general election, Nixon challenged Brown indirectly in a battle of favorite son candidates in the California presidential primaries. The vice president faced no opposition, but his camp wanted a large Republican turnout to embarrass Brown, who was running against George McLain, a longtime old-age pension promoter. GOP strategists mailed a broadside aimed at Brown to Republican voters, claiming that unless Nixon received more votes than Brown,

> Khrushchev will interpret the vote as an indication that the [Eisenhower] administration's tough attitude toward Communism is not supported by the American people. And Chou En-lai will take it as the first step by the United States in the admission of Red China to the U.N.[7]

The Republican faithful came out in significant numbers, as Nixon garnered 1,517,652 Republican votes, compared to Brown's 1,354,031 on the Democratic side (cross-filing had been eliminated in 1959); McLain received almost half as many votes as the beleaguered Brown, who was suffering from a storm of public protest over his short-lived reprieve of the death penalty for the vicious rapist, Caryl Chessman.[8]

Having "defeated" Brown, Nixon proceeded to turn back a challenge by Nelson Rockefeller at the Republican National Convention and won the nomination. At the end of his tough but relatively clean campaign against Kennedy, the vice president held on to Republican voters in his home state and corralled enough Democrats to win there by six-tenths of 1 percent. He succeeded in overcoming strong opposition from the state's Kennedy organization by having a solid campaign team of his own and by spending much time in California, particularly in the final days of the race.[9] Victory in his home state, of course, did not reflect the national results, as Kennedy edged by Nixon in the closest presidential election of the twentieth century. Consequently, with his political career up in the air, and after fifteen years in Washington, Nixon returned to southern California.

The pressure for him to run for governor began almost as soon as he arrived in Los Angeles, shortly after the end of his service as vice president. State Republican leaders wanted a well-known candidate who could win back the governorship, and whose coattails might help the party regain control of the state legislature. Urged to run by national Republican figures as well, and swayed by a number of movements to draft him, Nixon dutifully but unenthusiastically declared his candidacy for governor in September.[10]

His entrance into the race did not sit well with the other Republican gubernatorial candidates. Goodwin Knight, who still harbored ill will toward Nixon due to the fiasco of 1958, had earlier announced his intentions to seek the governorship. Hepatitis would force Knight out of the race in January 1962, but not before he took some serious shots at Nixon, including the charge that the latter had tried to "bribe" him with the job of chief justice of the state Supreme Court if he would drop out of the primary.[11] Nixon also faced opposition from former lieutenant governor Butch Powers but, embittered by his inability to generate much organizational or financial support, he withdrew from the race in March and eventually endorsed Brown (as did Knight). At that point, only the conservative and relatively unknown state assemblyman from Los Angeles, Joseph C. Shell, remained to challenge Nixon in the primary. Shell resented the fact that Nixon had not stuck to his earlier personal assurance that he would not be a candidate for governor.[12]

Shell touted his campaign against Nixon as an ideological "crusade from which there will be no turning back."[13] His decision to enter the race, however, stemmed largely from the fact that his Hancock Park residence had been gerrymandered into a "safe" Democratic Assembly district, which made another run for the Assembly appear futile.[14] Nevertheless, Shell's gubernatorial campaign commitment to make "absolutely essential cuts in the cost of government" to save the state from "economic collapse" did reflect a crusading conservative spirit.[15] Pledging to clean up the "mess in Sacramento," Nixon had a similar but less anxious view of the state's economic stability. Shell called attention to Nixon's lack of experience in state government and to the probability that the former vice president would use the governorship as a stepping stone to the 1964 Republican presidential nomination.[16] While both these points proved troublesome for Nixon throughout his campaign, his biggest challenge would be in appealing to the staunch right wing of his party, which had found its champion in Shell.

Captain of the University of Southern California football team that won the Rose Bowl in 1939, Shell appeared to have been a rugged all-American boy turned politician. He learned to fly at age fifteen, served as president of the student body in high school, married his college sweetheart, and piloted planes for the Army and Navy in World War II. His campaign literature as well as reporters often mentioned that he was "trim and supple" or "tall and strongly built." Mindful of this, Shell, in a rare display of humor, vented his frustration over Nixon's refusal to debate him, stating that "I am in better shape than Nixon," so "maybe he would [instead] like to wrestle."[17] Despite the occasional one-liner and his attractive appearance and background, Shell's militant message limited his appeal to the Republican right. In addition, though amiable and upstanding, he lacked charisma. A prominent conservative and close friend joked that "not to know Joe is to love him. . . . [H]e ha[s] no personality at all." A member of the California Young Republicans (CYR), a large activist group, recalled a campaign speech by the assemblyman at the 1962 CYR convention "that was so bland it seemed to matter only that Shell was giving it."[18]

Shell may not have been a compelling candidate, but for many steadfast conservatives, particularly those on the far right, his campaign was inspiring and in some ways served as a dry run for the Goldwater crusade two years later. Echoing Reagan's by-now polished diatribe against "big government," Shell thundered, "I'm tired of more laws, more bureaucrats, more forms to fill out, more confusion and more waste." He declared, "when the first budget is returned to me as Governor, I shall regard myself as expendable." He professed a willingness to eliminate "unnecessary appropriations," even if that meant sacrificing his reelection, to save the state from the economic ruin of "dictatorial" and "socialistic" policies.[19] This selfless commitment to principle indicated that Shell did not consider himself to be a career politician like Nixon, though he had served almost ten years in the Assembly. Shell's experience in office meant that he could not campaign as a virtuous outsider—despite often sounding like one—as Reagan would do so effectively in 1966. Reagan's carefully crafted "citizen politician" image was not unlike that of the charming, do-good congressional novice in the film *Mr. Smith Goes to Washington* (Sacramento, in this case), minus his blatant naiveté. Shell projected a similar concerned-citizen image—"He is not a politician in the accepted sense of the word," his literature avowed—but he lacked Reagan's considerable attributes and a propitious political climate for his grassroots campaign.

Shell did not pose a threat to Nixon in terms of actually defeating him in the primary, yet the former football star's criticism of Nixon strained the latter's efforts to mollify disgruntled right-wing Republicans. Nixon took the high road against Shell, choosing not to attack him but Brown instead. Brown, however, faced no serious opposition in the primary. Thus he could focus much of his campaign rhetoric on the Nixon–Shell confrontation, which he exacerbated by labeling the former vice president a pawn of the "Stone Age ultraconservatives."[20] This created a dilemma for Nixon. He could ignore or skirt Brown's assault on the Republican right and suffer the consequences of not defending that faction; on the other hand, if he did stand up for this contingent, he would seemingly validate Brown's barbed assertion that the man who had barely lost the presidency had become a browbeaten apologist for the California far right.

The issue of Republican extremism hampered Nixon's campaign mainly due to Shell's candidacy and the rise of the JBS. While disapproving of Welch's more outrageous statements, Shell was otherwise uncritical of the Society, taking the position that its members harbored the views and concerns of "dedicated" Americans.[21] Nevertheless, he made clear that he did not belong to the group and avoided embracing it, for polls revealed a lack of support for the JBS, even among Republicans. Shell's own pollster advised him that in southern California the political climate "is [generally] very warm for the candidate who favors anti-communistic societies," but warned that support would cool if Shell's name became strongly linked to the "radical" JBS.[22] Shell therefore strongly backed the maintenance of loyalty oaths for state employees and favored outlawing the Communist Party in California, but attempted to steer clear of directly associating his views with those of the Birchers and other extremist groups.

Cautious in his initial criticisms of the JBS, Nixon believed he had to do more than just disassociate himself from the group given Welch's defamation of Eisenhower and his secretary of state, John Foster Dulles.[23] At the 1962 California Republican Assembly (CRA) Convention, therefore, the former vice president and Thomas Kuchel led an effort to have the CRA formally censure the Society, but settled for a compromise resolution condemning Welch. Nixon described the Birch leader as "dictatorial and totalitarian," and as having "rendered immeasurable harm to the cause of individual liberty." He realized, however, that his attack on the JBS and Welch "was a no-win proposition."[24] When a speaker reminded those disenchanted with the resolution that as a congressman Nixon had "put a real, honest-to-God Communist behind bars," hisses echoed throughout the convention hall.[25] The invocation of the defining episode of the candidate's early political career could not redeem him in the eyes of the dissenters.

Nixon's excoriation of the JBS also alienated two of his close friends and political associates, congressmen John Rousselot and Edgar Heistand. As members of the Society, both men refused to denounce Welch. Nixon lost "not only their support but the support of their friends in two heavily Republican districts."[26]

Battling Nixon for the CRA's endorsement for governor, Shell led the fight against the anti-Birch resolution. "We're being presumptive and insulting," he proclaimed, "when we tell the people they can't belong to . . . the John Birch Society." While Shell stated that he welcomed the support of "all citizens regardless of their affiliation," he made clear that he was not soliciting the support of the JBS or any similar organization. Murray Chotiner, who had suggested the compromise resolution, responded to Nixon's call that the party's Birchers resign from the Society by comparing that request to asking Republicans "to change their [party] registration simply because they may differ with statements made by its leaders." Reflecting the sentiment of many at the convention, Chotiner found much to commend in the purpose of the JBS and in the loyalty of its members.[27]

Nixon's most comprehensive biographer stated that in regard to the JBS matter at the convention, "Nixon had maneuvered through a delicate maze without collision."[28] On the contrary, though his anti-Birch pronouncements may have temporarily toned down some of Brown's campaign trail thunder, the initial resolution condemning the JBS ran into a phalanx of opposition from the right. Shell had hoped that the extremism issue would not be belabored at the convention, and believed that Nixon's insistence on a resolution showed he did not understand the depth of the empathy for the Society in the conservative ranks.[29] Indeed, if Nixon had limited his formal assault to Welch in the beginning, the intraparty acrimony might have been minimal. Instead, he had adamantly insisted that the initial resolution be passed intact and publicly expressed regret over the compromise. While clearly justifiable, Nixon's explicit condemnation of the JBS at the convention failed to strike the right balance between placating an important faction in his own party and defusing a Democratic issue. A "no-win proposition" to be sure, his stand nonetheless evinced ill-conceived calculations and an uncharacteristic lack of political savvy.

Senator Kuchel strongly backed the anti-Birch resolution as well, which intensified the hostility of the right-wingers by providing one more reason for them to despise him. The senator's "liberal" voting record was anathema to the many conservatives who booed him at the convention when he declared, "I was the first member of Congress who arose to denounce the John Birch Society. . . ." Referring to his hecklers as "my courteous friends," Kuchel averred "that anyone who followed the Society's tenets, whether a member or not, is not qualified for public office."[30] These statements could not have come as a surprise to his staunch opponents; so Kuchel, who had never been considered a conservative like the Nixon of old, probably made few new enemies at the convention.

Nevertheless, the senator faced vigorous opposition from two right-wing Republicans in the primary, Loyd Wright and Howard Jarvis. Wright, a lawyer and past president of the American Bar Association, charged that Kuchel was a "Fabian Socialist," intent on vilifying the "patriots" who "rise above the complacent and sound the clarion call of warning" about the encroaching communist threat.[31] Jarvis, a businessman who accurately described himself as being "to the right of Barry Goldwater," contended that "[t]o save our free system, we must maintain militant liberty through political Americanism."[32] Evidence of the appeal of the superpatriotic messages of Kuchel's two opponents, at least at the convention, could be found in the CRA's endorsement vote, as Wright and Jarvis together won as many votes (220) as the senator.

Nixon also won the CRA's endorsement, but in less than impressive fashion given his stature. In keeping with the outsider image he promoted, Shell declared the 263–176 vote to be "a major move in breaking the old established party machine in California. . . ."[33] While he fell well short of dismantling the machine of the "kingmakers," he did cause it to sputter, for much right-wing money went to Shell. Nixon had hoped to do some TV telethons during the primary, along the lines of his election eve broadcast in 1960, but he lacked the funds. Though Nixon had wealthy supporters, they and his Southern California Finance Committee did not raise the kind of money he needed for the media campaign he desired.[34] The tight budget meant he had to engage in much small talk in crossroads towns, in addition to stepping up speeches and glad-handing at rallies and banquets.

Fairly wealthy himself, Shell received campaign contributions from friends associated with and in the oil business, in which he had worked prior to (and during) his time in the Assembly. His connections began with his father-in-law, Harold Morton, a powerful oil company attorney, known as "Mr. Big" in Republican fundraising circles. Cy Rubel, the CEO of Union Oil, backed Shell through the primary, and it seems certain that the assemblyman received significant support from former Werdel backer Hub Russell, a Bakersfield farmer who became rich from the oil tapped on his property. Shell may also have received money from Morton's chief client, Superior Oil president William Keck, another ex-Werdel supporter who later became a major contributor to Goldwater's presidential campaign.[35] Though he would strongly endorse Nixon in the general election, Walter Knott backed Shell in the primary, stating in a letter soliciting donations that the assemblyman "has had the courage to ... fight for the conservative cause" and "is a qualified electable candidate."[36]

In addition to a shortage of money, Nixon lost the support of the Los Angeles County Young Republicans (LACYR) shortly after the CRA convention. An important conservative group, the LACYR voted to censure the former vice president for disrupting party unity by attacking Republicans who belonged to "some patriotic organizations."[37] The head of the LACYR, Robert Gaston (son-in-law of Charles Jones, CEO of Richfield Oil), was a strong Shell supporter, and in February had narrowly lost to a moderate Nixon supporter in the election for president of the California Young Republicans. The acrimony attendant to the Nixon–Shell contest was evident in the factionalism within the Young Republicans and affiliated groups, such as the Young Americans for Freedom, throughout the primary and into the general election campaign. In 1963 Gaston would succeed in securing the leadership of the CYR, and thereby devoted the group to the Goldwater presidential crusade.

The animosity within the Republican ranks was not confined to rancor between the two factions, for senate candidates Jarvis and Wright took numerous shots at each other as well. In March, Jarvis charged that Kuchel supporters had encouraged Wright to enter the race to split the conservative vote.[38] He also attacked Wright's campaign chairman, Ronald Reagan, for not formally joining the Republican Party until January, and for his onetime membership in the left-wing United World Federalists. Reflecting the widespread suspicion that many conservatives harbored toward Hollywood, Jarvis stated that Reagan used "many pro-communist people on his General Electric show." Wright fired back that the actor "has been espousing ... the conservative cause to stop the Fabian Socialists in this country ... and the drift toward the welfare state."[39] Nixon, for whom Reagan had campaigned in 1960, offered to issue a statement on the actor's behalf, but the latter thought Nixon's support might increase the factional roil. Believing he held considerable sway with conservatives, Reagan did not wish to add to this animosity so that he would be better able to swing the right-wing behind Nixon after the primary, at which time he would seek a commitment from Shell to "unite to beat Brown."[40]

As the primary campaign wound down, however, it became clear that getting Shell to stand behind his victorious opponent after the election would be no easy task, given the rising stridency of his attacks on the former vice president. For example, in late May, before 15,000 supporters at the Los Angeles Sports Arena, Shell labeled Nixon a "loser" and declared that only he could beat Brown. Not lacking in pageantry, the assemblyman's appearance on stage had been preceded by patriotic hymns from a sixty-voice choir. Once at the podium the candidate was flanked by a bevy of pom-pom-waving cheerleaders known as Shell's Belles, whose ubiquitous presence throughout the campaign invoked the candidate's past gridiron glory. Amid the spectacle he proclaimed that "nothing solidifies Democratic voters like the name and the thought of Richard Nixon." In a statement that hovered between a threat and a warning, Shell remarked that "a large number of Republicans would not vote for Richard Nixon," and that of those who would, "a sizable part . . . would not get out and work for him," thus assuring his defeat.[41]

The assemblyman's words were echoed by other conservatives, some of whom confessed a desire to see the "liberal" Nixon lose to Brown, so as to provide a better opportunity for a right-wing candidate in the next gubernatorial election. Nixon's purported liberalism hurt him, particularly with those on the right who viewed the candidate and his ardent supporters as turncoats and "commie symps."[42] In this context, Jarvis's assertion that "Nixon's not as liberal as Kuchel" amounted to the distinction of the lesser of two evils.[43] Shell, of course, both capitalized on and contributed to this rising right-wing resentment toward the former vice president. Moreover, the assemblyman's description of Nixon as a loser was reinforced by the latter's precipitous drop in the California Poll. Two weeks before the primary election, Brown pulled ahead of Nixon for the first time, and Shell's share of the Republican vote had grown to roughly one-third.

Though Nixon campaigned with an eye on appeasing his party's conservative malcontents after the CRA convention, he encouraged Republican activists to help him "hold our Party on the proper course."[44] He rarely even mentioned Shell in his speeches and comments and tried to appeal directly to his opponent's supporters through his Shell-like vow to clean up the economic "mess in Sacramento." Nixon also attacked Brown as "soft on communism," hoping to rally wayward conservatives behind him with the theme that had served him so well in his early political career. Shell, however, declared that while "there is a communist problem in the state," that issue "beclouded" the larger matter of California's precarious fiscal situation, which he could handle better due to his experience in state government.[45] Indeed, Nixon's reputation as a national political figure preceded him on the campaign trail, as enthusiastic crowds greeted him with questions on Cuba and Kennedy rather than on state issues.[46] Nixon's instant recognition made him a celebrity to be seen and heard, but not necessarily a candidate to be embraced.

The results of the June 5 election made clear that the image of "Governor Nixon" did not have the pervasive appeal, even among Republicans, that the candidate and his strong supporters had expected when he entered the race.

Shell won a third of his party's vote, an impressive percentage not only given his opponent's prominence, but also because the assemblyman's poll numbers had been as low as 2 percent just seven months earlier.[47] Having acknowledged in the campaign's closing weeks that Shell would probably do as well as he in fact did, Nixon saluted him "for fighting a good battle," but obviously hoped the conflict would now end. Shell, however, proved less than conciliatory, declaring that his backers were "dedicated to a set of principles," and that "[t]o the degree Mr. Nixon varies from those principles he'll lose votes."[48]

Due to the lingering resentment of Shell and his sizable faction, Nixon and a coterie of state Republican heavyweights sought to win over the man who had become the party's newest power broker. (Contributing to Shell's lack of magnanimity was his belief that saboteurs working for the Nixon camp had tried to kill him by fouling the fuel supply of his airplane during the campaign, forcing him to make an emergency landing.[49]) As conditions for his support, Shell demanded from Nixon a promise to cut the state budget, and that, if elected, Nixon would allow the Shell wing to comprise one-third of the state's 1964 Republican Convention delegation. In a midnight meeting at the home of Henry Salvatori two weeks after the primary, Nixon and Shell achieved a rapprochement in which the assemblyman dropped his specific demands and formally endorsed Nixon. Apparently caving in to mounting pressure for party unity, Shell stated that "there were no requests made nor any offers tendered or received by Mr. Nixon or myself," and that "there is no real split between us."[50] Despite this modus vivendi, the wounds opened during the campaign would continue to fester, aggravated all the more by Brown's incessant attack on the Birchers and other "Stone Age" extremists and their dubious Republican bedfellows.

With assaults from the right subsiding after the truce with Shell, Nixon in the general election campaign would not face that factional gauntlet of criticism that had battered him during the primary, but the governor and the California Democratic Council (CDC) would escalate their attack, charging that the " 'old Nixon' is the real Nixon," that the master of the smear had returned to shamelessly denigrate good Democrats once again.[51] Thus the Brown camp sought to make it as tough as possible for Nixon to win essential Democratic votes, and at the same time tried to sharpen the rift within the Republican ranks. Unlike Kuchel, who had defeated Wright and Jarvis combined by an impressive three-to-one margin in the primary, Nixon was not making a reelection bid and therefore could not easily "run on his record." In a sense, though, he did just that when he decided to make communism in California the chief issue of his campaign. Hoping to exploit the anticommunist reputation he had gained through his prosecution of Hiss and in his celebrated "kitchen debate" with Soviet leader Nikita Khrushchev in 1959, Nixon set out in earnest to depict Brown as weak-kneed in dealing with the "red menace" in the Golden State.

The former vice president stopped short of calling Brown a communist, and actually asserted that the governor was "as much against communism as I am." Nevertheless he saw himself as better qualified to root out subversives, given his "14 years of experience" in fighting the dreaded foe, who now had militant legions "only 90 miles away from the American mainland." Describing Brown's record in battling communism as "dismal," Nixon stated that because no antisubversive legislation had been passed during the Brown administration, the state needed new laws to meet the mounting dangers. The conservative Democratic chairman of the Senate's Un-American Activities Committee, Hugh Burns, declared existing laws to be adequate, however. He called Nixon's contentions "both shocking and absurd" while praising Brown's "splendid cooperation" with his committee.[52] Though many reacted to Nixon's soft on communism charge with similar incredulity, he would not relent.

To bolster this allegation, Nixon managed to gain the backing of prominent right-wing figures in the press who had been cool toward him during the primary, but who despised the governor. These individuals included newspaper magnate William Randolph Hearst II, journalist and Goldwater disciple Ralph de Toledano, and columnist and commentator Fulton Lewis Jr., whose description of the CDC as "Pat Brown's Extremists" was widely circulated.[53] Even then, support from hard-line conservatives and the far right came more in the form of assaults on Brown and the CDC than in praise for Nixon; and while William Knowland endorsed his former Senate colleague in an editorial in the *Oakland Tribune,* he deemed "absolutely fantastic the claim that Brown is 'soft on communism.'" The governor himself, of course, went further. "My opponent is desperate," he declared, and, lacking "legitimate issues . . . must reach into his shabby bag of tricks for the old slander that has been his stock in trade for the last 16 years."[54]

In particular, Brown and the CDC scornfully highlighted Nixon's past negative campaign collaborations with his long-time chief strategist, Murray Chotiner, in an attempt to bolster the "Tricky Dick" image. Though Nixon later claimed that "no one was ever able to challenge" the facts in the Pink Sheet attack on Douglas,[55] he must have known in 1962 that the "anything-to-win" charges leveled during and after his Senate race would be fully revived when he questioned Brown's anticommunist credentials. Nixon's decision to assail Douglas's "Americanism" in 1950 was egregiously unethical but politically understandable. His vituperative anticommunist campaign reflected, exploited, and defined the intense Cold War fears of 1950, the year that saw the rise of Joe McCarthy. Twelve years later, however, those fears had been tempered by memories of the senator's ugly inquisition and by the fact that the two superpowers had found they could peacefully coexist, albeit uneasily. The "soft on communism" issue, then, appealed most to the right-wingers who already believed that Brown and the CDC were fellow-travelers or at least unwitting accomplices in the "great conspiracy." Ultimately Nixon's charge against Brown appeared to be geared toward appeasing alienated conservatives, the only group with whom the matter could qualify as one of the state's most pressing problems.

Many of the conservatives Nixon tried to assuage, particularly those on the far right, supported an anticommunist ballot proposition that he did not. Proposed by Republican Assemblyman Louis Francis, the measure provided for a constitutional amendment that would give judges, grand juries, and various government officials the right to designate organizations as "subversive," making members subject to severe legal penalties and social ostracism on that basis alone. In backing the proposition, Howard Jarvis declared, "I want the Communist conspiracy in America controlled, ruthlessly. . . ." Loyd Wright and James Utt expressed similar opinions. Nixon opposed the amendment, ostensibly because it was not tough enough. Ignoring the denial of due process, he stated he did not favor the proposition because of a "fatal technical flaw . . . which leaves a loophole by which communists and communist-front organizations may escape enforcement."[56] He seemed to be saying that like Brown, the Francis Amendment was "soft on communism." Apparently hoping not to upset his suspicious right-wing allies, he rejected the proposition on staunchly conservative grounds, rather than side with the moderate and liberal objections to the measure's unconstitutional aspects.

The CDC led the effort to defeat the Francis Amendment, undertaking a major campaign to alert voters to its "unconstitutional dangers." The Council, along with the American Civil Liberties Union, distributed much anti–Francis Amendment literature, as well as a tape of a debate between CDC president Tom Carvey and Francis. The Council's declaration that the proposition "is a threat to our civil liberties of the first magnitude" was echoed by the *Los Angeles Times*.[57] While supporting the intention of the amendment, the *Times* lamented the "monstrous denial of the basic American proposition that everybody is innocent until proved guilty before a trial jury." Even R.C. Hoiles's Santa Ana *Register* opposed the measure, essentially on the libertarian grounds that it would give unwarranted power to a multitude of state authorities.[58]

Aside from the denial of due process, liberals criticized the amendment (which became Proposition 24 on the state ballot) for superseding provisions already covered in federal antisubversive legislation, specifically in the McCarran Communist Registration Act of 1950 and the Communist Control Act of 1954. Furthermore, Proposition 24 would in effect overturn California's Levering Act, which instituted loyalty oaths for all state employees in 1950, but would retain virtually all of act's stipulations, while adding a wide-ranging guilt-by-association clause. Robert Kenny stated that the amendment was what the ancient Romans disparagingly called a *"lex satura* . . . a saturated law, a stuffed, crammed, glutted and gorged law."[59] Representing the liberal opposition, he appealed to the state Supreme Court to strike the proposition from the ballot on the grounds that Francis had added a provision to the measure after submitting it to state authorities for titling. The court declined Kenny's request without comment.

It seems certain that the constitutionality of the amendment would have been legally challenged if it had not been rejected by voters. Though 66 percent of the California electorate approved of the proposition at the beginning of October,[60] it was resoundingly defeated in November. The pervasive criticism of the amendment, which mounted in both Democratic and Republican circles as the election approached, doubtless led to the proposition's demise. Reflective of the distinct regional differences in California's anticommunist attitudes, 51 percent of Orange County voters supported the amendment, while 48 percent backed the measure in Los Angeles County; in the northern metropolitan counterparts to these two counties, San Francisco and Marin, only 24 and 23 percent of the voters, respectively, favored the proposition.[61]

While the campaign for and against the Francis Amendment was conducted outside the gubernatorial race, the rising tide of opposition to the measure could only hinder the effectiveness of the invective Nixon aimed at Brown's record on anticommunism. The crusade against alleged subversives became more closely associated with right-wing zealotry due to the debate over Proposition 24, creating a political climate conducive to the categorization of Nixon's charges as desperate and extreme. Furthermore, Nixon's attack on Brown became entangled with the more vitriolic campaign waged against the governor by the far right. This contributed greatly to the onslaught of allegations from Brown and the CDC that Nixon was following the "scurrilous" Birch Society "primer for political action."[62]

Nixon and other Republicans countered these charges with accusations that Brown and the CDC engaged in "dirty tactics" and smear campaigns of their own, but, more often than not, Republicans were on the defensive in this battle because they had dirtier hands than their opponents. When a bumper sticker asking "IS BROWN PINK?" appeared on vehicles in southern California, state Republican Party chairman Caspar Weinberger declared that the GOP did not participate in the distribution of the stickers.[63] He also denied party involvement in the circulation of a sensational booklet titled "California **D**ynasty of **C**ommunism," which attacked the CDC in particular, as well as Brown and other prominent Democrats. When reporters revealed that Jud Leetham, the GOP chairman in Los Angeles County, admitted that he and others had been distributing the booklet and would continue to do so, Weinberger declared that he could not control the actions of every campaign worker.[64] He believed that the extremist literature and stickers might well have been produced by the Democrats and "planted" at Republican meetings and offices. Brown's campaign manager, Don Bradley, however, contended that "Birch Society types" brought the smear material into local Republican headquarters in strongly conservative areas, and that he and others simply did their best to expose that fact.[65]

In the case of another booklet, Nixon's campaign manager, H.R. Haldeman, attempted to justify the use of a doctored photo that showed an applauding Brown next to a boldfaced statement supporting "Red China's" admission to the United Nations. (Brown was actually applauding a young girl crippled by polio, who was cropped out of the picture.) Haldeman, who later helped execute dirty tricks and the Watergate coverup in the Nixon White House, declared that the photo "is only illustrative of the actual statements made by Brown."[66] While the CDC did favor China's admission to the UN, Brown made clear he opposed that position. That fact held no moral suasion for Haldeman, who initiated a number of other unscrupulous efforts during the course of the campaign. Murray Chotiner, who had joined the Nixon camp after the primary as an unpaid advisor, encouraged such tactics, and Nixon at the very least did not disapprove. (In 1971, President Nixon told chief of staff Haldeman, "we were ratted on in the '62 campaign. But we never found out who it was, did we?")[67] To counter legal actions taken by Brown and the CDC on the distribution of smear literature, Haldeman would announce on November 1 that he planned to file a complaint with the Fair Campaign Practices Committee over a number of alleged unethical tactics by the Democrats.[68]

Countering the tactics of the Nixon camp, the Brown forces, under the guise of the "Independent Voters of California," circulated a copy of a restrictive covenant Nixon signed in 1951, which Nixon could not deny. By signing the covenant, he vowed not to sell his home to an African American or a Jew. Nixon chose not to respond to this revelation. Campaign aide John Ehrlichman suggested that Nixon's silence was rooted in "the premise that deep in their hearts most of the people who would vote for him approved of such covenants. . . ."[69] Given the overwhelming support for the repeal of the Rumford Fair Housing Act in 1964, Ehrlichman was likely right.

Yet racial concerns did not prove particularly salient or contentious during the campaign. Conservatives did grouse about certain race-related matters, such as Brown's creation of the Fair Employment Practices Commission in 1959,[70] but that was hardly a supercharged issue like the Rumford Act four years later, or the Watts riot in 1965. Moreover, Nixon, in keeping with the Modern Republican "proper" ideological course, had to counter Brown's charge that he was unsympathetic to the plight of blacks. In one of his late campaign telethons, the former vice president enlisted the support of Jackie Robinson, the ex-baseball star who in 1947 had broken the color barrier in the major leagues. "America needs to develop the talents of all our people," Nixon assured Robinson, "including the Negro people."[71]

On another front, Nixon had to defend himself from incessant accusations and questioning by Brown and other Democrats about a secret $205,000 loan Nixon's brother received from the Hughes Tool Company (owned by the millionaire aviator and entrepreneur, Howard Hughes) in 1956. When knowledge of the loan became public in 1960, critics asserted that a number of Hughes's companies, which did much business with the federal government, had received preferential treatment in the awarding of federal contracts during Eisenhower's second term. The incident proved troublesome but manageable for Nixon, and did not become much of an issue during his presidential bid. Nevertheless, Brown and others badgered him about the matter, despite his repeated claim that he was "never asked to do anything for Hughes."[72]

In a joint press conference on October 1—the closest the two candidates ever came to debating—Nixon declared that Brown and his "hatchetmen" had prodded certain newsmen to ask him about the loan. After poignantly defending his brother and mother, the latter having put up "practically everything she had as security for that loan," Nixon thundered that the governor "has the chance to stand up as a man and charge me with misconduct. Do it, sir."[73] Brown bumbled his way through a less-than-dignified rejoinder, sounding much like the "tower of jelly" that many Republicans thought him to be. Given Nixon's comments in his memoirs, this exchange seems to have been his most satisfying moment in an overwhelmingly frustrating campaign.[74]

Perhaps more than anything else, the statements and exchanges at the press conference reflected the absence of the discussion of substantive issues in the campaign. Though reporters contributed to this vacuity by focusing on purported smears, they merely followed the candidates' leads. Despite his later claim to have made every effort "to campaign on the issues," Nixon did this in earnest only in the telethons he aired toward the end of the race, and even then he tended to expound mainly on national and international matters.[75] Brown, in turn, did little to elevate the contest's discourse. Nevertheless, Nixon's soft on communism charge, along with the underhanded methods of Chotiner, Haldeman and others, provided ample fodder for the governor's almost daily assertion that his opponent lacked both integrity and an issue. Moreover, Nixon struggled when it came to detailing what he meant by the "mess in Sacramento," because the Brown administration's fiscal record contained no glaring problems that could be easily assailed or exploited. In fact the governor's master plan for higher education and his efforts to improve state infrastructure and water projects were widely commended. Nixon's campaign therefore became entrenched in hackneyed Cold War invectives and other standard Republican diatribes.

Further tapping the latter, the former vice president blasted the "Democratic trend toward big government . . . in Sacramento and Washington" in an address to the conservative California Real Estate Association (CREA) in mid-October. He received a standing ovation when he declared that government should not meddle in functions that could be done better by private enterprise.[76] The realtors' convention had gotten under way two days earlier with an inaugural address by an executive of the National Association of Real Estate Boards, who proclaimed that "the thwarted desire for ownership of land is essentially the reason for the turmoil in the world today."[77] In light of this pronouncement, it is sadly ironic that two years later the CREA, in leading the effort to repeal the Rumford Fair Housing Act, would seek to deny African Americans and other minorities the right to own land in the neighborhoods of their choice. Ronald Reagan, who would be strongly in favor of the Rumford repeal in 1964, delivered "The Speech" to the convention's opening-day audience with his usual panache. In addition to his diatribe on high taxes and bloated government bureaucracies, the actor proposed that the United States should blockade Cuba to stop the Soviet military buildup there. "We are very late on Cuba," he contended, "and we must not wait any longer."[78]

The wait did not prove to be long, for on October 22 President Kennedy announced that he had ordered a naval blockade of Cuba after reconnaissance photos revealed Soviet missile installations on the island. Across the country Americans reacted with considerable alarm, as the nuclear exchange that had long been feared loomed closer than ever to being triggered. Both Brown and Nixon declared their complete support for Kennedy's actions and asked all citizens to remain calm. The governor stated he would curtail his campaign activities in light of the crisis, and asserted that anyone who now suggested that "the leadership of either party is soft on communism" sowed the "fatal seeds of disunity and distrust."[79]

Nixon chose not to assail Brown directly but did so implicitly on October

24 with his familiar refrain that California needed a "forceful and positive [state] program to supplement federal action in the fight against communism." He also called for anticommunist courses to be taught in state public schools, and made clear that as governor he would take a personal hand in the selection of textbooks for such classes. Noting that his opponent had labeled him a would-be "dictator" for his proposed curriculum and personal involvement in it, Nixon declared, "I welcome this attack."[80] The Cuban crisis, then, afforded Nixon the opportunity to exhibit his bravado in combating communism. It also highlighted his national stature. In a special televised speech on October 27, Nixon used his oft-repeated "I know Khrushchev" line, and described Castro, whom he had also met, as "a hot-blooded maniac" compared to the "cold" Soviet leader. Reminding voters that he had greater experience in foreign affairs than Brown, he provided a detailed analysis of the Cuban dilemma.[81] Perhaps the best speech of his campaign, it nonetheless reinforced the "steppingstone" notion, making the former vice president's purported concern for the problems of Imperial Valley farmers or the logistics of state transportation plans seem all the more disingenuous.

In his address Nixon charged that California's civil defense program lagged "way behind New York," and made a number of proposals for improvements. "Under no circumstances," he declared, "should we have a 'panic' program."[82] The missile crisis did create some hysteria in California, especially in Los Angeles, where a frenzied rush of customers to local supermarkets occurred after the city's civil defense director stated that residents should have a two-week food supply. The *Los Angeles Times* described the tension in the city as greater than in the "early days of World War II," when concern over a Japanese attack did not entail "the deep, shapeless fear inspired by the thought of nuclear war."[83] This high anxiety would wane as October came to a close, with Kennedy and Khrushchev peacefully resolving the superpower confrontation. Despite this resolution, Nixon would continue to condemn Brown's "shocking attempts to hoodwink the people of California into a false sense of security."[84] The governor appeared credible and responsible, however, having gone to Washington during the crisis for "high-level" briefings, which facilitated his dismissal of Nixon's allegation as "nonsense." Regardless of "experience," in the contest to exploit the Cuban issue the advantage went to the incumbent, whose dutiful actions spoke louder than his opponent's alarming words.

Stumping the state to endorse the Republican slate of candidates, Joe Shell supported Kennedy's blockade of Cuba, but lambasted him for having vetoed air support for the failed Bay of Pigs invasion in April 1961. Indicative of the conservative resentment of Kennedy's decision not to fully back the Cuban exiles who attempted to overthrow Castro, Shell called the president's inaction a "crime against humanity." He declared that this "total lack of understanding put us in our present position."[85] On state matters, Shell repeatedly echoed Nixon's attack on the governor's tepid anti-communism and asserted that a Brown victory would mean increases in taxes and state expenditures and the expansion of the welfare state. "The Brown administration and [Kennedy's] New Frontier tend to teach the people to accept handouts," Shell stated. "We must make a right turn toward less government spending and more individual responsibility." Though never enthusiastic, his support for his former opponent was generally unequivocal. In addition, he provided a list of his campaign contributors to Republican officials to solicit for Nixon's general election battle.[86] Nevertheless, Democrats made certain that both the Birch matter and the assemblyman's accusation during the primary that Nixon had used "gutter tactics" would not be forgotten.

Late in the campaign a group of disaffected ultraconservative Republicans began a write-in drive for Shell's gubernatorial candidacy. The Draft Shell movement "exposed" Nixon and Brown as the Tweedledum and Tweedledee of California politics. Citing a Biblical admonition, "Let No Man Deceive You By Any Means," the Draft's flyer went on to list the purported identical and duplicitous positions of the Democratic and Republican candidates on issues of the utmost concern: both favored "Godless, socialistic one-world government" (i.e., the UN) as well as federal and state bureaucracies, while opposing student loyalty oaths and patriotic organizations. A vote for Shell, therefore, "will decide if we can regain [the privileges of] our Constitution and the Bill of Rights."[87] The assemblyman expressed displeasure with his allegiant supporters and disassociated himself from them. This movement's fervor for "correct" views, however, presaged the litmus test for ideological purity that would be applied to Republicans by many Goldwaterites in California in 1964, a "for us or against us" mentality that allowed no compromise. Unable to rally these Shell followers behind him, Nixon proved to be the first prominent "liberal" Republican casualty of the far right's fervor, followed later by Rockefeller and then Kuchel.

The origins of the write-in movement are uncertain, but it is clear that Goldwater loyalists participated in it in the hope of denying Nixon the strong political base the governorship would give him in a challenge for the 1964 presidential nomination. The draft effort doubtless gained further impetus from the pervasive loathing of Nixon's candidacy among important activists in the CRA and the Young Republicans. The latter's Los Angeles County branch, under the guidance of Gaston, not only declined to support

Nixon but sought to discredit him whenever possible. This Republican animosity, which proved widespread in southern California, stemmed mainly from the Birch issue and the rejection of Nixon's "middle-of-the-road" views.[88] Redolent of the Draft Shell circular, a Young Republican newsletter assailed the former vice president by stating that the "difference between a 'liberal' Republican and a 'liberal' Democrat is the difference between creeping socialism & galloping socialism."[89] Of the many Republicans who agreed with this statement, it is likely that more than a few did not vote for Nixon. At the very least, as Shell had maintained in his primary campaign, these right-wingers would hardly be inclined to do their part in the footwork and phone calling essential to Nixon's hopes of victory.

Contrary to Nixon's dilemma with intraparty discord, the Brown campaign unified Democrats in the course of vilifying their long-despised opponent. The governor and the more liberal CDC glossed over their differences so as to focus their combined energy on pummeling the "Prospector of the Potomac." Watching the Nixon–Brown contest with keen interest, President Kennedy had planned to visit California during the last week of October but had to cancel that trip due to the Cuban crisis. Members of Kennedy's cabinet, however, took to the stump for the governor, and the president made a few timely announcements about defense contract awards to California industries during the course of the campaign. Apparently wanting to see Nixon lose as much as anyone else, Kennedy told Brown and Don Bradley, "I killed the guy. All you have to do is bury him."[90] To the Democrats' delight, alienated Republicans, such as those in the CYR, assisted in that burial.

As the campaign came to a close, Nixon could look back on few high points. These rare moments would have included the fusillade he fired at Brown over the Hughes loan in early October, and a visit and ringing endorsement from Dwight Eisenhower shortly thereafter. In addition, he did appear to have a fair chance to win in mid October, as the California Poll showed the race to be dead even, but the numbers changed once again in Brown's favor after the missile crisis. While the specific impact of this event on the election results cannot be known, the conventional wisdom—supported by polling data—is that it helped incumbents. Nixon figured it killed whatever chance he might have had to beat Brown. Resigned to defeat by late October, Nixon plaintively recalled, "[w]e had to play the dreary drama through to its conclusion. . . ."[91]

The campaign ended in the mudslinging fashion in which it began, but with more frequent salvos and bursts of bombast. As if to settle the soft-on-communism matter once and for all, Brown trumpeted that "I am every bit as good an American as . . . Nixon and a whole lot better." Not to be outdone, Nixon declared that in the last days before the election, Brown's "professional hatchetmen . . . [will] launch the most massive campaign of fear and smear in the history of California elections."[92] This assertion, however, was tactical, and had no basis in fact.[93] While Brown had his moments of epithetical blather, it was Nixon, with help from his hatchetmen Haldeman and Chotiner, who engaged in the big smear, as he had in his earlier California campaigns. But the tactics that had politically eviscerated Voorhis and Douglas would not cut deeply into Brown.

The governor, therefore, emerged victorious on the first Tuesday in November. Nixon lost by almost 300,000 votes, a better showing than Knowland in 1958, but there could be little consolation in that dubious distinction. Kuchel, on the other hand, defeated his Democratic opponent, State Senator Richard Richards, by more than 700,000 votes, despite the fact that he did not return to California to campaign until mid October. Aided by a popular picture showing him helmet-clad as he entered an Air Force fighter jet for a speedy return to Washington during the missile crisis, Kuchel's impressive victory margin included the support of over 800,000 Democrats.[94]

There has been debate over whether Nixon lost due to his inability to corral enough Democratic support or because the Republican right largely abandoned him.[95] In all likelihood, Nixon lost critical Democratic votes *due* to the dissent and desertion within his party. The GOP feud cost Nixon important election workers and cast another shadow over his candidacy, which could not help but diminish his electoral chances. Moreover, he appeared to be red-baiting and pandering to the right with his soft-on-communism charge, offsetting the positive impact his denunciation of the JBS might have had with conservative and moderate Democrats unexcited by Brown. Combined with the revelations of deceitful campaign methods and doubts over Nixon's interest in being governor, the fallout from the Republican factional rancor alienated enough voters from both parties to bring about his defeat.

Conversely, difficulties of the sort that plagued the former vice president did not hobble Brown, whose best issue, other than Nixon himself, proved to be the state's great economic growth during his administration. He also capitalized on the Cuban crisis by fashioning a timely "in-charge" image to counter notions that he was an amiable bumbler. On the organizational level, the Democrats carried out an effective registration drive, and on election day shuttled to the polls many of the governor's supporters who otherwise might not have bothered to vote. These factors compounded Nixon's problems, further frustrating his hopes that he could "peak" during the final week of the campaign and overtake Brown.[96] Perhaps the most discouraging factor of all for Nixon was his press coverage, which he deemed unfair. This led to his famous "last press conference" the day after the election, in which he bitterly proclaimed to startled reporters, "[y]ou won't have Nixon to kick around anymore" due to his decision to end his political career.

Though not singling them out specifically, Nixon clearly aimed his diatribe at the *Los Angeles Times* and one of its political reporters, Richard Bergholz. The *Times* had embraced Nixon in his early political pursuits and throughout the 1950s, providing largely uncritical coverage and resounding endorsements, which played no small part in his initial ascent. This biased reportage began to change in 1960 when the paper's conservative publisher, Norman Chandler, turned over the corporate reins to his more moderate son, Otis. The latter set out to make the *Times* one of the country's best newspapers, and knew that to achieve that goal the publication's political coverage would have to be evenhanded. Therefore, Bergholz and fellow *Times* reporter Carl Greenberg—the only reporter to cover him fairly, Nixon stated—avoided favoring Republican candidates over Democrats in their stories.[97] As other authors have noted, members of the press merely reported what the gubernatorial candidates uttered, much to Nixon's chagrin and often to his detriment.[98] Responding to the former vice president's implicit blast at his paper, Chandler pointed out that the *Times* had endorsed Nixon in every one of his campaigns, including his run for governor. "We continue today to believe that he was the best qualified candidate for governor. . . ." (In 1971, Nixon stated: "Otis Chandler; I want him checked out with regard to his gardener. I understand he's a wetback.")[99] In fact, though the paper had taken on a more moderate tone, its political endorsements remained primarily Republican, but its editorial and news columns lost their ingrained conservative edge.

Nixon's loss left the California Republican Party in disarray, much as Knowland's defeat had four years earlier. As a whole, the party fared poorly in the election, winning only one important office on the state level outside the legislature. Furthermore, with Nixon—who joined a New York law firm in 1963—and Knowland qualifying as has-beens, Republicans lacked a clear-cut leader who could foster optimism. Nevertheless, Jud Leetham expressed confidence that the GOP would recover and dominate state politics in the near future. Speaking of an impending "Republican movement in California," Leetham stated that the next leader of the party would have to be able to represent all its factions, an obvious reference to Nixon's shortcoming in this regard.[100] The next commanding figure in state Republican politics, however, would be Barry Goldwater, who by 1964, if not earlier, had endeared himself to conservative Californians as rugged individualism personified, but whose appeal did not extend beyond the right.

Five

"How the West Was Won"

Though Republican candidates in California fared poorly in 1962, the party made a modest improvement on the drubbing it took four years earlier. Disappointed in Nixon's loss, Modern Republicans found some consolation in Kuchel's victory and in the defeat of both the Francis Amendment and the two avowed JBS members seeking reelection to Congress. Conservatives, many of whom supported Kuchel, though usually without enthusiasm, could take satisfaction in the reelection of Secretary of State Frank Jordan (who had survived in 1958 as well) and especially in the triumph of Dr. Max Rafferty, a combative "back-to-the-basics" right-wing educator who won the ostensibly nonpartisan race for State Superintendent of Public Instruction. Most importantly, fervid conservatives who opposed Nixon or voted for him reluctantly could take stock in Shell's strong showing in the primary and in Rafferty's victory as portents of a burgeoning crusade.

Indeed, the conservative movement gained greater force after the election, particularly through the newly formed United Republicans of California (UROC). Established by Shell and his gubernatorial campaign manager, Rus Walton, the organization aimed to take control of the party from its more moderate power brokers who were entrenched in the CRA and the Republican State Central Committee (RSCC). A "grassroots" operation along the lines of the CDC, the UROC, according to Walton, represented "democracy in action" because it did not have the "top down" hierarchy that typified the Republican machine of the "old smoke-filled room." In addition to Shell himself, the principal financiers of the organization included Hub Russell and former state senator Bruce Reagan (no relation to Ronald) of Pasadena, as well as others who had ardently backed Shell's challenge to Nixon.[1]

Walton stated that UROC shunned populism by "neglecting to bend to the wind and . . . whims of the people," but rather adhered to conservative positions and values on important issues. The UROC "Statement of Principles" proclaimed: "Complete centralizing of power destroys liberty and encourages tyranny, but the dispersion and decentralization of governmental power insure the freedom of each individual citizen." Affirming that "God is the source of the rights and freedoms of the individual," the organization averred, "[t]he threat of the evil of Communism must be met and overcome by a determination to achieve victory for the free way of life."[2]

Though issue-oriented like the CDC, the UROC became dedicated to Goldwater's anticipated presidential bid. To facilitate that effort, the organization militated against Modern Republicans with a zeal that exceeded the conservative support for Shell's bid for governor. The UROC proved instrumental in helping Robert Gaston win the presidency of the California Young Republicans (CYR) in 1963 by paying for much of his travel expenses during his extensive campaign throughout the state.[3] Despite protests from Caspar Weinberger and other moderate party officials that incursive tactics would ultimately hurt both party factions, the UROC did not relent in its attempt to "rebuild" the California GOP in accordance with conservative principles. The organization grew to be a significant force, enlisting approximately 20,000 members by 1964.[4]

Almost a movement unto himself, the staccato-speaking Rafferty rose to prominence in 1960 when he ran successfully for superintendent of schools in La Canada, a wealthy Los Angeles suburb. He gained considerable support from conservatives due to his strident criticism of "progressive" education and related "problems." In a June 1961 speech to his La Canada constituents, he assailed "the phoney sophisticates who clutter up our colleges," the "spineless, luxury-loving, spiritless creeps" who had come out of public school classrooms in the recent years. The blame for this lack of character, the superintendent contended, could be placed squarely on the shoulders of progressive educators who stressed "relative" values and dismissed notions of "eternal verities." Lambasting the idea that educators could "teach the child, not the subject," Rafferty proclaimed that such methods made even the best students more susceptible to "Red psychological warfare," and in the worst cases produced "unwashed, leather-jacketed slobs, whose favorite sport is ravaging little girls and stomping polio victims to death."[5] He would use the "unwashed ... slobs" castigation, or a variation of it, time and again to deride student demonstrators in the mid- and late 1960s.

In his speech, Rafferty focused on "a vanishing species—the American patriot," and lamented that the historical "hero" had been "debunked ... to make room for the [contemporary] jerk," as exemplified by the "vapid [textbook] ditherings" of "Dick and Jane." The superintendent's strident views doubtless alarmed some Californians. In addition to his castigations of progressive education, his celebration of the Founders and unabashed nationalism included a call for the "indoctrination" of the nation's school children through the illumination of the "glittering sword of patriotism." Yet this utterance, and others like it, stirred many conservatives, especially those among the ample legions of vehement anticommunists in southern California. Though inspired by Rafferty's devout praise for the likes of Nathan Hale and George Washington, right-wing indignation surely simmered when he asserted that "[p]atriotism feeds upon hero-worship, and we decided to abolish heroes."[6] The superintendent made it his mission to restore an unequivocal reverence for the nation's "heroic" past in California's youth, and to turn back the "evils" of progressive educational theory.

Rafferty became the "chosen" conservative candidate for state superintendent after Virgil Hollis, a school superintendent in Marin County, declined to enter the race. Shortly after Hollis's decision, a "draft Rafferty" office opened in Orange County. Eventually he was summoned to a "meeting of millionaires" at the California Club in Los Angeles. These individuals, who gave Rafferty their approval and sizable contributions, included at least nine heads or executives of major oil companies and leading state banking and real estate figures. Twelve of Rafferty's chief contributors had been backers of the right-to-work campaign as well.[7]

Rafferty touted his conservative agenda on the campaign trail in his pitched battle against Ralph Richardson, a liberal Democrat. During the campaign, Richardson declared that Rafferty possessed "one of the finest minds of the twelfth century," and appeared to be "running against the ghost of [progressive educator] John Dewey" in his quest to bring elementary education back to the days of the *McGuffey Reader*. Rafferty countered such assertions by making strident arguments for the time-tested fundamentals of learning rather than a specious "life adjustment" curriculum.[8] The outspoken views of each candidate, particularly Rafferty's, made this race a key contest in the state's liberal–conservative struggle. The Richardson camp noted that its opponent both appeared publicly and socialized with JBS members, and endorsed ultraconservative measures such as the Francis Amendment. For his part, the charismatic Rafferty warned that if Richardson won, a state-controlled education system based on a "European" model would wrest control from local school boards and dictate which textbooks and methodologies would be used in the classroom.[9] California voters found his argument convincing enough to give him a comfortable victory over his liberal adversary.

While Rafferty's victory and Shell's strong showing against Nixon provided a boost for conservative morale, the subsequent formation of the UROC and the right-wing takeover of the CYR provided the incipient organization in California for Goldwater's presidential candidacy.

Epitomizing Rafferty's patriotic hero of American history, Arizona Senator Barry Goldwater appeared to his devoted supporters to possess the steadfast American virtues of those who had earlier "conquered" both the harsh terrain and the Native Americans of the West. His admirers saw him as a plain-speaking defender of the "pioneer spirit" elemental to American life, and spiteful of the Washington beltway politicos who derided that spirit to promote big government. Critics, however, saw Goldwater's beliefs, and much of Western politics in general, as the stuff of nostalgia. Secretary of the Interior Stewart Udall, for example, stated that those who tenaciously clung to the creed of rugged individualism were afflicted by the "Zane Grey syndrome"—an "oversimplified world ... of individualistic 'good men' pitted against bureaucratic 'bad men.'"[10] This description, drawn from Udall's experience as a native Arizonan and bureaucrat, contained more than a modicum of truth.

Nevertheless, millions of Americans each week got caught up in the oversimplified world of television Westerns, willfully succumbing, if only momentarily, to the Zane Grey syndrome. Generally reflecting the yeomanly heroic past that Rafferty heralded, episodes from myriad Westerns enabled viewers to escape from the complexities of modern corporate society and vicariously experience the inflated thrills and simple satisfactions of life on the sagebrush frontier. By the early 1960s the weekly audience for TV Westerns was estimated at about 60 million. Writing in the *National Review*, William F. Rickenbacker explained this phenomenon by contending that "people would much rather live on the Old Frontier than the new one." Implicitly exhibiting the anti-Eastern animus harbored by many Westerners, he suggested that

> [i]f Wyatt Earp or somebody from Arizona or Texas with the glint of the Western mountains in his eye ... offers himself as a candidate on a platform of running the rascals out of town, 60 million of us westerners will put him into office.[11]

Movie Westerns held the same appeal as their TV counterparts, with a strong heroic component. Released in 1960, *The Alamo,* produced by and starring John Wayne, depicted the men who defended that Texas fort as gallantly dedicated to the cause of liberty, and contained many patriotic utterances and symbols. The fervidly conservative Wayne—who joined the JBS in the 1960s—wanted the film to be a "metaphor of America," to give patriotism a boost, because "we've all been going soft, taking freedom for granted."[12] Though *The Alamo* did not become the box office blockbuster Wayne and his associates hoped it would be, the star-studded *How the West Was Won,* in which Wayne played Civil War general William Sherman, proved to be the second most popular film of 1962. The movie celebrated the legendary individualism of the West, as stout settlers contended with the often inhospitable environment, "bad" men, and native inhabitants of the region, in pursuit of their "self-made" livelihoods. The film, in short, contained all the elements that helped Westerns permeate American popular culture.

Inextricably linked to this ruggedly romantic past, Goldwater's Western image fit the description of either Udall's anachronistic Zane Grey or Rickenbacker's righteous Wyatt Earp for critics and admirers, respectively. Embracing the Earp image, California conservatives, especially in the Southland, supported the senator mainly because he promised to struggle to renew the "old but true" American values and laissez-faire government. Politically rooted in the "rugged" conservatism of the Calvin Coolidge–Herbert Hoover era, but imagistically tied to the Western frontier, Goldwater and his devout followers celebrated the "100 percent Americanism" and unimpeded capitalism of bygone times.

Goldwater sowed the seeds for his 1964 presidential candidacy when he led the conservative opposition to the "liberal" party platform at the 1960 Republican National Convention. New York governor Nelson Rockefeller, the leading challenger to Richard Nixon, pressured the vice president into making the platform more moderate, particularly in regard to civil rights. Though Goldwater backed Nixon, this "treasonous" move outraged him and his fellow conservatives, whom he urged to "take this party back."[13] After Nixon's defeat, support for the senator's candidacy quickly coalesced, led by a formal draft movement headed by F. Clifton White, a savvy Republican campaign organizer.[14] By the summer of 1963, Goldwater had emerged as the favorite to win his party's nomination.

Never enthusiastic about pursuing the presidency, the senator became more uncertain about his desire in the waning weeks of 1963, after the assassination of President Kennedy. The two men had been friendly adversaries while Kennedy resided in the White House, and Goldwater believed that in a presidential campaign he could persuasively illuminate the virtues of conservatism in debates with his liberal opponent.[15] In the somber aftermath of Kennedy's death, however, Lyndon Johnson appealed to the grieving nation to honor the slain president by supporting the latter's liberal agenda, particularly on civil rights: "Let us continue," Johnson exhorted. Therefore 1964 would not prove a propitious year to win converts to conservatism; but before contending with this problem in the general election campaign, Goldwater had the more immediate task of overcoming considerable opposition to his quest for the Republican nomination, which he officially announced in January. The battle for delegates to the party's national convention reached its climax in the California primary.

After poor showings in the earlier Republican primaries, Goldwater needed to win the California contest in June to secure his party's nomination. Though he had amassed more delegates than any other Republican candidate, most of them came from nonprimary states in which he had no strong opposition. Following a defeat in the campaign's first primary in New Hampshire, the senator won in Illinois, Indiana, and Nebraska. These victories, however, were unimpressive because he did not face serious challengers. In light of this, Goldwater hoped to score a decisive victory in California over his leading opponent, Rockefeller, the only other candidate on the ballot. In this winner-take-all contest, the senator sought to add the Golden State's eighty-six delegates to his slate, which would give him more than the required number for the nomination.

Rockefeller hoped to sink Goldwater in California by pinning the extremist label on him. Despite a well-financed effort, the governor's attempt to depict the senator as a right-wing radical did not sway enough Republicans for him to triumph in the primary. In particular, Rockefeller could not generate enough support among conservatives. Though an avid anti-communist, Rockefeller's adversarial stance did not match the absolutely uncompromising views that had helped make the senator so popular among Southland conservatives. More important, as governor of a large Eastern "welfare state," Rockefeller represented the statism the Goldwaterites despised. A multitude of southern California Republicans, therefore, resented the scion of the Standard Oil empire. This resentment compelled them to work hard as volunteers in the Goldwater campaign, which proved invaluable to his success.

In some ways Rockefeller appeared to be a made-to-order opponent for Goldwater in California, where the Arizonan's campaign took on a brazen populist air in which the West of the stout pioneers challenged the East's "corrupt" power brokers. A short book by arch-conservative Phyllis Schlafly, *A Choice Not an Echo* (the title became a Goldwater campaign slogan), greatly aided this effort. Approximately a half-million copies were sold or distributed in California prior to the primary, and its thesis helped rally the state's right-wing Republicans. Schlafly charged that since 1936, powerful Eastern liberal Republicans had conspired with "left-wing" Democrats to assure that neither party's nominee would threaten the "hidden policy of perpetuating the Red Empire . . . to perpetuate the high level of Federal spending and control."[16] Schlafly declared that the Republican "secret New York Kingmakers" aimed to deny Goldwater the presidential nomination because he intended to put an end to this "conspiracy."

The senator's political life did appear to be dedicated to that goal, as his strident conservatism thrust him into the vanguard of the Republican right.

By the late 1950s he became the leading voice of that faction, filling a void created in 1953 upon the death of Robert Taft. Goldwater, however, leaned further to the right than Taft. Unlike Goldwater, Taft had not called for the virtual elimination of extant New Deal agencies and legislation. In Taft's vision of America, the federal government had regulatory and fiscal obligations in social and economic matters, albeit limited; in Goldwater's, it did not.

Reflecting the sentiment of his liberal, "vital center" colleagues, Richard Hofstadter described Goldwater as a pseudo-conservative who espoused beliefs well to the right of Taft's. He borrowed the term *pseudo-conservative* from sociologist Theodore Adorno's book *The Authoritarian Personality,* and drew upon Adorno's assertion that pseudo-conservatives, "in the name of upholding traditional American values ... and defending them against more or less fictitious dangers, consciously or unconsciously aim at their abolition."[17] Despite the condemnation of the intelligentsia—indeed, in no small part because of it—the senator developed a substantial and devoted following.

Goldwater's California devotees were led initially by Shell and Gaston, among a few others. Shell's clash with Nixon had foreshadowed an early but important confrontation between Rockefeller backers and Goldwaterites over the control of the party in 1963 at the annual convention of the CRA. The organization had always been dominated by moderates, but conservatives now posed a serious threat. The moderates declared that a conservative victory would also be one for the group's extremist ally, the JBS. Amid considerable acrimony, retired Navy commander Harry Waddell, who had described Birchers as "good Americans" and welcomed their support, lost to William Nelligan, a San Francisco labor union official, in the CRA presidential election. With this victory Rockefeller backers seemed well positioned to steer the CRA's endorsement to their man at the 1964 state convention. Outgoing president Fred Hall triumphantly proclaimed that the election of Nelligan "is the turning point against the conspiracy of the John Birch Society and its supporters to capture control of the Republican Party."[18] Conspiratorial or not, the "good Americans" returned to the 1964 CRA convention as part of the strong conservative bloc.

The Rockefeller forces commanded the CRA and all its machinery in early 1964 but were outmaneuvered in parliamentary procedure by the Goldwaterites, and ultimately lost control of the organization at the convention in March. Conservatives from Orange County, a haven for the JBS, now dominated the CRA's leadership, and the senator received the group's endorsement for the presidential nomination.[19] Given that he had also received the backing of the UROC and the state's Young Republicans, both of which had unofficial ties to the JBS, the issue of Birchism flared up once again. Before stepping down as CRA president, Nelligan warned that "fanatics of the Birch variety have fastened their fangs on the Republican Party's flanks and are hanging on like grim death." Spurning this takeover, one progressive Republican group fought the JBS through biting and cathartic humor by forming the FAB Society—the acronym stood for "Fuck A Bircher"—at the convention. Goldwater tried to downplay the extremism matter by deploring those who "conjure up phantom issues . . . as the one about the extremist take-over of the Republican Party in California."[20] He had been hurt, however, by his image as an extremist in earlier primaries, particularly in New Hampshire. The senator likely knew this problem would continue in California, given that he, like Harry Waddell, had judged Birchers to be upstanding citizens.

Heightened by the conservative triumph in the CRA, the fear of extremism spurred a strong "stop Goldwater" movement within the GOP in California and across the country. Hoping to rally moderates and liberals, Republican National Committeeman Joseph Martin Jr. declared that he had joined the Rockefeller campaign "to do my part to prevent the Republican Party from becoming a branch of the John Birch Society. . . ." Martin did not view Goldwater as an extremist but believed he "simply doesn't understand the forces behind him. They'll ruin the party." The *New York Times* echoed Martin's concern: "[the senator] might not believe in the extremism of the right in either foreign or domestic policy; but those who do would vastly profit from his victory."[21]

Though the number of Birchers among California's Republicans in 1964 is uncertain, Los Angeles and Orange counties ranked as the Society's premier urban strongholds. While most Southland conservatives were not members of the JBS and did not subscribe to the more outlandish contentions of Robert Welch, their "pro-American" views did reflect anticommunist and antistatist tenets and goals broadly similar to those of the Birchers. To these people, therefore, membership in the JBS did not necessarily come with an extremist opprobrium.[22] Goldwater, while generally supportive of the JBS, rejected Welch and his convoluted conspiracy theory. Indeed, he called for Welch's resignation, but to no avail: "I wish he would step out so the fine, responsible people who are members could take charge." His denunciation of Welch put some—though ultimately not enough—tangible distance between him and the "kook" element of the far right. He also received support from some of the nation's leading conservative thinkers who had denounced Welch, including Professor Russell Kirk and William F. Buckley Jr. (The latter frequently lauded Goldwater in the *National Review* and syndicated newspaper commentaries, but did develop a rocky relationship with the senator's chief advisors during the course of his campaign.)[23] The senator received additional support, though often qualified, from a number of prominent GOP congressional colleagues; including Everett Dirksen, the Senate minority leader. All these factors doubtless contributed to the widely held belief among Southland Republicans that Goldwater was a true conservative—a true Republican, for that matter—and not a radical right-winger.

Ultimately, Rockefeller's effort to portray Goldwater as an extremist failed in the south because the senator's opinions were either not seen as radical by the vast majority of the region's Republicans, or were deemed extreme but necessary to remedy the ills of and threats to the nation. (The latter belief was later reflected in Goldwater's acceptance speech at the Republican Convention.) Despite this prevailing sentiment, conspicuous support from the JBS would have been problematic for the senator due to the organization's negative public image. The Society, therefore, did Goldwater the favor of foregoing a formal endorsement, but members worked hard for him during the campaign.[24]

Voter anxieties also blunted Rockefeller's depictions of Goldwater as an extremist. A poll of those likely to vote in the Republican primary revealed that Castro's Cuba and the fear of Soviet subversion and espionage, both Goldwater issues, ranked among the top concerns of the state's party members. Anticommunism as a campaign issue, however, was not the senator's high trump card due to Rockefeller's strong anticommunist record. Though less zealous than Goldwater, the governor had opposed Kennedy's nuclear test ban agreement with the Soviet Union in 1963, and firmly promoted a strong defense policy. He also had proposed in 1959 that a bomb shelter be built in every American home. Anticommunism aside, it seems that Rockefeller, one of the "agents of the Kingmakers," was hurt most in southern California by the perception of New York as a big welfare state with high taxes. Moreover, he appeared to be the candidate to whom the baton of Modern Republicanism—whose powerful exponents had declined to repudiate the New Deal—had been passed. These factors led many California conservatives to view Rockefeller as an Eastern advocate for wasteful bureaucratic government. This plagued him greatly, for federal spending and the national debt concerned the state's Republicans most of all.[25]

Determined to present himself as a "mainstream Republican" during the California campaign, the senator toned down his fulminations against costly liberal federal programs. He still maintained that the government had to withdraw entirely from farm subsidies, public housing and urban renewal, and substantially cut back aid to education. He also stated that federally controlled public power agencies, particularly the Tennessee Valley Authority, should either be eliminated or be turned over in large part to private enterprise. To the many conservative Southland Republicans holding these beliefs, Rockefeller in contrast appeared to be a taxmonger and a spend-thrift.[26] Goldwater, however, had been and continued to be attacked for his stand on Social Security. Long an advocate of the actuarially unsound position that the system should be made voluntary, the senator had been hurt in previous primaries by this position, especially by elderly voters. To reverse this trend, his campaign ads in California declared: "I say strengthen the security in Social Security."[27]

Beneath this rhetorical expedient Goldwater believed that "one of the great evils of Welfarism . . . [is that] it transforms the individual from a dignified, industrious, self-reliant spiritual being into a dependent animal creature without his knowing it."[28] The liberal welfare state, the senator intoned, violated the American principle of rugged individualism that he often extolled through references to the country's "pioneer spirit." In California, Goldwater's camp smartly portrayed him as the quintessential rugged American to appeal to those individuals they saw as being of a similar ilk. One of the Arizonan's top advisors, F. Clifton White, wrote in his campaign memoir that most of the California Goldwater enthusiasts "are rugged individualists of the old stamp," but in the same paragraph he rightly acknowledged that "their livelihood might be dependent upon jobs directly or indirectly created by government money."[29] Clearly, those who held jobs created "directly or indirectly" by the government could not truly qualify as rugged individualists of the old self-made stamp. White's observation suggests that rugged individualism endured more as a state of mind than of reality in Goldwater's inner circle. In this sense, the largely mythical self-reliance and economic independence of the Old West permeated the new.

The history of the Western states is, in fact, one of dependence on the federal government. While rich in natural resources, California could not have prospered without federal aid. Funds for transportation and harbor improvements, in addition to subsidies for ranchers and the timber industry, helped the state boom. The greatest benefit, however, came from federal construction of dams and irrigation systems, especially during the New Deal. The chief beneficiaries of these efforts proved to be large-scale farmers who generally opposed the New Deal. In addition, hydroelectric power and other water projects enabled the Los Angeles basin to absorb a postwar population explosion. Yet, as historian Patricia Limerick has noted, many Western politicians "took advantage of programs that helped their local interests, and then spent much of their remaining time denouncing the spread of bureaucracy and the give-away quality of the New Deal."[30]

This criticism of big government went on unabated into the 1960s and flourished in the Goldwater campaign. Cochairman of the senator's California crusade, Ronald Reagan established himself as the chief rhetorician of Goldwaterism (better than the senator himself), speaking to likeminded voters across the state. He lambasted the New Deal legacy of "welfarism," bloated bureaucracy, and the resultant usurpation of individual freedom. Reagan never publicly acknowledged, perhaps not even to himself, that he and his family had been bailed out by the New Deal.[31] He also seemed oblivious to the fact that the Pentagon, the biggest bureaucratic behemoth of all, underpinned the southern California economy.

Indeed, California had more lucrative defense contracts than any other state, as well as the highest military and civilian Defense Department payrolls. Concentrated in the south, the various defense contractors, military bases, research laboratories and test ranges constituted a large metropolitan-military complex. Its employees, as political analyst Kevin Phillips has stated, "logically tended to support Pentagon, patriotism and paycheck."[32] Rockefeller posed no significant threat to the latter, having long been an advocate of a strong defense policy regardless of the cost. Nevertheless, Goldwater charged that the governor would pirate California's defense contracts for New York industries.[33] The senator's greatest advantage in the military realm, however, sprang from his shirtsleeve Westernism and war-tested patriotism. This appealed not only to the metropolitan-military ranks, but, more importantly, to the legions of others who identified patriotism with the military and its attendant individual bravado. Rockefeller could not compete with Goldwater on this macho level.

Having logged many hours as an Army cargo pilot in World War II, Goldwater still served as a major general in the Air Force Reserve and continued to fly planes and military jets, facts often highlighted in his campaign literature. Rockefeller, on the other hand, had served faithfully during the war, but from behind a desk in the State Department. Furthermore, despite his pronouncements for a strong defense, the governor still had the air of his silver spoon and limousine upbringing. In contrast to Goldwater, then, Rockefeller had not been subjected to the spartan elements, a rite of passage critical to the attainment of what Rough Rider Theodore Roosevelt—to whom some compared the senator—called the "sturdy virtues" of manhood. Goldwater, "the descendant of an Arizona pioneer family," had these politically charismatic virtues, and was often portrayed in the California campaign simply as "THE MAN."[34] As one of the senator's admirers put it: "Barry appeals to both men and women; his appeal is personal, animal, sexual, magnetic."[35]

Acclamations of Goldwater's manliness and ruggedness could be found in the printed word and the visual image. One campaign circular urged

Republicans to vote for "THE MAN for President of the United States." "HERE IS THE MAN," another flyer proclaimed, "as dynamic, strong and solid as the modern West he loves." The emphasis on "modern" served to ward off notions that the senator's ideas hearkened back to bygone eras. A circular with a similar intent proclaimed that "He's a space-age man with a victory plan," and came with a picture of Goldwater in a jet pilot suit. Another photo presented the senator in his military reserve uniform survey-ing the Berlin Wall with a vigilant gaze, while yet another showed him wearing a cowboy hat while camping with his sons in the Arizona moun-tains. It appeared there could be no doubt that Goldwater constituted "A COURAGEOUS MAN, A FIGHTING MAN" and, of course, "AN ALL-AMERICAN MAN."[36]

This cult of manhood received an additional boost from the prominent public support the senator received from Hollywood actors notably associ-ated with macho and/or law-and-order roles. These actors included Robert Stack (government agent Elliot Ness in the TV show *The Untouchables*); Clint Walker (Sheriff Cheyenne Bodie in the TV Western *Cheyenne*); Efrem Zimbalist Jr. (detective Stuart Bailey in the TV show *77 Sunset Strip*); Rock Hudson (macho, his fluffy films with Doris Day notwithstand-ing); and the cinematically definitive man and patriot, John Wayne (Davy Crockett in *The Alamo,* among numerous other roles). Though not necessar-ily macho, Reagan was the most visible of the Hollywood stars and the most vocal. He used his considerable speaking skills to spread Goldwaterism through "The Speech," as this castigation of bureaucratic "tyranny" neatly reflected the free market focus of the senator's campaign. Reagan's mes-sage, as Garry Wills has aptly noted, was that "a slow invisible tide of socialism was engulfing America, held back only by a few brave business-men."[37] In this vein, Reagan warned that these men alone could not pre-serve truly free enterprise much longer. The nation therefore needed THE MAN in the Oval Office, and many Californians became fiercely dedicated to that end.

To help foster this dedication, Goldwater's staff gave his campaign the air of a patriotic revival. For example, before the campaign's $100–a-plate "Kickoff Dinner" at the Los Angeles Sports Arena on March 19, the *Gold-water For President Campaign Newsletter* noted that Ronald Reagan de-clared "you've never heard the Star Spangled Banner 'til you hear it Thursday [at the dinner]." The event's chairman, Bruce Reagan, promised there "won't be a dry eye in the place by 7:30." To lighten this moist-eyed celebration, at least 100 "Goldwater Gals," decked out in gold and white Western wear, were guaranteed to give "a debut to end all debuts." Offic-ially, the Gals received instructions to "just SMILE" and corral potential voters to whom they could spout the aphorisms of the senator's manifesto, *The Conscience of a Conservative,* and other campaign literature.[38] There was no shortage of devotees to join in this task in southern California. Half of the 70,000 petition signatures to put Goldwater on the ballot (only 13,702 were required) came from Los Angeles County, as did most of the volunteers in the senator's crusade. These workers obtained enough signatures by noon of the first day of the petition drive.[39] The Rockefeller camp, in contrast, had to pay its petitioners, who took two weeks to get 44,000 signatures, of which 22 percent proved invalid.[40]

Most of Goldwater's financial support came from those living in the suburban hills and valleys of Los Angeles and Orange counties. Henry Salvatori, the Senator's California finance chairman, donated much money himself and successfully appealed to other wealthy Goldwaterites to make four-figure contributions. Utilizing a populist approach, Salvatori claimed that through advertising, the liberal "writers' and commentators' hatchet job will be nullified" by presenting the senator "directly to the people."[41]

Enthusiasm for Goldwater often proved overwhelming. "The evangelistic fervor of [Goldwater's] rallies," the *Wall Street Journal* reported, "at times embellished with choir singing and prayers, lifts most audiences to high emotional pitch."[42] Individual emotion matched this mass ardor. Pivotal in swinging the CRA behind the senator, Dick Darling recalled that

> Goldwater had a group of dedicated, hard-working people, many of whom neglected their business [*sic*] and many of whom went broke, but they felt so strongly about the issues in that campaign that they were willing to lose tremendous amounts of money, to lose their business [*sic*]. Many of them, really, almost destroyed themselves.[43]

This zeal sustained the crusade when defeat seemed imminent.

Goldwater appeared headed toward victory in the June 2 primary until May 15, when Rockefeller scored an upset win in Oregon over Nixon's vice-presidential running mate in 1960, Henry Cabot Lodge. Not a serious candidate in that primary, Goldwater had been counting on a Lodge victory to deny the governor momentum heading into the final weeks in California. The senator feared that Rockefeller now had a "great springboard" for the state. The Harris Poll showed Goldwater had reason for concern. He fell from a 9 percent lead over Rockefeller shortly before the Oregon contest to an 11 percent deficit five days after it.[44] Though this trend must have been disturbing, Goldwater might have found some consolation in the fact that the polls had been wrong in previous Republican primaries.

Rockefeller's momentum got another boost on May 25 when he received a roundabout endorsement from former president Eisenhower, whose description of the "ideal Republican presidential candidate" implicitly rejected Goldwater. Attacking the latter for his opposition to civil rights legislation in particular, the governor tried to capitalize on Ike's statement the next day in San Diego by declaring that the senator "is outside the framework of responsible Republicanism which has been defined by President Eisenhower." The *New York Times* contended that Eisenhower's position "may well be the decisive factor" in California. Goldwater, however, asserted that "New York newspapers tried to pressure" Eisenhower "to take a stand against me." Though clearly stung by Eisenhower's remarks, Goldwater stated that if the former president did not want him to run he would have let him know personally.[45] Rockefeller also presented himself as the "stop Goldwater" proxy candidate of potential nominees Nixon, Pennsylvania governor William Scranton, Michigan governor George Romney, and Lodge (a Bostonian), none of whom was on the California ballot. To many Goldwater supporters, it must have seemed as though Rockefeller and other "secret New York Kingmakers" controlled the strings of the nomination process once again.

·Despite such suspicions, feelings of impending doom began to fade during the last days of the campaign. Ironically, a Goldwater statement that initially hurt the senator may have helped turn the tide in his favor. On May 24, he reminded the nation of his seemingly nonchalant attitude toward nuclear arms with a nationally televised comment on ABC's *Issues and Answers* about the suggestion that "low-yield nuclear weapons" could be used for defoliation of the forests in Vietnam. Attempting to capitalize on the alarming reaction to this statement in the press, the Rockefeller camp quickly mailed a flyer containing bellicose Goldwater quotes on foreign policy to all registered California Republicans, which asked: "Whom do you want in the room with the H-BOMB?" Voters were urged to "Reject Extremism" or suffer the dire consequences: "[t]he very life of your Republican Party—and, perhaps, our nation's—is up to you." The flyer caused a backlash, journalist Theodore White remarked, "as much for its cost and size as well as its shrill tone."[46]

A number of other factors bolstered the spirit and confidence of the Goldwater forces. Nixon, Romney and Scranton, for the sake of party unity, contradicted Rockefeller by making clear that they did not favor either candidate in the California contest, though Lodge maintained his support for Rockefeller. In addition, Eisenhower, incensed that his much publicized "ideal candidate" description was taken as an anti-Goldwater maneuver (which it essentially was), told reporters on June 1: "You people tried to read Goldwater out of the party, I didn't."[47]

The senator also certainly benefited—how much is conjecture—when Rockefeller's second wife, Happy, had a baby boy on May 30, drawing attention to the governor's recent divorce. According to the Harris Poll, Rockefeller lost several points to the undecided column the day after the birth. The final Harris tally the day before the primary had Rockefeller leading Goldwater by two percentage points, with 18 percent undecided. Before the birth of the governor's son, political scientist Eugene Burdick reported that only a "handful" of the California voters he interviewed recalled that Rockefeller had been divorced.[48] The newly highlighted divorce may have accounted for the Catholic vote not going as heavily to Rockefeller as had been expected.[49]

Perhaps as important as any act, event or repudiation, Goldwater seemed to shake his post–Oregon primary doldrums in the campaign's final days. He exhibited this rejuvenation best on May 30, Memorial Day, before an estimated 25,000 supporters at Knott's Berry Farm. In a setting that was a cross between a carnival and a revival, the senator received rousing endorsements from Ronald Reagan and John Wayne. Goldwater then took the stage and lambasted President Johnson's foreign policy, invoked the memory of the Alamo and other heroic moments in American military history, and listed Khrushchev as among those in the "stop Goldwater" movement. While leaving the attacks on Rockefeller to others at the rally, the senator proclaimed to his rapt audience that he felt victory "in my bones," but "I do not say we have won it."[50] The momentum, though, had indeed changed.

The Goldwater campaign's ad blitz in the two days before the primary, particularly in the *Los Angeles Times,* aimed to further this momentum. The Rockefeller camp did not match this effort, fearing that heavy advertising would draw negative attention to the governor's wealth. This proved to be a miscalculation, for many Republicans remained undecided, and some likely needed another nudge in Rockefeller's direction. The day before the primary, the *Los Angeles Times* carried four full-page ads for Goldwater; two ads, no more than a quarter-of-a-page each, appeared for Rockefeller. Given the quantity and size of these promotions compared to Goldwater's, the governor seemed to be running for county supervisor while the senator sought the presidential nomination. Numerous ads for Goldwater also ran on television and radio, but none aired for Rockefeller.[51]

The senator's ads emphasized that he favored "a sound Social Security system," and a goal of "peace through strength," which could be achieved *"without war."* In addition, ads indirectly spotlighted Rockefeller's divorce by touting Goldwater as "a true family man." A full-page ad in the *Times,* attributed to the Committee of Mothers for Barry Goldwater (CMBG), gave this theme a visceral Western and religious appeal. The CMBG pronounced that the senator "is a living symbol of the heritage of the pioneer spirit of the West," and that he could keep the country strong, "spiritually, economically and militarily," and in the process set an example of good character for the nation's children. Therefore, "It is our prayer that thousands of other mothers and housewives will join us at the polls on June 2nd to assure the California nomination of Barry Goldwater. . . ."[52] Their prayer was answered, as California Republicans gave the senator a narrow victory over Rockefeller. Likening Goldwater's triumph to an epilogue in a formulaic Western, *Time* magazine declared, "[t]he good guys vanquished the bad guys and the Grand Old West was once again made fit for decent folks."[53]

Though Rockefeller won 45 of 58 counties, including all those in the populous San Francisco Bay area, Goldwater triumphed with 51.4 percent of the vote.[54] The governor failed to minimize his losses in southern California, despite frequent campaign appearances there. His engaging grin, incessant handshaking and apocalyptic warnings about the potential consequences of a Goldwater victory did not help in the key counties of Los Angeles and Orange, where he lost by a combined 207,000 votes. With the exception of Santa Barbara, Goldwater won all the southern California counties. He won by only 16,000 votes in San Diego County, a smaller margin than expected, but not surprising due to the large amount of money spent by the local Rockefeller organization.[55] The Goldwater effort focused on the Southland megalopolis. In Los Angeles County, where nearly 40 percent of the state's Republicans resided, the senator won by 158,000 votes. The tireless door-to-door effort by Goldwater workers in the county's thousands of precincts doubtless contributed to this margin.[56]

Rockefeller, who had hoped to hold Goldwater to a 100,000-vote margin in the Southland, won in the region's racially mixed metropolitan areas, but Goldwater won by landslide margins in the Los Angeles basin's conservative Republican strongholds, the largely white middle- and upper-middle-class districts and suburbs. This trend led some analysts at the time to claim that race was the deciding factor in the campaign.[57] Broad ideological differences over the role of the state, however, divided Republicans more than civil rights or any other single issue. Moreover, the senator's opposition to the landmark 1964 Civil Rights Act was consistent with his antistatism and did not hinge on racism, though racist implications could not be avoided.[58] (Still, racial factors did roil California politics in 1964, especially the opposition to the Rumford Act. The latter, and the mounting impact of racial matters in general, will be assessed in the following two chapters.)

With Goldwater's victory, Southland conservatives could proclaim that they had triumphed over the "un-American secret New York Kingmakers" and the group's quasi-Eastern liberal sympathizers in the California Republican Party. The "kingmaker" thesis of Schlafly's *A Choice Not an Echo* appears to have had a considerable impact in obtaining votes and volunteers for the senator. Goldwaterite Gardiner Johnson, Republican National Committeeman for California, declared that the book "was a major factor in bringing victory to Goldwater against the terrific assault of the press, the pollsters, and the paid political workers of the opposition." Goldwater advisor Stephen Shadegg noted that in certain precincts in San Francisco, volunteers distributed copies of the book to voters who indicated a preference for Rockefeller. He reported that the "book precincts" went 20 percent stronger for the senator than in other area precincts with residents with the same educational, occupational, and economic background.[59]

The power of Schlafly's book came from its "history as conspiracy" message. Much as significant earlier works with the same theme, such as *Cato's Letters,* which agitated American revolutionaries in the eighteenth century, and *Coin's Financial School,* which helped rally populists in the late nineteenth century, the tract vilified self-serving power brokers and decried their legacy of deceit. The anti-Eastern theme that had pervaded populist literature was in full force in Schlafly's work. She called on "grassroots Americans" to work to elect Goldwater so the "Liberal Establishment"—especially the kingmakers—could be ousted and their policies reversed. Seeing themselves as grassroots upholders of true American values and civic virtues, southern California conservatives found this a compelling appeal. Perhaps second to only Goldwater himself, *A Choice Not An Echo* helped renew the conservatives' shared sense of mission in 1964 by targeting the liberal and largely Eastern enemy.

Seeming to speak for the state's disgruntled "Eastern sympathizers," the *San Francisco Chronicle* editorially lamented that Goldwater "didn't really win California at all, but only part of California, the Los Angeles basin." Likening the senator to actor Rudolph Valentino's "sheik" movie character, the *Chronicle* asserted that Southland Republicans were "singularly willing to be swept up and carried away in the enchantment over the handsome stranger."[60]

Goldwater, however, was no stranger to California, having made at least 500 speeches there between 1958 and 1964.[61] Much better known and more admired than Rockefeller, the casually charismatic "Man of the West" attracted hordes of dedicated volunteers, in stark contrast to his Eastern opponent. Goldwater's troops labored to reach every registered Republican in the state with at least one mailing, one phone call, and a visit from a precinct worker. On the day of the primary, the senator's volunteers made a minimum of two door-to-door checks of known supporters in Los Angeles County to make sure they had voted.[62]

In the end, this dedication to Goldwater and his message appears to have made the difference. While Rockefeller's newly publicized divorce, the paucity of his late campaign advertising, and the all but complete dissolution of the "stop Goldwater" movement helped the senator's cause, Goldwater won mainly because he inspired a vast network of Southland supporters to get the vote out. Unable to counter the rugged Western symbolism and effusive patriotism ("Americanism") of the senator's campaign with an equally compelling theme and image of his own, Rockefeller could not muster the devoted staff and legions to match his opponent's forces; nor could he sufficiently ameliorate the aversion of conservative voters to his candidacy. As the *New Republic* noted, California's progressive Republican leaders were unsuccessful in their "attempts to derail Goldwater because of their coolness toward Rockefeller's candidacy." In this same vein, the *Los Angeles Times,* which had endorsed the governor, asserted that he had the "impossible task of sustaining the mixed loyalties of a large voting segment that preferred someone else."[63]

Goldwater's victory made him the presumptive favorite to win the nomination in San Francisco in July, but his intraparty battles did not cease. Rather than lining up uniformly behind the senator, many Republican liberals and moderates throughout the country held out hope that William Scranton might yet prevent what George Romney called the "suicidal destruction of the ... party."[64] To preclude this fate, Scranton dutifully declared his candidacy on June 12, proclaiming that he offered a "real choice," not an "echo of fear and reaction." His decision virtually assured that the gathering in San Francisco would be, as one prominent Republican put it, "the bloodiest damn convention you've seen in a long, long time."[65]

The lingering acrimony among California Republicans provided ample evidence that this prognostication would prove correct. Tom Kuchel outraged many conservatives by hailing Scranton as the savior "who can yet prevent the holocaust" of the Republican declension into nineteenth-century theories.[66] Goldwater supporters who had loyally supported Kuchel in the past were particularly miffed by his remarks (and no doubt remembered them during the senator's doomed primary battle against Max Rafferty in 1968). Other targets of this conservative wrath included former national committeeman Joe Martin, San Francisco mayor George Christopher, and Caspar Weinberger. Though officially neutral during the primary, Weinberger led a successful effort shortly after it to block an "extremist" takeover of the Republican State Central Committee at a "reorganization" meeting slated for August.[67] This contributed to the continuing clamor over extremism. Heated debate over the latter sustained factional acrimony in California and elsewhere, and led to a debacle at the Republican Convention.

Unable to generate strong support among moderates, Scranton's challenge to Goldwater was reduced to a cantankerous formality by the time the convention got under way. Scranton's backers made modest efforts to sway Goldwater delegates to their side but met with steadfast resistance. The senator's California chairman, William Knowland, declared that even if he and his delegates had not signed a personal pledge to Goldwater, "[w]e of the West have lived up to the code that a person's word is as good as his bond." He then assailed Scranton's eleventh-hour campaign as a "kind of super-Madison Avenue approach," directed by Eastern hucksters.[68] Indicative of the adamant opposition to attempts to derail the Goldwater juggernaut, the senator's faithful supporters held fast not only to their candidate, but to the conservative principles embodied in the party platform.

Despite the efforts of Scranton and others, the Goldwaterites succeeded in having the convention adopt their conservative agenda without amendments. The most rancorous moments in the arguments over the platform came when a Scranton supporter proposed to the delegates an "antiextremism" plank that singled out the Ku Klux Klan and the JBS. Boos and catcalls filled the convention hall after this proposition, and escalated when Rockefeller took to the podium to defend it.[69] Goldwater's managers marshaled their forces to vote down the antiextremism measure, but were embarrassed by the ugly spectacle that had taken place during Rockefeller's speech. Frequently drowned out during his oration, the governor and a coterie of likeminded Republicans eventually walked out of the convention. While many Goldwaterites undoubtedly saw the Rockefeller incident and the convention on a whole as triumphs, others, such as Holmes Tuttle, thought differently. Tuttle believed that Goldwater missed an opportunity to unify the party by declining to ask Scranton to be his running mate, and that the uncivil zealotry of many of the senator's supporters had turned the convention into "a fiasco."[70]

Scranton's resolute though ill-fated challenge to Goldwater, however, all but eliminated a potential Goldwater–Scranton ticket and seriously hindered any rapprochement between the conservatives and the Modern Republicans. Opting for geographical but not ideological balance, the senator chose New York congressman William Miller as his running mate. Miller, who also served as chairman of the Republican National Committee, had opposed Eisenhower policies even more than Goldwater. Moderns considered the selection of Miller to be not only another snub, but politically imprudent. The senator sought to appease the malcontents at a gathering of party leaders in Hershey, Pennsylvania, in mid-August. If elected, he promised to follow the Eisenhower–Dulles foreign policy, support Social Security, and enforce the mandates of the impending Civil Rights Act. He also sought to assuage the fears and dismay created by his acceptance speech proclamation that "extremism in the defense of liberty is no vice." He therefore repudiated extremist groups, but he avoided specifically mentioning the JBS.[71] Nevertheless, the Hershey declaration merely produced a veneer of Republican harmony, as many prominent figures continued to voice lukewarm support for the senator at best.

Providing no indication that the Republican Party was irremediably fractured, more than 53,000 people filled Dodger Stadium in Los Angeles on September 9, as Goldwater officially launched his campaign. World War II hero James Doolittle introduced the senator as "the leader of the modern American Revolution," which brought a ten-minute foot-stamping ovation from the crowd.[72] Doolittle, along with ex-actor and U.S. Senate hopeful George Murphy, had been introduced by Ronald Reagan. In his opening remarks, Reagan regaled the faithful with repeated sallies at Lyndon Johnson and Pat Brown, but the night ultimately belonged to Goldwater, who reveled in what would be his campaign's greatest display of mass adulation. Declaring that only Republicans were "speaking for freedom," the senator delivered the antistatist diatribe that had initially endeared him to Southland conservatives. Earlier in the day, before a large crowd at the Los Angeles International Airport, Goldwater thanked the many Angelenos who had worked so hard for him in the primary, for they had "achieved a political miracle."[73]

Many activists in the senator's campaign, however, believed too much in that "miracle" and had more of a myopic faith in the righteousness of their crusade than a realistic grasp of the practicalities of electoral politics.[74] Committed to ideological "purity," Goldwater's most conservative followers, who came to control his California campaign, would not tolerate Republican "infidels" within their ranks. Weinberger, for one, made his services available shortly after the convention but was shunned until the senator, upon learning of this exclusion in late October, insisted that he be allowed to be an active backer.[75] On the other hand, the ineptitude and dogmatism of Goldwater's campaign led the conservative George Murphy to keep a noticeable distance from his party's presidential candidate by early October, even in southern California.[76] Weinberger's marginality and Murphy's disassociation provided clear indications that the "modern American Revolution" had largely succumbed to its excesses at a time when inclusiveness and moderation were critical.

Even though the problems afflicting the Goldwater effort in California could be found in most other state organizations as well, the ultimate responsibility for the campaign's woes rested with the senator himself and his chief advisors. They too seemed more intent on making a conservative statement than shaping a pragmatic electoral strategy. They had managed to do both just enough to win the nomination, but with Goldwater trailing Johnson by 35 to 40 percentage points in virtually every poll in early September, there seemed to be nothing left but the ideological crusade. Always pulsating with that fervor, the senator's campaign fostered a staunch devotion to a larger cause for many conservatives, which helped mitigate the impending disaster on election day.[77] Yet Goldwater, who had understood his dim prospects of winning from the outset, did want a respectable showing, primarily for the sake of providing the conservative movement with firmer footing in the American political landscape.[78] Nevertheless, as the campaign approached its final weeks, the polls still predicted one of the greatest presidential election landslides ever.

Cognizant of the fact that Goldwater was heading toward an ignominious defeat, some of his influential California supporters sought to at least salvage his message. Thus began the effort to have Ronald Reagan deliver "The Speech" on national TV on the senator's behalf. The idea sprang from the response to his keynote address on the alleged evils of liberalism and the "welfare state" at a $1,000-a-plate dinner (an unheard-of amount for that time) in Los Angeles, organized by Holmes Tuttle and Henry Salvatori after the convention. Besieged by requests from that audience to put the actor's speech on film for widespread distribution, Tuttle and Salvatori arranged to have a film made of Reagan's address to an audience at the University of Southern California. Distributed to numerous local Goldwater organizations across the country, the film increased contributions to those groups, which in turn gave greater impetus to the effort to show the speech on national TV.[79] Deeming it too negative on Social Security, several of Goldwater's closest aides persuaded him to ask that the address not be shown on a national network, but Reagan successfully appealed to Goldwater to allow it to be aired.[80]

Broadcast on October 27, Reagan's speech proved to be the most effective statement on the senator's beliefs in the entire campaign. The actor delivered the address, entitled "A Time for Choosing," with characteristic aplomb, balancing a scathing attack on Johnson's Great Society with a reverent invocation of the nation's constitutional principles. Reagan proclaimed that the "Founding Fathers ... knew that ... when a government sets out to [control society], it must use force and coercion to achieve its purpose." Establishing freedom versus tyranny as his underlying theme, he assailed liberal foreign policy for negotiating with communist "slave-master[s]," and declared that Socialist Party leader Norman Thomas was right in stating that as president, Goldwater "would stop the advance of socialism in the United States." Goldwater's election, Reagan concluded, could begin the process of reversing this socialist trend, and save "our children" from taking "the last step into a thousand years of darkness."[81]

The address received a torrent of accolades from Republicans and brought in more money to the senator's coffers than could be spent in the remaining week of the crusade.[82] Praise for Reagan's rhetorical skills could even be found in the "liberal" media. Though not necessarily agreeing with The Speech's substance, *Time* magazine called the actor's oration "the one bright spot in a dismal campaign."[83] Reagan's shining moment, of course, would hardly be enough to propel the Goldwater–Miller ticket to victory, given the depths from which it had started and remained. In contrast to Reagan's congeniality, the senator's Wyatt Earp image proved more threatening than reassuring, more reactionary than virtuous. Campaigning in the West in mid-October, Lyndon Johnson stated, "[w]e here in the West know how the West was won. It wasn't won by the man on the horse who thought he could settle every argument with a quick draw and a shot from the hip."[84] Most Americans agreed.

Johnson therefore buried Goldwater on November 3 in a huge landslide. While it is unlikely that any Republican could have defeated the president in the wake of Kennedy's martyrdom, the senator's crushing loss could not help but be humiliating to conservatives. Nevertheless, Goldwater had been largely responsible for building a firm base for the Republican right, and Reagan offered hope for the future of the movement. In California in particular, many right-wing Republicans believed they had found what they had long been seeking: a truly conservative yet electable candidate for governor, and perhaps a future occupant of the White House.

Six

"A Great White Light"

Though Goldwater's defeat qualified as an electoral catastrophe, California conservatives began to extricate their movement from the debris of his campaign shortly after the election. Many of the senator's supporters no doubt agreed with the bumper sticker that proclaimed "27 million Americans can't be wrong," but that was a dubious declaration considering Johnson's 43 million votes. The Goldwater minority nonetheless could not be dismissed, especially in the Golden State. Conservatives there were heartened not only by the epiphanic Reagan speech, but by two major successes at the polls in 1964: the election of George Murphy to the U.S. Senate, and the overwhelming repeal of the highly controversial Rumford Fair Housing Act.

A former Hollywood actor and dancer, Murphy beat his Democratic opponent, Pierre Salinger, despite Murphy's association with Goldwater and Fred Schwarz's Christian Anti-Communist Crusade. His victory hinged in part on his neutral stance on the Rumford Act. Salinger strongly supported the measure, but voters repealed it by approving "Proposition 14" by a two-to-one margin. Though hardly clear at the time, the success of Proposition 14 and Murphy presaged the election of Reagan as governor, for candidate Reagan would skillfully rouse the same white middle-class resentments of liberalism that the Rumford Act stirred; and Murphy, like Helen Gahagan Douglas before him, proved an actor could be elected to a prominent public office in image-conscious California.

Lacking Reagan's polished speaking skills, Murphy nevertheless possessed his fellow actor's congeniality and fervid opposition to communism. Friends from their early days in Hollywood, Murphy and Reagan testified about alleged communist infiltration in the film industry in 1947 before the House Un-American Activities Committee.[1] At roughly the same time, both men also became leading figures in the Motion Picture Alliance for the Preservation of American Ideals, which aimed to ferret out subversives in Hollywood unions and guilds. Unlike Reagan, Murphy was a prominent player in the California GOP and worked hard for the party's nominees in the 1950s and early 1960s, regardless of their ideological inclinations. Consequently, after the "former song and dance man" (his most common description in the press) won in the 1964 primary, Republicans as divergent in their views as Tom Kuchel and William Knowland promised to campaign in his behalf, and many Democrats warmed to his glib charm. As the candidate's northern California campaign manager, Arch Monson, stated, "[e]verybody likes George Murphy."[2]

The same could not be said of Salinger, who at the eleventh hour decided to vie for the seat vacated by the seriously ill Democrat, Claire Engle. The former press secretary for Presidents Kennedy and Johnson, Salinger became locked in a fierce primary battle with one of the founders of the CDC, State Controller Alan Cranston. Salinger's political foes—Democrats and Republicans alike—questioned his eligibility to be a candidate, and whether the native Californian even qualified as a resident for voting purposes, given his long absence from the state. Secretary of State Frank Jordan, the chief elections officer, led the effort to deny Salinger the opportunity to run for office. Though ultimately unsuccessful, the attempt to keep Salinger off the ballot contributed to the notion that he was mounting a "carpetbagger candidacy."[3] Supported by the powerful state assembly leader Jesse Unruh, Salinger edged out the Brown and CDC–backed Cranston in the primary. Cranston's defeat portended the weakening of the CDC and increased factional animosity among California Democrats.[4]

In addition to being relatively unscathed by factional rancor, Murphy did not have to contend with the charge that he was an opportunistic outsider—an accusation that he effectively hurled at his opponent. Implicitly emphasizing Salinger's carpetbagger image, Walt Disney praised Murphy in a widely run newspaper ad, declaring that "this outstanding American is truly qualified to represent California—as a Californian."[5] Murphy's campaign manager, Robert Finch, stated that the carpetbagger matter and Democratic infighting remained salient issues throughout the campaign. Finch also believed that Murphy had the right combination of positive recognition, both as an actor (he never played a "bad guy") and Republican activist.[6] A frequent speaker at party events, he proved especially popular with Republican women. Straddling the bounds of flattery, Murphy declared that the "ladies" campaigned for him "all over . . . like a pack of muskrats."[7]

Murphy also received strong support from the state's influential agricultural industry, as he vowed to renew the controversial Bracero Program, which allowed Mexican immigrants into the U.S. to harvest fruit and vegetable crops at a minimal cost to mostly large-scale agricultural operations. Justifying the program by invoking a racial stereotype, Murphy claimed that unlike white Americans, "Mexicans are really good at that [kind of work].

They are very low to the ground . . . so it's easier for them to stoop." On the state's most heated issue, Proposition 14, he carefully avoided prejudiced utterances, or even a position, stating that the matter was a moral issue and had no place in politics.[8] Conversely, Salinger, over the objections of his advisors, frequently stressed his opposition to Proposition 14 and labeled Murphy an "arch-conservative of the same stripe as Goldwater, but [who] hasn't the courage to express his honest convictions."[9]

Murphy, however, differed with Goldwater on the Civil Rights Act and on foreign aid cuts, which helped him win over more moderate voters from both parties. At the same time, his longstanding and vehement anticommunism, along with his antistatist rhetoric, kept the Republican right behind him.[10] Forming a right–center coalition during the course of his campaign, Murphy steadily gained ground on Salinger, who had been a heavy favorite at the contest's outset. Salinger could not overcome his carpetbagger image and convince enough voters that his affable opponent harbored extreme views. In addition, Proposition 14 hurt Salinger not only because he was electorally on the wrong side of the issue but also because as his campaign wound down, so did his workers and funds, siphoned off by the escalated effort against the repeal of the Rumford Act. All these factors helped Murphy upset the former White House press secretary on election day, a rare Republican triumph in a Democratic year. At a star-studded victory celebration at the Hollywood Palladium, Murphy broke into a brief tap dance with Reagan, the man many believed would be the next actor to seek a high public office in California.[11]

The divisive Proposition 14 campaign came about after the passage of the Rumford Act in 1963. Consonant with the Kennedy administration's push for civil rights legislation in the latter half of that year, the Democratic-controlled state legislature, at the behest of Brown and behind the leadership of assembly speaker Jesse Unruh, passed the Act in September. In the debate over the bill on the assembly floor, opponents vowed they would seek to repeal the bill through an initiative the following year. Coordinating the incipient juggernaut of opposition, the California Real Estate Association (CREA) quickly responded with a petition drive to have a referendum on the act on the 1964 ballot. Petitioners had no trouble getting more than 1 million signatures, far more than required.[12]

Though Murphy had taken no position on Proposition 14, Reagan and other notable California Republicans vigorously backed the measure. Like Reagan, individuals and organizations actively campaigning for the repeal of the Rumford Act generally predicated their position on the "sacredness" of property rights and individual freedom. Officially supporting the proposition, the CRA resolved that "the right to own and manage property . . .

[is a] God-given right not to be retracted by the whim of the government." Acknowledging the measure's discriminatory aspects, CRA president Nolan Frizzelle proclaimed that the "essence of freedom is the right to discriminate." Putting the matter even more bluntly, Robert Gaston stated that "Negroes are not accepted [in white neighborhoods] because they haven't made themselves acceptable." In the same vein, the "Committee For Home Protection" declared that "[p]eople give property its value" and reminded voters that "majorities as well as minorities have rights."[13]

The effort to approve Proposition 14 also had the avid backing of the UROC and the JBS, whose members and literature promoted the notion that communists had infiltrated the civil rights movement and shaped its agenda, a recurrent charge of the far right. For example, in a March 1964 open letter to the U.S. Senate, the secretary of a Southland UROC chapter claimed that liberals, following the "CommUNist line," were behind the 1964 Civil Rights Act, "which will impose slavery on Americans." Citing a 1928 "official CommUNist" pamphlet titled "American Negro Problems," the secretary averred that "[e]very major . . . method . . . being used today to stir up racial riots and *to advance* the *CommUNist course* through *racial agitation is listed in this pamphlet.*" She therefore maintained that civil rights statutes threatened "Private Property Rights . . . [and the] Right to the Pursuit of Happiness."[14]

Emphasizing the sanctity of property rights, CREA, in cooperation with the National Association of Real Estate Boards and likeminded groups, raised a war chest of funds, organized a large speakers bureau and launched a formidable ad campaign. Billboards, bumper stickers and literature abounded. Red, white and blue pamphlets, invariably emblazoned with "FREEDOM," a buzzword for supporters of the proposition, trumpeted the right to "rent or sell to whom you choose" and featured sketches of happy white middle-class families outside their cherished suburban homesteads.[15] The message was clear: the Rumford Act threatened the lily-white suburban life that had seemingly become part and parcel of the American dream.

Believing the Rumford Act could help all Californians fulfill their aspirations to live in the communities of their choice, most prominent Democrats opposed Proposition 14, along with the League of Women Voters, the State Bar Association, and numerous church groups and clerics. Imploring voters to not "legalize hate," opponents of the proposition faced major problems. In addition to a shortage of funds relative to the coffers of the supporters of the repeal, "NO on 14" activists found that many blacks and Mexican Americans, the two groups that would be most affected if the proposition passed, were initially for the measure because they did not fully understand it. There was in fact a fair amount of confusion about the proposition among all voter groups, primarily because voting "yes" on the measure meant "no" to the fair housing law. Moreover, lower-income white voters, though traditional Democrats, proved cool to the arguments against the proposition.[16]

Though not necessarily pervasive, blatantly racist attitudes fueled the Proposition 14 campaign and proved pivotal to the successful repeal effort. As one anti–Proposition 14 organizer in southern California stated, proponents of the proposition whom she dealt with "were very, very bigoted people."[17] Indeed, many active supporters, as noted earlier, made openly or thinly veiled racist remarks in couching their case for the repeal. While only a few extremist pamphlets touted the proposition as a hedge against the "mongrelization of the races," fears of interracial dating and miscegenation surely concerned some residents in white neighborhoods, especially parents who perceived their daughters as "vulnerable."

A measure of the animus toward African Americans among extremist members of the Republican right during the Proposition 14 crusade could be seen at the California Republican Convention in August, when a plank to "send the blacks back to Africa" was introduced (but quickly tabled).[18] Despite such outlandish proclamations by the far right, many Californians favoring the repeal doubtless did not despise blacks. It is even likely that a fair number generally supported the 1964 Civil Rights Act in broad principle given the strong support for Johnson's civil rights agenda outside the South; but the idea of the sacredness of property rights, or more specifically, property values, proved paramount. For white suburbanites in particular, an influx of blacks into their neighborhoods meant a market depreciation of their homes. In what amounted, therefore, to a contest between real (estate) and seemingly abstract values, concerns over property eclipsed the ostensibly venerated principle of equality.[19]

The negative reaction among white Californians to the Rumford Act was similar to that of the nation's Southern whites to the U.S. Supreme Court's decision in *Brown vs. the Board of Education of Topeka,* the landmark 1954 school desegregation case. Opposition to the Rumford Act, however, unlike the reaction to *Brown* in the South, generally was not publicly predicated on overtly racist themes spread by prominent politicians. And in most cases, Californians who attacked Proposition 14 in a bigoted way were not as malicious as the white supremacists denouncing *Brown* and civil rights in the South, where lynchings of blacks still occurred into the 1950s. The main similarity between Southerners and Californians steadfastly opposed to *Brown* and Rumford, respectively, is that both groups sought to preserve the status quo—the maintenance of Jim Crow segregation in the South, and de facto restrictive covenants in California.[20]

Choosing not to openly harness the backlash to the Rumford Act during his presidential campaign, Goldwater urged his California supporters who displayed both "Yes on 14" and Goldwater bumper stickers to remove the former from their vehicles. In doing so he sought to mollify Republicans who backed civil rights legislation in principle.[21] Seeking to avoid criticism on a related front, the senator decided not to show the controversial film entitled *Choice* on national television to promote his campaign. Put together by public relations director Rus Walton, the film proclaimed: "Now there are two Americas." It focused on student unrest, inner-city riots, rising drug use, and liberal sexual attitudes, all of which were linked to Lyndon Johnson, who was shown, as Walton put it, "in his black Lincoln careening over the fields of Texas throwing beer cans out the window." Narrated by the actor Raymond Massey (who had reprised his popular role as Abe Lincoln in *How the West Was Won*), the film linked Goldwater to patriotic images and depicted blacks working contentedly in cotton fields. The film closed with John Wayne asking voters to choose between the "two Americas."[22] Though well received by Republican audiences, the widely read columnist Drew Pearson derided the film as "racist." Against the recommendation of some of his advisors, Goldwater declined to make the film a formal part of his campaign, stating "I'm not going to be made out as a racist."[23] The California Young Republicans (CYR) and other groups, however, showed the film in both public and private settings.

In his campaign, Goldwater made an effort to differentiate his libertarian opposition to mandated civil rights from the politics of prejudice. A onetime member of the Urban League and a contributor to the NAACP, the senator in *The Conscience of a Conservative* maintained that "it is both wise and just for negro children to attend the same schools as whites, and that to deny them this opportunity carries with it strong implications of inferiority."[24] (Ironically, the latter concern was integral in the Supreme Court's *Brown* decision, a ruling Goldwater deplored.) Still, Goldwater's moral opposition to racist policies and practices did not dissuade him from utilizing race as a campaign issue. As Goldwater biographer Robert Alan Goldberg has noted, though the senator "never explicitly linked blacks to urban violence and street crime, his words and images were charged with innuendo."[25]

Despite Goldwater's moral support for racial integration, racists, particularly in the Democratic South, backed him because he staunchly opposed government intervention in such matters. Indeed, George Wallace, who had entered the 1964 presidential campaign as the South's segregation candidate, dropped out mainly because of Goldwater's position on the segregation issue.[26] Amid the emotional debate in California over the Rumford Act *and* federal civil rights legislation, the senator's opposition to the latter, in addition to his insinuations regarding urban unrest, could not help but make him appear as a bigot to civil rights supporters who did not know or understand the reason for his position, or dismissed that reason as less than earnest. The outcome of the vote on Proposition 14, however, indicates that Goldwater probably was not hurt much, if it all, by his stand against civil rights in the general election in California, except among black voters, but he was hardly courting them.[27] Rather, he suffered primarily from the myriad other statements he made over the course of his senatorial career and presidential campaign.

After the election former Goldwater Committee members in California wasted no time in regrouping for the purpose of advancing the conservative movement. Frustration over the senator's loss aside, by the end of November the Citizens for Constructive Action (CCA) had been organized, with the aim of "affirm[ing] certain fundamental [American] principles." In "The California Declaration," the group espoused, in condensed form, the political credo found in *The Conscience of a Conservative.* Headed by Walter Knott, the group included founding members Joe Shell, Henry Salvatori, Ronald Reagan, William Knowland and Republican activist Gardiner Johnson. Seeing the political battle as being between "deceptive socialists" (liberals of both parties) and "Americanists," members of the CCA claimed they represented "fed-up people" who opposed big government, a conciliatory foreign policy, and apologists for the "heritage of America."[28]

Lasting only a short time in its initial form, the CCA was important in that it served as a way station for numerous principal Goldwater backers prior to the formation of the Friends of Ronald Reagan.[29] Many Goldwaterites, in California and elsewhere, proved eager to make donations of both time and money to continue the conservative cause; and the CCA had most, if not all, of their names. Though ostensibly dedicated to a set of principles as opposed to a slate of candidates, CCA members by early 1965 began to focus more on Reagan's potential gubernatorial bid. In fact, it appears that no more formal gatherings of the organization took place after Salvatori announced to members that meetings had been held between Reagan and a small group of southern California supporters regarding the actor's candidacy.[30] Most members then became involved in the nascent Reagan campaign, displaying the same enthusiasm and commitment as they had for the Goldwater crusade.

Other Republican organizations, such as the CRA and the UROC, continued their active efforts to forge a right-wing base for the party in California. Conservatives remained in complete control of the CRA in 1965, prompting state party liberals and moderates to form the "California Republican League" for fundraising and public relations. Recruiting drives for new members for both the CRA and the UROC proved successful. In this regard, Goldwater's loss seemed to encourage members of these maverick groups to try harder. While the foot soldiers of the right-wing organizations maintained their vigilant sense of commitment, their tactics became less militant. As a conservative Republican state official explained, during the Goldwater crusade the senator's workers "would ring a doorbell, and if the man answering it said he didn't like Goldwater they had the impulse to grab for his throat. You don't find that today."[31] Bellicose zealots surely remained, but by and large the Republican right had learned the virtue of the soft sell.

In addition, fundraising efforts of UROC and CRA members continued to be frequent and fruitful. A prominent UROC activist, for example, held cocktail parties at which she charged guests for drinks, with the proceeds going to the organization. Similarly, one of the top recruiters for the CRA held swimming pool parties where prizes were raffled off. Though both groups worked for the perpetuation of right-wing ideals and objectives, CRA and UROC members maintained a somewhat competitive relationship, and the groups differed at times in terms of their linkage and obligations to the party. Individuals in both organizations, however, harbored scorn for the party's formal apparatus, which was purportedly controlled by liberal Eastern interests.[32]

The JBS also remained strong and in high profile, and attempted to establish control of the Republican volunteer organizations and committees. The John Birch Society Chorale, attired in red and white striped blazers, often regaled crowds at conservative functions, where Society members sought to exert their influence. The JBS succeeded in placing at least 20 members, and perhaps as many as 50, on the Los Angeles County Republican Central Committee.[33] In addition, three members of the JBS were elected officers of the CYR at the organization's convention in February 1966, where support for Reagan proved widespread. Though the group did not formally endorse any gubernatorial candidate, the election of the Birchers, along with other CYR problems, stirred the extremism issue when the primary campaign got under way.[34] Successful in taking over the UROC in 1966 as well, the JBS clearly became more powerful organizationally in California after Goldwater's defeat, though it does not appear that the group's membership increased to any appreciable extent, if at all.[35] Rather, Birchers found it easy to gain more clout in the conservative organizations in which they had significant membership from the outset (e.g., UROC), or in groups taken over by conservatives (e.g., CRA) in which members of the Society were part of the invasive force.

The JBS enjoyed success in California despite a multi-pronged attack in October 1965 from the premier conservative periodical, the *National Review*. While making clear that from the Society's earliest days the *Review* agreed with the group's general purpose of fighting communism, editor William F. Buckley Jr. noted that his magazine had long taken exception to the "fog of confusion that issues from Mr. Welch's typewriter." Ultimately, the "distortions" of Welch, and his hypnotic grip over many JBS members, "disqualified" him and his organization from being effective in fighting communism. Within the pages of the *Review*'s attack, Joe Shell concurred with its editors, stating that "[t]hose who follow any person without question place blinders on reason." Providing the final comment, Goldwater called upon JBS members to resign, given that Welch's statements "have generally been wrong, ill-advised and, at times, ill-tempered."[36]

The growing division among conservatives over the legitimacy of the JBS seemed to indicate that the organization would be at least as much of an albatross to right-wing Republican candidates in 1966 as it had been two years earlier. Furthermore, there were concerns among conservatives about the lingering stigma of "Goldwaterism," which opponents could and would use to cast the senator's former fervent backers as extremists and as primitives within the Republican Party. Moving away from Goldwater's name but not his ideals, the conservative movement in California nevertheless grew stronger in 1965 and 1966 as the nation's political center moved further to the right, helping offset the issue of extremism. This rightward shift in public opinion came mainly from the white backlash, opposition to protests against the Vietnam War and other campus unrest (especially at the University of California), and from the growing discontent with government bureaucracy. The challenge for the state's Republican right was to gain an electoral advantage through these issues.

A multitude of conservatives, of course, believed that in Reagan they had found the right man for that job, but the actor himself hedged on entering the gubernatorial race. While he angrily declared shortly after Goldwater's defeat that the California Republican Party "will have no more of those [liberal] candidates who are pledged to the same socialist philosophy as our opposition," he gave little hint that he would run for any political office. In addition, some of the same people who were trying to convince Reagan to run in early 1965 had been unsuccessful in an attempt to get him to challenge Thomas Kuchel in the 1962 primary.[37] If Reagan's own words are a proper measure, however, he seemed to believe that, in addition to the ever-present Soviet threat, freedom faced more peril from Johnson's Great Society than it had from the corporate liberalism of Kennedy's New Frontier. Always apocalyptic in their tone, the admonitions in The Speech by the time of the Goldwater campaign, and in the succeeding year, became more exigent than in earlier variations. In 1961, for example, Reagan warned that "we have 10 years . . . to win or lose [the battle against communism]—by

1970 the world will be all slave or all free." In 1965, with the "enemy at our gates," he declared, "[y]ou and I have reached a moment of truth. . . ."[38] For Reagan, that moment manifested itself in the decision to run for governor.

That decision did not come without considerable pressure from the founding members of the Friends of Ronald Reagan. Pivotal in convincing him to run, Holmes Tuttle, an automobile dealer, and oil man Henry Salvatori—both millionaires—met with the actor in early 1965 to make their case for his candidacy. Working in conjunction with fellow millionaire Cy Rubel and Tuttle associate Ed Mills, Tuttle and Salvatori told Reagan that the group would handle the finances for his campaign.[39] Reagan agreed to think it over, considering no doubt that upon declaring his candidacy he would have to stop hosting the popular television show *Death Valley Days,* as well as give up a number of lucrative endorsement contracts. Uncertain of the extent of his appeal, but aware of the "disastrous state of the party" (and, given The Speech, the country), Reagan, about a month after an overnight visit by Tuttle and his wife, decided to launch an informal campaign by going on an extended speaking tour of the state. If the reaction proved favorable he would announce his candidacy at the beginning of the new year.[40]

With his gubernatorial ambitions all but washed up by the wave of conservative support for Reagan's bid, an embittered Joe Shell still believed he deserved to be the candidate of the party and particularly of the faction he had faithfully served for so long. Hoping Shell would back out gracefully, Reagan convert Vernon Cristina tried to "talk some sense" into his old friend, telling him, "[y]ou don't have the ingredients to win." Goldwater attempted to get Rus Walton to persuade Shell not to run; but Walton, while understanding Reagan's appeal, declined out of loyalty to the man whose 1962 primary campaign he had managed.[41] Rubel, Salvatori and Tuttle on numerous occasions tried, without success, to convince Shell that Reagan was the best candidate. Having been Shell's finance chairman during his challenge to Nixon, Rubel felt especially bad about deserting him. Shell harbored the greatest resentment for Tuttle, however, for he rightly believed that the latter had spearheaded the drive to draft Reagan and had been active in the effort to convince Nixon to run for governor. Though never an actual candidate, Shell did not hesitate to publicly criticize Reagan during the primary campaign.[42]

In early 1965, Shell, Reagan and Max Rafferty were considered the leading conservative candidates for the Republican gubernatorial nomination. A California Poll at that time showed that of the three men, Reagan had the highest "excellent" rating among California voters in terms of being a good candidate, but also had the highest "poor" rating. After breaking down the categorical numbers, Shell appeared to be a somewhat stronger candidate than Reagan or Rafferty, but moderates Tom Kuchel and George Christopher had the best overall ratings.[43] Kuchel would soon decide to stay in the Senate, while Rafferty opted to seek reelection to his superintendent office. With Shell moping on the sidelines, by early spring it became clear that the Republican race would be between Christopher, who saw himself as the least objectionable candidate, and Reagan.

To help make the actor less objectionable, a close friend of the "triumvirate" (Rubel, Salvatori and Tuttle) sought the services of Bill Roberts and Stuart Spencer, the best Republican campaign management team in the state. The two had established their company in the mid-1950s and compiled an impressive record of 34 victories in 40 efforts. (One of their losses was Rockefeller's 1964 California primary campaign.) Fearful that Reagan had become too associated with the extreme wing of the party and functioned as its "martinet," Spencer and Roberts initially hedged at the request. Reagan, however, dispelled these qualms upon meeting with the two men. Knowing that the actor had more than adequate financial backing and good name recognition, they agreed in April 1965 to manage his campaign. They had earlier turned down a request to manage the Christopher organization and subsequently miffed and dismayed his backers by going with Reagan.[44] But Christopher had lost in two earlier attempts to win a statewide office, making him less attractive than Reagan. Moreover, as Roberts explained, "[a] candidacy [for statewide office] from northern California is not the most substantial candidacy at any time under any circumstances."[45]

Soon after taking over Reagan's campaign, Roberts crafted a fundraising letter, asking prospective "club members" of the Friends of Ronald Reagan to donate $100 or "such amount as you care to invest. . . ." Using a "time for choosing" as both the opening and closing words of the appeal, "the question was, and still is: Will the people control the government or will government control the people?"[46] While the triumvirate alone could have easily financed Reagan's effort, the fundraising letter, which proved very successful, helped broaden the base of Reagan's serious supporters.[47] The wording of the letter clearly intended to evoke the memory of the actor's popular speech for Goldwater, but made no mention of the senator or his 1964 crusade. In extracting this oratorical silver lining from the dark cloud of Goldwater's defeat, Reagan and his handlers avoided any direct linkage with the senator. Similarly, the actor's autobiography, *Where's the Rest of Me?*, opportunely released in late 1965, made no mention of Goldwater, but The Speech could be found in the book's appendix. Thus Reagan sought to jettison the looming image of the wild-shooting cowboy conservative, at the same time retaining the essential elements of the Arizonan's creed in a relatively soft-spoken yet assertive manner.

Indeed, the main task facing California conservatives after 1964 was to blunt the shrill edge of Goldwaterism without losing the driving force of the senator's philosophy. To that end, the smooth yet dynamic Reagan was a godsend. On balance, as journalist and author Lou Cannon has noted, "Reagan inspired where Goldwater tended to terrify." The senator's modern-day gunslinger remarks, such as "let's lob one [an A-bomb] in the men's room of the Kremlin," may have gone over well in a dusty Arizona town, but to the majority of Americans the remark, and others like it, made the senator appear dangerously cavalier and trigger happy. In addition, whereas Reagan's remarks on being a political novice had an endearing, homespun essence, Goldwater had hardly inspired confidence in his leadership abilities with such declarations as "I haven't really got a first-class brain."[48] His opponents' efforts to taint him notwithstanding, Reagan was relatively unhindered by ill-advised comments or by the gruff intensity that often gripped the senator, and he transcended his intellectual limitations with a flair Goldwater sorely lacked. In describing the Reagan phenomenon, Jud Leetham proclaimed: "[t]here's a messianic thing about him—a great white light."[49] For Goldwaterites, then, the savior of not only the conservative movement, but of the Republican Party and California government, had arrived.

Appropriately enough, in early January the actor-turned-politician announced his formal candidacy for governor in a half-hour prerecorded television film. In an in-person question-and-answer session after the film, Reagan sounded his familiar warnings on the encroaching control of both the state and federal governments. When asked whether he would accept the backing of the JBS, he maintained that he would not "submit a loyalty oath" to those who chose to vote for him. "There is a place in any party," he contended, "for anyone who feels they can support the goals of that party." As if somehow seeking to rise above the usual fray of the political arena, Reagan declared that he was a "citizen politician," but as a Republican would "campaign on the basis that the opposition is the administration in Sacramento." In stating, "I will have no word of criticism for any Republican," Reagan invoked Republican State Central Committee chairman Gaylord Parkinson's eleventh commandment, which helped maintain party solidarity and, for the most part, limited Christopher's criticisms of Reagan to his political "inexperience."[50]

Seeking to turn this lack of experience to the actor's advantage, Spencer and Roberts fashioned the "citizen politician" image. "The founding fathers of this country were not professional politicians," Reagan observed. "They were citizen politicians." He contended that individuals outside the realm of government service should "make their talents available to help solve the state's problems that baffle professional politicians."[51] He ignored the fact that running the largest state in the country in the 1960s was a more complex task than governing the new nation had been in the late eighteenth century. Still, the implicit connection between Reagan and the founders put him in revered company without making any absurd direct comparisons and reinforced the connection, albeit facilely, that conservatives had long made between their cause and "constitutionalism."

Despite his many attributes as a candidate, Reagan did have a major liability at the outset of his campaign; as he later stated, "I did not know anything about the organization of state government."[52] To remedy this problem, Spencer–Roberts and the triumvirate hired psychologists Stanley Plog and Kenneth Holden of the Behavior Science Corporation (BASICO) to function essentially as a briefing team for the candidate. The two wrote careful position papers on the state's most pressing issues which Reagan, with his thespian flair, recited to reporters and audiences. (With the exception of a line here and there, he continued to write his own speeches.) Professing that government should utilize "the full creative talent of all our people," Reagan's general philosophy was packaged under the title of "The Creative Society." Though developed by Holden and Plog, the phrase and general idea came from the Reverend W.S. McBirnie, a fiery right-wing radio commentator. McBirnie believed that Nixon had lost in 1962 because he had no cohesive program like the Creative Society, and therefore his candidacy lacked "excitement."[53] Influential in the Goldwater campaign and in the fight for Proposition 14 as well, McBirnie was one of the many "extremist" Reagan backers cited during the general election campaign by the Brown camp in the attempt to discredit the Republican opposition.

The governor, however, had more immediate concerns than Reagan or Christopher due to the dissension and challenges within his own party. While these problems were evident in 1964, they grew more serious the following year, as CDC members quarreled over Lyndon Johnson's escalation of the war in Vietnam. Led by the Council's president, Simon Casady, the CDC voted at its 1966 convention to condemn Johnson's Vietnam policy, much to the chagrin of Brown. Believing that Casady had used his position irresponsibly in disparaging LBJ and members of California's congressional delegation,[54] the governor led a successful effort to oust him. Nevertheless, hecklers greeted Brown when he addressed the convention, and several hundred delegates walked out after he asked for their endorsement votes. Though he won the CDC's backing by a comfortable margin, more than 700 of the Council's 1,800 delegates abstained, highlighting the acrimonious split within the Democratic ranks.[55] The tumultuous convention hurt Brown in his continuing power struggle with Jesse Unruh and strengthened the gubernatorial candidacy of the conservative Democrat Sam Yorty, who had been elected mayor of Los Angeles in 1961.

Republicans relished the Democratic infighting, but, despite the eleventh commandment, had their own matters of pointed disagreement. In particular, debate lingered over civil rights, with Reagan and Christopher on opposite ends. While appearing with Christopher at the state convention of the National Negro Republican Assembly, Reagan was asked how black Republicans could "encourage other Negroes to vote for you after your statement that you would not have voted for the civil rights bill?" Defending Goldwater's opposition to the bill and his own, Reagan responded that he favored the aims of the act but could not support "a bad piece of legislation." Christopher made clear that he had supported the bill and contended that "the position taken by Goldwater did more harm than any other thing to the Republican Party.... Unless we cast out this image," he concluded, "we're going to suffer defeat." To the surprise of most everyone, the former mayor's assertions prompted Reagan to shout: "I resent the implication that there is any bigotry in my nature. Don't anyone ever imply that I lack integrity." He then stormed out of the hall. Though he eventually returned, Reagan had jeopardized his level-headed image and provided Christopher with the opportunity to express his "sympathy in this moment of [Reagan's] emotional disturbance." Believing that his opponent had inferred he was a racist, Reagan apologetically told the audience, "[f]rankly, I got mad."[56]

The actor clearly did not see himself as bigoted in any way, as evident in his autobiography. In the latter, he recalled that his father would not allow him to see the film *The Birth of a Nation* because it glorified the Ku Klux Klan. His father, Reagan stated, believed "that all men were created equal and that the man's own ambition determined what happened to him after that."[57] Those words apparently left a lasting impression. In 1946 Reagan participated in a radio program called "It's Happening Here," which assailed the Klan and racism in general. In the broadcast he proclaimed, "mobs are being stirred up; hopped up by racial hatred that is deadlier than marijuana. . . . I have to stand and speak, to lift my face and shout that this must end. . . ."[58] He participated in a few other projects of this sort and, while president of SAG, worked to improve the conditions for black actors until the red scare cast suspicion on such actions.[59]

While certainly no civil rights crusader, Reagan indeed was not a bigot. Yet at the time of his 1966 campaign he prominently displayed civic awards in his mountain ranch home from Orval Faubus and the unreconstructed racist Ross Barnett, two Southern governors who had resolutely blocked federally mandated integration in public education institutions in their respective states.[60] Though Reagan professed on the campaign trail that "freedom can't survive in a nation that tolerates prejudice or bigotry," one wonders how he could make such a statement and still proudly exhibit awards from two men who not only tolerated racism but promoted and defended it. Reagan's "Mr. Magoo style," as Garry Wills has called it, evokes imagery that facilitates an understanding of this conundrum: similar to the bespectacled Magoo, Reagan saw what he wanted to see; in the cases of Faubus and Barnett, this was two dedicated defenders of states' rights.[61] He proved smilingly resistant or oblivious to anything ignoble about individuals or causes he liked when these undesirable realities threatened the rudiments of his worldview. His one outburst notwithstanding, this mindset in effect insulated him from being truly rattled by the many charges during the campaign that he was exploiting the white backlash.

Reagan, of course, also had to deal coolly with accusations that he represented the forces of extremism, serving as their "martinet," as Roberts had once feared. Ironically, the issue had become especially contentious in September 1965, when a Shell supporter told reporters that Reagan had praised John Rousselot as a "terrific fellow . . . willing to do anything from calling me names in public to endorsement—whatever we want."[62] Shell, and the Brown camp as well, used this statement, and the fact that Reagan had spoken at a fundraising dinner for Rousselot in 1962, to place the actor arm-and-arm with him and the JBS. Reagan countered these depictions by maintaining his strong criticism of Robert Welch and some of the Society's positions, but refused to issue an outright condemnation. Privately, Reagan apologized to Rousselot for "my attempt to get a laugh" and assured him, "I'll keep my words in line with yours" in downplaying the matter. In defending his position on the JBS, he repeatedly stated that if members of the Society supported him, they "will be buying my philosophy, I won't be buying theirs." He later noted that neither the FBI nor the California Senate Sub-Committee on Un-American Activities had found the JBS to be subversive.[63] While not defusing the extremism matter, his position constituted a middle-of-the-road approach that helped him avoid alienating the far right yet distanced him enough from the JBS to be acceptable to moderate and conservative voters of both parties.

Well behind but gaining on Reagan in the polls, Christopher told delegates at the 1966 CRA convention that the Republican candidate for governor could not win "if our nominee refuses to reject the radical right as well as the radical left."[64] His remark brought a chorus of boos from the largely conservative delegates, reminiscent of the negative response to efforts to condemn the JBS at the 1962 convention. Reagan easily won the CRA's endorsement, though one of the Assembly's subcommittees had recommended endorsing a dark horse candidate to avoid adding to Reagan's "extremist" image. The recommendation was overruled by the parent committee, and the CRA proceeded to back Reagan and pass numerous conservative resolutions. Among other things, the organization expressed its support for a proposed constitutional amendment to allow voluntary prayer in public schools as well as for federal legislation to make anti–Vietnam War demonstrations acts of treason.[65]

As the war in Vietnam escalated, so did student protests against it, much to the disgust of many Americans who supported the war or who at least believed in "my country, right or wrong." Reflecting this loathing at the CRA convention, Reagan excoriated "the beatniks and malcontents" at the University of California, Berkeley (UC), who had given "aid and comfort to the enemy" in Vietnam. He also castigated the "vulgarity and obscenity" of the students in the rebellious "Free Speech" movement at UC, which began in the fall of 1964 when a civil rights advocate violated university policy prohibiting the distribution of literature at a popular campus location. Reagan proclaimed that "a leadership gap, a morality gap and a decency gap in Sacramento" had unleashed these radicals.[66] Continuously inundated by questions about how he would respond to the "mess" at Berkeley, Reagan turned the student unrest at UC into one of his best campaign issues, to the pleasant surprise of Spencer and Roberts. Spencer recalled that campus unrest did not show up as a major public concern in their polls, but that apparently it was "a sub rosa emotional issue with people," which Reagan "escalated" into a major issue. Brown campaign advisor Fred Dutton later stated that "Berkeley, in our polls, was the most negative word that you could mention."[67]

Though Reagan had found a major issue in Berkeley, problems arose for him in early May when the JBS took over the leadership of the UROC. Providing potential fodder for assaults on Republican extremism, the takeover occurred at the group's convention despite resistance from Rus Walton and other less zealous members. Walton, the organization's executive director, had minimal contact with other UROC officers during 1965 because for most of that year he had been working in Washington, D.C. Upon his return to California there were indications that members of the JBS aimed to gain command of the UROC's leadership and agenda. Walton wasted no time in publicly venting his displeasure with these individuals, protesting that the UROC should not become an extension of the JBS or any other group.[68] The battle lines were drawn for a showdown at the organization's 1966 convention.

Though still ultraconservative, the UROC had moderated its positions and tactics somewhat after Goldwater's defeat. The group's more extreme members, however, perhaps energized by Reagan's candidacy, managed to elect Joseph Crosby, the husband of a prominent Bircher, as president, and placed other Society members on the board of governors. Crosby triumphantly proclaimed that conservatives had thwarted the attempt by "liberals" take control of the organization. A disillusioned dissenter declared, "[w]e have witnessed the triumph of the disoriented," of those "who must relate every ill to Communism."[69] Walton's disagreements with the Birchers, some of whom were friends, were more strategical than ideological. Nevertheless, he denounced the extremist takeover as a victory for "rigid militance over those who learned our lesson in 1964." While Walton would later play a significant role in Reagan's gubernatorial administration, he had no part in the 1966 campaign. His prominent association with the UROC had brought the enmity of the Reagan high command. The actor's advisors had debated whether their candidate should even attend the UROC convention and accept the group's endorsement.[70] Not willing to run the risk of snubbing important right-wing supporters, Reagan did address the delegates and accept their backing, but Christopher took to the podium as well. Steering clear of the extremism issue, the moderate San Franciscan helped give the convention at least some semblance of a bifactional Republican function, as opposed to an ultraconservative pep rally. Promoting the former image, a Reagan spokesman pointedly stated that Christopher, who did not directly repudiate the UROC Birchers, must have wanted the group's endorsement or he would not have spoken at the convention.[71]

Christopher surely knew he had no chance of winning the UROC's backing but opted to address the convention to promote party unity and to show that he was a team player. In addition, he would need at least some conservative votes to win in the primary. As the campaign headed into its final stretch he had reason to be optimistic, for polls showed that by May he had cut Reagan's lead from 13 percent (in January) to 6 percent. Moreover, surveys also indicated that Christopher would beat Brown decisively in the general election, while Reagan was either a bit behind the governor or narrowly ahead, depending on the poll.[72] Citing the surveys that showed Christopher as the stronger Republican candidate against Brown, William Bagley, a Republican assemblyman from the San Francisco Bay area, made a hopeless appeal to Reagan to withdraw from the gubernatorial race and throw his support and finances behind Christopher. Less than a year earlier Bagley had remarked that "not one in ten thousand takes the Reagan movement seriously."[73] A visceral miscalculation, the statement reflected the assemblyman's gut-level hatred of "bug-eyed" and "blithering" right-wingers. Nevertheless, after the primary, Spencer and Roberts convinced him to become an honorary chairman of Reagan's campaign. Believing that the lack of support from Shell backers had defeated Nixon, Bagley made this magnanimous move to avoid being "in the same bag with them."[74]

Keenly aware of Christopher's strength against Brown in the polls, the governor and his chief campaign aides feared the former San Francisco mayor more than Reagan. The governor's aides therefore set out to discredit Christopher by dredging up his 1939 misdemeanor conviction for violating a then-controversial milk-pricing statute as a Marin County farmer. Though Christopher initially assailed the Reagan camp as the source for the attack, it soon became clear that Brown advisors had done the dirty work by leaking the old story to syndicated columnist Drew Pearson. The latter immediately disparaged Christopher in his widely distributed column, and even appeared at press conferences in Los Angeles and San Francisco with a blown-up picture of Christopher emblazoned with "WANTED" under his face.[75] The issue hurt Christopher especially with southern California voters who, unlike Bay area residents, had never heard of the matter before. The former mayor's poll numbers dropped precipitously as Reagan's lead grew to 17 percent in the final days before the election.[76]

While the governor and his inner circle achieved their goal of mortally wounding Christopher, it came at the expense of Brown's "nice guy" image. Consequently, he yielded the tactical high ground to Reagan and gave Democratic voters another reason not to support the governor or to reconsider their support. An increasing number of disillusioned Democrats expressed their frustration with Brown by backing Yorty, who echoed Reagan in charging that the governor had become beholden to "left-wingers," particularly to the CDC.[77] Struggling to maintain an image as a beacon of moderation, Brown called Yorty a right-wing "fright peddler" and contended that the man who could not effectively govern Los Angeles could hardly be trusted to run the entire state.[78] The mayor's popularity with conservative Democrats, however, continued to rise. As Brown aide Fred Dutton noted, the fact that Yorty, "a transparently hack politician whose main talent was to always keep running," could mount a significant challenge to the governor revealed the latter's "serious weakness."[79]

The candidacies of Reagan and Yorty received a boost on May 10, when the State Supreme Court ruled the repeal of the Rumford Act to be unconstitutional. The mayor, a one-time New Deal liberal, had opposed Proposition 14 in 1964 but changed his position after the measure passed overwhelmingly. Though not adamant in his new-found opposition to fair housing, Yorty benefited from the ire of the Democratic voters who had favored the proposition. Certain that the judicial decision would be appealed at the highest level, Brown declared that "Proposition 14 would be the law of the land until the Supreme Court in Washington acts." While Christopher urged Californians to accept the ruling and "get on with our business," Reagan declared that "[a]ll of us are losers if we allow this precedent [for the rights of property owners] to be established." Using the decision as a rallying cry, the *CRA Newsletter* declared that "a clear expression of the people's will" had been subverted by the "Brown-appointed political hacks on our State Supreme Court."[80]

Championing the "people's will," Reagan further contributed to the widespread indignation over the court's ruling by reminding voters that in 1964 Brown had called the petitioners for Proposition 14 "the shock troops of bigotry."[81] While Brown's statement had clearly been impolitic, bigotry of course had played no small role in the opposition to the Rumford Act. Moreover, the devastating riot of August 1965 in Watts, an impoverished African American section of south central Los Angeles, no doubt bolstered the view among whites that blacks "haven't made themselves acceptable" for white neighborhoods, as Robert Gaston had asserted during the Proposition 14 campaign. Contributing to such views, and at the same time offending blacks and others, Los Angeles police chief William Parker compared the behavior of the rioters in Watts to that of "monkeys in the zoo." On an earlier occasion, Parker had linked the "type of Democracy" favored by the National Association for the Advancement of Colored People to the communist agenda "represented by *The People's World*."[82]

A near-riot occurred in Watts during the primary campaign in March, reigniting the fear of urban unrest among white Angelenos and others, including African Americans themselves. This incident once again made "arson and murder" in Watts a salient issue for Reagan in the course of excoriating the governor's lack of leadership.[83] It was Brown's bad luck that he had been out of the state during the initial outbreaks of violence in Watts in both August and March, and Yorty made voters well aware of those absences (though the mayor had his own problems in this regard). The recurrent trouble in the black community, combined with the court's decision against Proposition 14, made it much harder for Brown to skirt the race issue or ignore the backlash rhetoric of Reagan and Yorty.

Reagan, however, could afford to ignore an eleventh-hour attack by the fading Christopher. A week before the primary, the former mayor let loose with a fusillade of questions and assertions about the actor's past affiliations with left-wing and "communist dominated" organizations, such as the United World Federalists and the Americans for Democratic Action. In so doing he violated the eleventh commandment, which he had at least marginally abided by to that point. Christopher declared that Reagan's ideological swing from left to right had occurred so quickly, "it might indicate instability of some sort," which, among other things, the Brown camp would readily exploit if Reagan won the nomination.[84]

Reagan pointedly stated that his autobiography had provided the fodder for Christopher's attack, but that the book also explained how the actor discovered the alarming truth about the politics of the far left.[85] In the book, Reagan declared, "I was a near-hopeless hemophiliac liberal" during the 1930s and World War II, and "not sharp on communism." (He once called George Murphy an "archreactionary.")[86] His naiveté about communism, he contended, accounted for his membership in certain groups with communist connections. He began his move to the right in the late 1940s—along with millions of other Americans—when he became aware of the "communist plan" to take over the Hollywood film industry to establish "a world-wide propaganda base." During this time Reagan became very active in Hollywood politics as president of the Screen Actors Guild (1947–1953) and began to associate liberal "big government" with the "planned economy" attendant to socialism.[87] His antistatism therefore grew with his anticommunist fervor. His objections to government bureaucracy in the aftermath of the Roosevelt and Truman years were not unusual, but by the early 1960s the vehemence of that opposition would put him squarely and quite visibly in the ranks of the Goldwater conservatives.

Reagan's swing to the right was neither rapid nor as extreme as Christopher had suggested, and certainly did not indicate emotional "instability." Other influential conservatives had in fact journeyed much further along the ideological spectrum. For example, former members of the American Communist Party, as well as former party sympathizers, could be found among the editors of the *National Review* from the periodical's inception. Several of the editors who experienced the transmogrification from militant Marxist to ardent free marketeer defended conservative tradition with a Christian moral angst—in line with Buckley's devout Catholicism—integrating reason with faith in God though not necessarily in contemporary humanity.[88] But their anxiety over the wayward drift of modern liberal society did not qualify as neurosis or instability.

In moving from New Deal liberalism to Goldwater conservatism, without discarding his admiration for FDR, Reagan skimmed the intellectual surface of liberal and conservative theory; he had neither the desire nor the capacity to plumb the theoretical depths of his convictions like his right-wing brethren at the *National Review*. Nevertheless, at the outset of Reagan's primary campaign, the erudite Buckley, who by now had achieved celebrity status, pronounced Reagan a "true conservative, who recognizes limits of political action. . . ."[89]

Given the lack of headway in President Johnson's War on Poverty,

Reagan's diatribe against big government on both the federal and state levels increased in appeal. In addition, his cheery demeanor and polished aphorisms helped give his conservative commentaries a positive ring, in contrast to Goldwater's crusty grousing and the often foreboding critiques of democracy and human nature made by conservative intellectuals. Reagan also benefited, as one Christopher aide resigned to defeat put it, from being the photogenic "glamour boy" of the Republican Party, with inexhaustible funds.[90] For the "money bags" who provided those funds, the actor proved to be the charismatic candidate they had envisioned, destined for the governor's mansion in Sacramento, and perhaps even the White House.

With so many factors in Reagan's favor, it came as no surprise that he defeated Christopher on June 7 in a landslide, overwhelming the former mayor in southern California in particular. Displaying the modesty and charm that had endeared him to so many, Reagan declared that in victory he was "very proud but very humble," and preached on the importance of party unity. Brown, on the other hand, beat Yorty by a margin closer than expected. Stating "I like a tough fight," Brown promised a "hard-hitting, fighting campaign" against Reagan, "based on the record." Still convinced he would be battling another Goldwater, the governor contended that the real issue "will be the ultra-conservatism of the Republican Party" and his opponent.[91] While the Brown organization and like-minded Democrats would labor to make Republican extremism the pivotal issue in the election, they would learn painfully that, at least in terms of political skills and vulnerability, Reagan differed from Goldwater, and that most voters had lost faith in the governor's "responsible liberalism."

Seven

Triumph of the Right

The issues that proved to be obstacles to Pat Brown in his reelection drive did not reflect well on the state of liberalism in California or the rest of the nation. Though the backbreaking squeeze would not come until 1968, liberalism was caught in an ever-tightening vise by the summer of 1966, with the "New Left" on one side and a growing number of conservatives—especially on social matters—on the other. The "counterculture" would not fully emerge until the following year (with the "summer of love"), but the antiestablishment politics of young student activists and like-minded others coalesced around opposition to the escalating war in Vietnam. Generally supportive of that battle against communism and ardently against protesting students, conservatives vented their anger over President Johnson's War on Poverty through polemics that could be summed up in good part by the buttons and bumper stickers that proclaimed: "Join the Great Society—Go on Welfare!" His legislative accomplishments as president notwithstanding, Johnson's vision of a Great Society had withered in two short years due to a lack of nurture in a nation that was coming apart rather than together. Ironically, the resentful and divisive "us against them" rhetoric that had helped spur New Deal liberalism under Roosevelt—his "forgotten man" versus the callous "economic royalists"—would now be used by conservatives against "nonproducers" to undermine the kindred liberalism of the Great Society.

Leading this assault in California, Reagan pledged to "listen to the people, not lecture them." He attacked the policies of both Johnson and Brown, but made sure he "was offering positive alternatives," as outlined in the Creative Society.[1] Still, his disarming amiability proved to be his greatest asset, as it usually concealed, at least partially, the grating negativity of conservative resentments over civil rights and the growth of government bureaucracies. Assiduously rehearsed yet seemingly natural, Reagan's ability to at once charm and chastise enhanced his gravitational pull on Republican moderates who had supported Christopher. One week after the latter's defeat, his leading financial backers pledged their support to Reagan at a public meeting for party unity attended by the hierarchy of the Friends of Ronald Reagan. Christopher backer Thomas Pike, who had served in the Eisenhower administration, stated that the actor's philosophy "comes very close" to that of the former president.[2] Clearly an overstatement, Pike's assertion nonetheless portended that if Reagan lost to Brown, it would not be due to Republican factionalism. Deciding to beat up on Democrats instead of themselves, the Republican right in California—which now accounted for almost half the state's party membership—and the Modern Republicans at long last declared a truce. As Henry Salvatori happily proclaimed, "[t]he GOP has finally come through in one piece."[3]

The quest for party solidarity, however, was not entirely successful because Thomas Kuchel made clear he would not endorse Reagan. Openly backing Christopher in the primary election, Kuchel nonetheless agreed during that campaign to be a cochairman of a Republican "unity" dinner in Los Angeles on June 23, but declined to actually attend due to "official duties."[4] In a well-publicized letter shortly before the primary, Gaylord Parkinson urged him to reconsider his decision not to attend the dinner and "endorse the ticket from the bottom to the top," for the sake of the party and his own political future. "Frankly, Tommy," Parkinson warned, "you have a lot of fences to mend in this State." The Republican State Central Committee chairman declared, "[y]ou could do more to solidify our Party . . . and undo more damage by this one action than anything I know of."[5] Kuchel responded with an undiplomatic rhetorical query: "Who the hell is Parkinson?" He stated that he chose to exercise his right as "a free, independent American" in making his decisions, and considered Parkinson's letter to be a form of "intimidation."[6]

Though leading state Republicans predicted that Kuchel would eventually "come on board," that did not prove to be the case. A moderate in the progressive tradition of Governor Warren, the senator generally appealed to all but the most conservative Republicans, as well as to many Democrats. His popularity across party lines arguably made him the most powerful Republican in the state, and Reagan very much wanted his support. In early October, Reagan asked John McCone, a former CIA director and chairman of Knowland's 1958 campaign, to try to arrange a meeting where the actor could make one last effort to win Kuchel over. Briefing McCone with the requisite information for the latter's mission as intermediary, Reagan described the matters that had led to "a lack of understanding between the senator and myself."[7]

Reagan was certain that Kuchel held a grudge against him for serving as the "Honorary Chairman" of Loyd Wright's campaign for the Senate in 1962. "I have regretted [that decision] many times since," he confessed, "because I realize I have been in a position where I could make a contribution to [party] unity, and I endangered it in that campaign. . . ." The actor also contended that he had no hand in any Wright literature attacking Kuchel, nor, contrary to press reports, had he ever repudiated him.[8] He also stressed that he was not involved "in the despicable attempts to blacken" the senator's name, in which a false affidavit, circulated in 1963, detailed the arrest of Kuchel and another man in a drunken-driving and homosexual incident. Reagan stated that Kuchel believed that the wealthy corporate executive Patrick Frawley, a major contributor to right-wing causes in southern California and elsewhere, had a hand in that smear.[9] Despite attempts by opponents to link Frawley to his organization, the candidate declared that he "is not a part of my campaign, didn't support me in the primary, and has not contributed one dime to my campaign at this moment." (But he later recalled that Frawley "was always a supporter . . . as a fund-raiser.") Finally, Reagan conceded that "the Senator and I probably don't see eye to eye with regard to the Birch Society," but described Robert Welch as "utterly reprehensible" and excoriated JBS members who "seek to subvert a political party to the purposes and goals of their organization. . . ."[10]

Kuchel and Reagan never met during the fall campaign to attempt to settle their differences. The senator's refusal to endorse Reagan surely qualified as a significant disappointment to the candidate and his backers, but should not have come as a surprise. Given his equivocal position on the JBS, Reagan could hardly have expected an endorsement from the senator, whose strident criticisms of ultraconservatives made him one of the most vocal Republican opponents of right-wing extremism. In addition, Reagan's high-level association with Wright and Goldwater, and his assault on civil rights legislation, which Kuchel had strongly supported, may have ruled out an endorsement regardless of Reagan's position on the JBS. Furthermore, Leon Panetta, Kuchel's chief aide, believed that Reagan was not only too far to the right, but a political lightweight as well. After attending a postprimary National Press Club Luncheon at which Reagan spoke, Panetta reported to his boss that the amiable actor was simply "Goldwater in a prettier package" and possessed "sort of a Kiwanis Club approach to state problems." Other progressive Republicans in the state urged Kuchel not to endorse Reagan, claiming that if the Reagan forces took over the party, the progressive wing would no longer have a place in it. Though Kuchel had an amicable relationship with Reagan as late as 1961, that apparently had long since dissipated and with it the chances of the senator's endorsement.[11]

Unlike 1964, however, when many moderate Republicans deserted Goldwater, Kuchel now appeared to be an intractable party renegade. While adding to the longstanding enmity that fervent conservatives harbored for the senator, his refusal to endorse Reagan doubtless rubbed many other Republicans the wrong way as well, which in turn contributed to his eventual political demise. Max Rafferty, who defeated Kuchel in the Republican primary Senate race in 1968, challenged the incumbent on the premise that the latter had become about as welcome in the Republican Party "as a skunk at a picnic."[12]

Ardent Brown backers likely felt the same way about Sam Yorty's presence in the Democratic Party due to his backlash-based conservatism and strident attacks on the "Brown machine." Moreover, his lack of support for the governor after the primary did not bode well for the latter's prospects in the general election. In a staged exhibition of comradery, Brown invited the mayor to his office in mid-June and allowed him to try the governor's chair out for size. Yorty then coaxed Brown into promising to ask the state legislature to approve an antiriot law that he had authored along with his controversial police chief, William Parker. The law granted police the power to arrest anyone suspected of using inflammatory rhetoric in a public place—implicitly, blacks in riot-scarred neighborhoods.[13] Continuing to evoke harrowing images of urban unrest, Yorty kept the weight of the race issue on Brown's weary shoulders.

The governor also had to face the fact that he had fared worse than expected against Yorty not only among white voters, but among blacks and especially Mexican Americans. The governor's advisors attributed his poor support from these minorities in good part to Yorty's efforts to integrate Los Angeles city government and to Brown's apparent inattention to a number of important minority issues. They believed, however, that with hard work and the right overtures, Brown could win back most of the alienated voters within these groups.[14]

Though it is unclear whether Yorty would have endorsed the governor under any circumstances, the chances of an endorsement seemed to dissipate when the antiriot bill became law in October, but in an "emasculated" form, according to the embittered mayor.[15] The latter's harsh criticism of the bill reinforced notions that Brown was weak-kneed on crime, and delivered another serious and perhaps fatal blow to the governor's effort to court Yorty's conservative Democratic bloc.

The Brown camp also faced problems in gaining support from progressive Republicans, who they believed would be unwilling or reluctant to vote for Reagan. Realizing he may have alienated these potential backers, Brown hoped to minimize the repercussions from the Christopher smear at a "peace conference" with the former mayor in late June. He apologized for any hand his managers had in providing material to Drew Pearson and claimed they had acted without his knowledge. Having linked the governor directly to the smear for several weeks, Christopher announced that he had accepted Brown at his word and would not name him in a libel suit filed against Pearson, who had earlier sued Christopher on the same grounds.[16] The damage had been done, however. As one campaign advisor acknowledged, the potential fallout from the smear had not been properly calculated.[17] The governor found dubious relief in not being named in the libel suit, but, due to his staff's actions, surely lost some support within the ranks of a Republican constituency that had often been an ally during and since his challenge to Knowland in 1958.

To keep Republican moderates in the fold, Reagan sought to avoid distinct reminders of that faction's anguish during the Goldwater crusade. To this end, he declared at the outset of his challenge to Brown that he would have no one from outside the state actively campaign on his behalf. "An election of this kind," he contended, "is between the California people and their candidate."[18] The press interpreted this statement to mean that Reagan sought to keep Goldwater away from his campaign. Though he would never admit it, Reagan clearly did not want the Arizonan stumping the state for him. Denying any implication of such sentiments, the actor privately apologized to Goldwater for any misunderstanding of his reasons for not seeking his active support.[19]

Nevertheless, shortly before the primary, the senator informed Reagan that he would be speaking to a Republican women's group in Los Angeles in late June, and continued to offer his services for the general election campaign.[20] Responding to Goldwater after his landslide victory over Christopher, Reagan saluted him in a letter, stating, "[y]ou set the pattern and perhaps it was just your fate to be a little too soon. . . ." Tributes and pleasantries aside, he did not even mention the senator's offer to help on the campaign trail. As for Goldwater's upcoming California visit, the candidate suggestively stated that "I know such trips are usually fast, in and out," but hoped that the two might have a chance to briefly chat.[21] Consequently the man who had in effect, though inadvertently, launched Reagan's political career—and had given force to the movement behind it—was relegated to the sidelines in the gubernatorial quest of his star disciple.

Despite his distance from Goldwater, citizen politician Reagan followed the senator's style in applying the populist, common-man touch to his rhetoric and descriptions of his background. While Goldwater constructed a rugged image of himself as the "son of a pioneer family," Reagan's campaign literature depicted him as having been an industrious all-American boy, cut out for leadership: he had been "President of the [Eureka College] Student Body"; "Captain [of the] swimming team"; and had "Worked [his] way through college." The actor's "Three years [of] varsity football" may have reminded voters of his film role as the legendary Notre Dame gridiron star, George Gipp. (The latter's reported deathbed utterance, ". . . win one for the 'Gipper,'" was one of President Reagan's fondest invocations.[22]) His college degree notwithstanding, the candidate sought to exude an intuitive intelligence that deduced "common sense answers" to "problems that baffle professional politicians."[23] Moreover, he effectively and ever affably reduced conservative and liberal differences to invidious distinctions. Repeated complaints about the "intellectual clique in Sacramento" provided a clear "us against them" dichotomy when he assailed the growth of state government. Derivative of frontier populism as well as conservative attacks on liberal intellectual "eggheads" during the Eisenhower years, Reagan's antiintellectualism also lent itself to diatribes against the activities of the rebellious coterie at UC.

Indeed, campus unrest at Berkeley provided Reagan with a matrix through which he ably exploited and intertwined the key issues of antiwar protests, race and morality. Though the Vietnam War itself did not prove to be a contentious matter between the two candidates, Brown could not afford to vehemently attack campus antiwar activists given the rising opposition to U.S. policy in Indochina among his left-leaning Democratic constituents. Reagan therefore gained an advantage in terms of unabashed patriotism, for he could and freely did castigate those dissenters. Not lacking help from his supporters in this regard, Reagan experienced a vintage campaign moment in the small town of Lakeport, when a uniformed G.I., his face scarred by a shrapnel wound, placed a California flag in the candidate's arms and exhorted: "You go get yourself some of those Berkeley Cong, Mr. Reagan."[24] Conflating salient issues more subtly, the actor helped contribute to the controversy over a black power rally scheduled at UC in late October, declaring, "we can not have the university . . . used as a base to foment riots from."[25] Concerns about sexual immorality on campus provided Reagan with another potent UC issue. When he spoke of "sexual orgies" there, "so vile I can not describe them to you,"[26] he surely touched a nerve among the many middle-class parents whose children attended or planned to attend Berkeley or one of the other UC campuses.

The moral aspects of the unrest at Berkeley had also been exploited to the hilt by Max Rafferty en route to his easy reelection victory in June. (He won more than 50 percent of the nonpartisan vote, eliminating the need for a November runoff.) Facing nominal opposition in that electoral contest, Rafferty had long derided the UC dissenters in speeches such as "The Meaning of Berkeley." He promoted the notion that the Free Speech Movement had turned into an effort to condone "filthy speech." The campus protesters' "talk is a modern thieves' jargon," he contended, "relying strongly upon scarcely described obscenity and intelligible mainly to other members of the cult."[27] A month before the primary Rafferty stated that the proper course of action at UC would be to dismiss students who belonged to the discontented faction, along with the "many professors"—that intellectual clique in Berkeley—who had plotted to "take over control of the university."[28] Though the tone of his language remained the same as in his earlier diatribes, Rafferty's attack on UC protestors could only improve his image because he now at least seemed to be a determined defender of the ivied campus status quo, and not just a popular iconoclast fighting against it in the realm of progressive education.

Given that Rafferty and Reagan held essentially the same views on UC concerns, Charles B. Garrigus, a Democratic assemblyman and college instructor, warned against "a new set of three Rs for education—Reaction, Raffertyism and Reaganism."[29] Though the superintendent did endorse Reagan, the two men appeared together only a few times during the course of the campaign, and then only at functions concerning matters of public education. Despite Rafferty's popularity at the polls, Reagan and his staff avoided being too closely linked with him or other controversial right-wing figures, Californians or not. Furthermore, from the outset of his informal candidacy, the actor cordially declined invitations to speak to certain ultra-conservative groups he had addressed in the past, to avoid adding to his right-wing image and stirring his arch-conservative supporters to a more fevered pitch. He turned down, for example, an invitation to speak at the Americanism Educational League's annual banquet in 1965, contending that it was time to give others an opportunity to address the group. Seeking especially to appease moderate Republicans, Reagan, in a letter to George Murphy, expressed optimism in mid-August that the party would remain "glued together, if only we can keep some of the kooks quiet."[30]

Brown's campaign managers, however, would do all they could to depict Reagan as joined at the hip with some of those "kooks," particularly prominent individuals connected to ultraconservative organizations. In July, Hale Champion, one of the members of the governor's campaign "troika" (along with Bradley and Dutton), sent a memorandum to other top officials in the Brown organization suggesting "that we just don't talk about Reagan who is a very pleasant fellow, but always about Reagan and the people behind him." He maintained they could use "the stereotype of the spoilers and the barons just as Yorty used the stereotype of the [political] machine." "The conspiratorial theory of history still runs deep," Champion contended, so "[w]e have to get these other people into the fray . . . in case [Reagan] turns out to be relatively immune to our direct move on him."[31]

Though semi-retired, Harry Lerner, a longtime Brown associate and public relations agent, headed an investigative team that worked full-time on compiling negative material on the actor.[32] Citing the findings of these and other Democratic investigators, Roger Kent, a San Francisco lawyer who served as cochairman of Brown's reelection organization, announced in late August that recently released studies revealed that Reagan's campaign was financed and directed by JBS members and sympathizers. These individuals, he contended, in addition to harboring extreme political views, qualified as bigots, anti-Semites and anti-Catholics.[33] These charges initially appeared in late July in a "white paper" on the JBS issued by Alan Cranston. At the Republican State Convention a few weeks later, Reagan called the document "a propaganda piece that appealed to prejudice itself."[34] Nevertheless, certain actions at the convention seemingly gave weight to the accusations in the white paper. Reagan, Gaylord Parkinson, and other powerful party members helped quash a modest effort at the convention to pass a resolution condemning extremism. At the same time, delegates approved a statement demanding the "repeal or amendment" of the Rumford Act, over strong objections from black Republicans and others in the party's progressive faction.[35]

Given the pervasive resentment of the Rumford Act, the Brown camp downplayed the race issue as the campaign heated up and instead, following Champion's advice, pinned its hopes on the question of the "conspiratorial" forces behind Republican extremism. Hoping to fully revive the waning fears of Reagan's purported alliance with the far right, the Democratic State Central Committee and the CDC circulated a pamphlet, "Ronald Reagan, Extremist Collaborator: An Exposé," complete with footnoted "facts" and figures, detailing how Reagan functioned as the "extremists' collaborator," especially with the "super-secret" Birch Society. "It is true that genuine conservatives also support Reagan," the publication claimed, but they only "bring respectability to a campaign whose true nature . . . will dismay moderates and conservatives of both parties."[36]

Describing how "California 'Fright-Wing' " money flowed to the actor, the report listed members of the Friends of Ronald Reagan who had connections with the JBS or other ultraconservative organizations. The publication also named members of "Reagan's Rightist 'Brain Trust,' " which included Henry Salvatori and Walter Knott, as well as prominent figures providing "Out-of-State Extremist Cash." A litany of episodes from the candidate's "pro-extremist" past detailed his right-wing associations, while in succeeding pages he was shown to be in "violent conflict" with leading Republicans, such as Everett Dirksen and House minority leader Gerald Ford, who had repudiated the JBS.[37] Reagan essentially ignored this onslaught, maintaining his well-established position on the extremism issue:

he would not refuse the backing of anyone who supported *his* ideas, even if those individuals held certain views that strongly clashed with his own.

Reagan did indeed accept money from persons active in the JBS and similar groups, but he and his staff made every effort to avoid direct interaction with these people. His advisors, for instance, made arrangements to change the location of a Reagan reception in Pasadena upon learning that the host, who had offered his home for the gathering, belonged to the JBS.[38] And it does not appear that anyone on his Southern California Finance Committee belonged to the Society, though some, such as Knott and UROC head Joseph Crosby, had participated in events sponsored by the JBS. Despite the ultra-conservative activities of Knott, Crosby and a number of other significant Reagan supporters, the Democratic effort to expose his campaign as a Trojan Horse, replete with right-wing fanatics, did not have the impact that Brown and his backers had hoped. Such efforts ran headlong into Reagan's winsome responses, his proficient campaign staff, and an increasingly disinterested electorate. Outside of the state's coastal urban areas, it appears the extremism issue fell flat because the JBS was almost unknown.[39]

The Birch matter remained generally under control throughout the campaign, but anxiety that it would not periodically rippled through the ranks of Reagan's strategists. This trepidation was stirred when the manager of The Spirit of '76 House, a Birch Society literature hub in Massachusetts, informed the actor and his staff that he was writing a "fast-paced, gripping biography" of Reagan for distribution during the campaign. In addition to extolling Reagan, Richard Jennett, the manager of the book store and author of the biography, stressed "the *fact* that Thomas Jefferson if he were alive in 1964 would have been for Goldwater" (emphasis added). Requesting any material that the candidate or his staff might contribute for the book, the ardent Goldwaterite was certain the biography would be a "best-seller, given the highly dramatic promotional campaign we have in mind for it." William Roberts responded with some alarm, telling Jennett, as diplomatically as possible, that "while we can not stop you from publishing a book, I'm sure you can understand that we are concerned about what you might say."[40]

The "gripping" biography turned out to be a sixteen-page tabloid entitled "The Story of Ronald Reagan—The Next Governor of California." It seems that most of Jennett's biographical information came from *Where's the Rest of Me?* For instance, in showing Reagan's patriotic and "unselfish" concern for others, Jennett described the actor's contribution to America's World War II effort: He "found himself drawn into a top-secret military mission . . . as closely guarded as the A-bomb project." In his autobiography, Reagan stated that his job as narrator of bomber pilot training films for raids on Tokyo "was [part of] one of the better-kept secrets of the war, ranking up with the atom bomb project." Jennett: Reagan "knew that a slip of the tongue in a public place where an enemy agent was listening could trap bomber crews into an ambush." Reagan: "We knew the bomb targets well in advance, including the proposed time of the bombing raid.... It was enough to make us all fearful of talking in our sleep, or taking an extra drink."[41]

For the most part, then, Jennett's brief biography did not prove any more embarrassing than Reagan's own written recollections in overdramatized passages, such as the description of his role in the "secret" military project. While the actor's services as a war-time film narrator clearly qualified as important,[42] by the time of the Tokyo raids (spring 1945) there was little doubt about where American bombers were going to strike and limited resistance from the ravaged Japanese military. Therefore, Reagan's concern over spilling secrets about forthcoming air raids took on an element of suspense and peril beyond the actual dangers to those flying the bombing missions or to the success of the raids. To dwell on such matters, however, misses the point. The powerful appeal of Reagan's war stories, regardless of their accuracy, became quite evident in his later political life. At the outset of his political career, the autobiographical account of his dedicated service during the war, along with other altruistic aspects of his life, could only facilitate his all-American, nice-guy image—promoting the notion, as Jennett declared, that Reagan was destined "To Serve Others Unselfishly!"[43]

Nothing in "The Story of Ronald Reagan" itself should have caused much distress to Roberts or others in the candidate's high command. Jennett's trumpeted linkage of Reagan and Goldwater in an accompanying solicitation, however, along with his affiliation with the JBS, provided fodder for the Democrats' "Exposé" and poked an unwelcome far-right finger in two sore spots in the actor's public image. Indeed, Reagan's high-profile participation in Goldwater's presidential campaign and his refusal to disavow support from the JBS troubled a significant number of voters.[44] It is therefore no surprise that Democrats tried to exploit the extremism issue. But in making such a relentless and shrill attack on Reagan, Brown's strategists made a mistake similar to that of Rockefeller's advisors in 1964 in terms of the overkill on Goldwater's "extremism." Given that the issue of extremism had lost some of its resonance by 1966, the tidal wave of accusations against Reagan and certain conservative supporters probably inured voters to such charges more than they "shocked" them. The attacks also had considerable potential to offend the public's sense of issue priorities and, as with the Christopher smear, fair play. In smaller dispensations, the assault on Republican ultraconservatism might well have worked to Brown's advantage, but the all-out offensive against the congenial Reagan proved to be another miscalculation on the part of the governor's campaign staff.

Kuchel's defection notwithstanding, GOP unity in the Golden State played no small role in blunting the Brown camp's barbs on extremism. With the party no longer torn asunder by factional differences, the latter could not be readily exacerbated by exposés and the like. Moreover, former prominent Christopher supporters not only endorsed Reagan, but actively campaigned on his behalf. Among the ten initial members of the Kitchen Cabinet, the elite group of millionaires closest to Reagan at the start of his political career, four had been avid supporters of Christopher.[45] After backing Christopher in the primary, Los Angeles lawyer William French Smith went on to become Governor Reagan's personal attorney (and later served as President Reagan's first attorney general). Tire manufacturer Leonard Firestone had served as the former mayor's finance chairman in southern California, while San Francisco businessman Arch Monson had worked as state coordinator of his campaign. Both men became major Reagan fundraisers. Taft Schreiber, an executive at the Music Corporation of America and Reagan's Hollywood agent since 1938, had ardently backed Christopher but swung behind his onetime client after the primary. Reagan and Holmes Tuttle credited Schreiber with helping to get moderate Jewish voters to back the "citizen politician," which they deemed critical to securing the support of Christopher Republicans.[46]

Other than grumblings about the millionaire status of the businessmen in Reagan's inner circle, Brown's literature contained few fusillades against the men who became members of the Kitchen Cabinet. The only one to be specifically assailed as an ultraconservative was Henry Salvatori, whose involvement in "numerous extremist" anticommunist organizations qualified him to be in the "Exposé." Salvatori had indeed been involved in many right-wing causes, but he never belonged to the JBS nor was he active in any other truly far-right fringe group.[47] In addition, the large sums of money he donated to conservative endeavors often funded anticommunist projects at distinguished academic institutions such as the University of Southern California and Stanford University. Unlike Patrick Frawley, it does not appear that Salvatori made contributions to radically conservative organizations, but all his political commitments and considerations did revolve primarily around his fierce anticommunist convictions.[48]

Two other members of the Kitchen Cabinet, while surely dedicated anticommunists, nonetheless were most concerned about government encroachment in the free market. Retired banker Leland Kaiser, calling himself a "card-carrying capitalist," and fellow San Franciscan Jaquelin Hume, head of a produce company, helped rally Bay-area Republicans behind Reagan and assisted in fundraising efforts.[49] Not entirely opposed to government intervention in the marketplace, Hume harbored the Wilsonian belief that the main function of government was to ensure that "the economic game is played fairly." Upset by the "socialistic programs" begun by Franklin Roosevelt, Hume became disillusioned with Dwight Eisenhower because he did not roll back the liberal "welfare state."[50] In 1964, both he and Kaiser enthusiastically backed Goldwater, Eisenhower's best-known Republican critic.

While Hume's views on Eisenhower and Roosevelt reflected the usual right-wing complaints and resentments regarding the two presidents, most, if not all, members of the Kitchen Cabinet had actively campaigned for Ike. A strong backer of the World War II hero, Tuttle even tacitly supported Franklin Roosevelt, believing that the former president would "turn over in his grave" if he knew how bloated some of the agencies he had started had become. (Tuttle's view of Roosevelt resembled Reagan's, which may explain in part why the auto dealer became Reagan's closest "citizen advisor."[51]) On the whole, then, the Kitchen Cabinet was a small consortium of wealthy conservatives and moderates, a group of "citizen capitalists," relatively balanced in terms of Republican philosophy.

The views of these "self-made men," however, clearly drew upon social Darwinist ideas of public welfare and personal responsibility. While such beliefs at the very least fostered rather stoic attitudes toward racism and the plight of the poor, it would be wrong to assume that Reagan's elite backers were uniformly indifferent to these problems. Concluding that they were, Haynes Johnson declared that a "bedrock belief in a laissez-faire approach to society's problems was shared by virtually all those who initially formed behind Reagan." As a "perfect" individual example of this vestigial social Darwinism, Johnson cited Kitchen Cabinet member Justin Dart. While statements made by Dart certainly showed strains of Darwinian logic, Johnson overlooked the fact that in 1964 he had been the California finance chairman for Rockefeller, who had ardently backed the Civil Rights Act in his battle against Goldwater. Reflecting on his philosophy of government, Dart asserted that he "always [had] been for everything the government could do for the people that . . . [it] could afford to do. . . ."[52] The Friends of Reagan, of course, were dedicated to the creed that government could not afford a liberal agenda, economically or otherwise, in the realm of social welfare programs like those of the Great Society. By 1966 public opinion gravitated toward that belief. Capitalizing on this shift, Reagan's inner circle matched their dedication to the principle of limited government with a commitment to the moderation and party harmony essential to defeating Brown.

Recognizing the threat Republican unity posed, the governor persisted in his attempt to resurrect the rancorous GOP battles that the actor and his wealthy backers considered to be bygone. Buoyed by a late August poll that put him only three percentage points behind Reagan, Brown sent Reagan a long telegram on September 10, as the campaign actively got under way. He asked Reagan to repudiate the JBS and "disassociate yourself from the extremists," or "the Democratic Party will continue to produce documented evidence day by day of your deep involvement with the radical right. . . ." "The choice is yours," Brown declared. "All I ask is that you take a strong stand against extremism similar to that taken by the leaders of your own party. . . ."[53]

Obviously calculated to give as much exposure to the extremism issue as possible, Brown's telegram, which was released to reporters, came the day before he and Reagan appeared on NBC TV's weekly news forum, *Meet the Press*. During the separate questioning of each candidate, the governor charged that his opponent's refusal to withdraw his support from Birch members vying for legislative seats made him "almost the last protector of this secret right-wing society." Reagan countered with his patented response, and stated that "a candidate in my position has a sort of obligation to support the entire ticket of his party."[54] While this mediated exchange on extremism between the two candidates may have been news to Americans living outside California, few citizens of the Golden State could have found interest in these now redundant incantations.

By the end of September, however, Reagan added a counterattack to his standard rejoinder to assertions that he was an agent of the extremists. Foreshadowed earlier in his campaign, he assailed the governor's link to the CDC, stating in a radio ad that "Mr. Brown seems to be taken over by this group . . . whose positions parallel those of the Communist Party." The statement referred in particular to the CDC's opposition to the bombing of North Vietnam and its support for admitting "Red" China to the UN. Clearly outside the mainstream of public opinion, the Council's positions on these issues saddled Brown with unwelcome baggage and helped Reagan turn the tables on the governor. "Perhaps extremism *should* be an issue in this campaign," Reagan remarked. "I leave it to your good judgment to decide who is extreme."[55]

In addition to accusing Brown of skirting real issues in favor of the extremism "bugaboo," Republicans mocked his preoccupation with the matter. For instance, in a stinging editorial, the *Orange County Republican* declared that the "little old lady who was supposed to see Communists under every bed has been replaced by the little old man in Sacramento who sees a Bircher behind every tree."[56] Brown backers may have scoffed at such proclamations, but the incessant Democratic attacks on Reagan and the JBS did have a frantic and somewhat paranoid edge. Those characteristics were perhaps best exemplified in a charge made by Thomas Pitts, a state labor union official, who claimed that Reagan had "plotted" with the National Association of Manufacturers for "an extremist takeover of California."[57] Laden with fears of a right-wing conspiracy, Pitts's statement proved only slightly more shrill than the alarmist utterances and tracts coming from the governor's headquarters and on the campaign trail.

By early October it became clear that the Democrats had failed to convince enough voters that Reagan was an exponent of the radical right. The California Poll showed that the Republican candidate's three percentage point lead at the beginning of August had grown to 7 percent.[58] Nevertheless, the realization that the extremist label would not stick to Reagan did not bring an end to the use of negative material, much to the chagrin of some of Brown's advisors. Indicative of the dissension within the governor's inner circle, one insider recalled that "no matter how often decisions were made . . . that we weren't going to pursue that [negative] effort anymore, the [Lerner-led] operation continued to flourish."[59] Amid a palpable air of desperation, the Brown campaign now aimed its attack at Reagan's lack of political experience, in addition to charging that he was "riding the white backlash."[60]

Having adroitly defused the extremism issue, an increasingly confident Reagan decided to establish a joint ticket with the moderate Robert Finch, to aid the latter's come-from-behind effort in the lieutenant governor's race.[61] The arrangement proved beneficial to both candidates. Finch would benefit from the increased exposure in ads and in the press, as well as from the actor's coattails, while Reagan strengthened his image as a centrist and unifier of the Republican Party. Large newspaper ads urged voters to "Elect California's new team," a duo with "common sense and integrity," committed to dealing firmly with "Beatniks, taxes, riots, crime," and other pressing problems.[62] The two candidates did disagree on some matters, most notably on Proposition 16, an antipornography initiative. A cause célèbre of ultraconservatives like Patrick Frawley, the initiative aimed to empower private citizens with the right to determine what qualified as "obscene," and to shut down publications with an affidavit alone in the course of further legal actions.[63] Finch, a lawyer, stated that the initiative "plunges into the murky waters of censorship" and would eliminate all local antipornography laws. While Brown opposed the proposition on similar grounds, Reagan favored it in the hope that it would provide a voter "mandate" on smut.[64]

The brainchild of Republican assemblyman E. Richard Barnes, Proposition 16 was promoted in a muddled manner as the "CLEAN" campaign.

(The acronym stood for the "California League Enlisting Action Now.") An eleven-page advertisement appearing in many California newspapers the Sunday before the election claimed that due to a lack of legislative action, the state had become the "Smut Capital of the World." The proposition, according to the ad, would help protect young women in particular from the "degradation" of pornography. "What kind of woman do you want your daughter to be?" the ad asked; "What kind of woman do you want your son to marry?" Certainly not one whose moral "decency" had fallen victim to "salacious stories." The ad stated that such "obscene" literature had a "directive-like effect on some men" in provoking sexual violence toward women.[65] (Ironically, that assertion presaged the unlikely antipornography alliance, albeit indirect, in later years between feminists who subscribed to that Pavlovian theory, and the CLEAN-inclined religious right—two groups otherwise at diametrical and vociferous odds.)

Touting the initiative as a "carefully written document," the ad further asserted that "obscenity is not within the area of constitutionally protected speech and press,"[66] but ignored the fact that even "filth peddlers" had the right to due process of law, which the proposition aimed to subvert. Another frightening aspect, as Finch noted, was that "any eccentric," after deeming a publication obscene, could "sue any prosecuting attorney who did not agree with him and press charges."[67] Though few would argue against contentions that pornography posed a serious problem, the concern over the initiative's unconstitutional aspects, along with its potential to unleash book burners and other self-ordained censors, led to its resounding defeat at the polls.

While Reagan backed Proposition 16, "it was never something that we hung our hat on," observed Tuttle.[68] Reagan's support for the initiative, however, worked well with the moral emphasis of his campaign. In explaining the principles undergirding his Creative Society, he declared that "morality should be one of the basic motivating forces" in American life. In ads targeting Brown and Berkeley, he stressed the importance of "leadership and morality" in the course of berating "vietniks, beatniks, and filthy speachers *[sic]*."[69] He also called some of the Brown camp's tactics "immoral," such as notices in state employees' paychecks suggesting a "minimum contribution" to the governor's reelection fund.[70] When compared to the tacit moral tone of Goldwater's presidential crusade, Reagan's campaign stands out as having had an overtly moral theme.

Reagan's emphasis on "moral decency" played well with some traditional Democrats, as exemplified by the labor union member who was tired of Brown's tolerance of "the filthy, long haired . . . scum at Berkeley" and his "whitewash of the negroes arrested for rioting in San Francisco. . . ." A union member for forty years, he and others in the Brotherhood of Railroad

Trainmen (BRT) had decided to "vote against a Democrat" for the first time.[71] In stark contrast to these disillusioned BRT members, the Southern California District Council of the International Longshoreman's and Warehouseman's Union found fault with Brown's principles from a left-wing perspective. The council expressed "indignation at the retreat on your part in the face of the Regan *[sic]*, Yorty offensive or the so-called Anti-Riot Legislation." The council urged him to end this retreat, dispel "the apathy and negative moods" of the many people "who once were your most ardent . . . supporters," and "fire the imagination" of labor, minorities, and liberal and "middle of the road" groups.[72]

Seeking to win back the waning support of labor's increasingly factious ranks, Brown aide William Becker devised an approach to reveal the right's "conspiracy to divide labor, by using the race issue. . . ." He informed the governor's campaign hierarchy that when courting labor votes, Brown should cite the litany of liberal legislation and programs had that had contributed to the "good life" enjoyed by the "working people of America." Given that the "old reactionaries" knew they could not kill these programs, they could only win with Reagan "by frightening some white workers on the issue of civil rights" in an attempt to "divide and conquer . . . the working people."[73] Becker exposed not necessarily a conspiracy but rather a trend-setting conservative Republican strategy that grew out of Goldwater's success in the South in 1964. The exploitation of the race issue clearly divided labor's Democratic ranks in California in 1966, irremediably for Brown. His roundabout use of Becker's approach proved inadequate as Reagan and others, bolstered by urban unrest and related "disorder" at Berkeley, continued to exploit racial tensions. Reagan went on to win around 40 percent of the labor vote. Though Brown had won 78 percent of the vote from white union households in 1958, this support dropped to 57 percent by the Fall of 1966.[74]

The last weeks of the campaign were increasingly dominated by discussions and analyses of the white backlash. Most liberal pundits and politicians echoed Brown's lament that the backlash would have a considerable impact at the polls in California, and that Reagan would be a prime beneficiary.[75] Denying that a backlash even existed, Reagan maintained that the race issue reflected "nothing more than the concern people have for . . . extremists in the civil rights movement. . . ." In regard to this "extremism," he criticized the nascent black power movement, and hoped that the "more responsible segments of the Negro community" would repudiate those black leaders who had broken away from the passive and "orderly process of appealing wrongs through legitimate channels."[76] Believing that communists had created or at least thoroughly infiltrated the civil rights movement, many conservatives feared black political activism in any form. In addition to literature, widely distributed filmstrips, such as "The Watts Riot," presented graphic images of urban violence and dire commentaries that helped fuel the backlash that had begun in earnest in California with the resistance to the "infamous Rumford Forced Housing Act."[77]

The growing concerns among whites over the civil rights movement and inner city problems, along with the uncompromising opposition to the Rumford Act by Reagan and the California GOP, helped Republican candidates corral the burgeoning backlash vote. Throughout the campaign Reagan continued to speak of the threats to property, explicitly from the fair housing law, but more implicitly in references to unrest in black urban areas. Imbued with an almost Lockean lexicon, he emphasized the "sacred . . . human" right of the individual to the "possession and the disposition of his own property."[78] Concurring with Reagan on the right to "freedom of choice by the owner in housing sales and rentals," State Senator John Schmitz of Orange County declared that "Proposition 14 was . . . struck down by the California Supreme Court in an act of judicial tyranny. . . ."[79] Reflecting this resentment, conservatives mounted an ultimately unsuccessful retainment referendum against the three justices up for reelection who had voted to invalidate Proposition 14. Reagan took no public position on this effort, but it seems at the very least he would have agreed with Schmitz's statement on the Supreme Court's action.

Not surprisingly, the Reagan campaign made virtually no effort to stir support in black neighborhoods. As Roberts put it, "there were no votes there to speak of." During the mid-1960s, the Republican Party in California made a nominal attempt to appoint a token number of blacks to executive committees in the party in the hope of generating more minority support. Gaylord Parkinson recalled, however, that among black Republicans, "[u]nfortunately I found . . . a lot of 'Uncle Toms.'" They would go through "Amos and Andy" routines at party meetings, "passing resolutions for motherhood and this sort of thing."[80] In reducing most black party members to racist stereotypes, Parkinson revealed yet another of the difficulties African Americans faced in trying to fit in with the Reaganites of the GOP.

In terms of working with minorities, Parkinson preferred "the Mexicans because they were more family oriented, much more responsible" than blacks.[81] The notion that African American families suffered from incohesiveness was not unique to Republicans of Parkinson's ilk. In the influential "Moynihan Report" of 1965, Assistant Secretary of Labor Daniel Patrick Moynihan bleakly described the instability inherent in lower-class black families during and since slavery. The recent familial breakdown, Moynihan concluded, stemmed from endemic urban poverty, which shamed the un- or underemployed male parent in particular, often leading latter to desert his family. Though liberal Democrats and conservative Republicans could agree on the precarious state of poor black families, their respective remedies for this problem differed drastically. Reflecting the statism, if not the specific prescription, of most liberal Democrats, including Brown, Moynihan recommended government programs to create jobs for African American men in addition to incentive allowances for black parents who lived with their families.[82] Reagan viewed this sort of government intervention as an attempt to "exchange one odious form of paternalism for another." He contended that "private enterprise has more to offer [blacks] than Big Brother government,"[83] ignoring the fact that the private sector had done very little for the majority of African Americans struggling to cope with the pervasive problems within urban ghettos.

Believing that Brown had not done much of late in this regard either, Dr. Carlton Goodlett, a black physician and newspaper publisher, had declared his candidacy for governor in March. Essentially running as a protest candidate, Goodlett declared that he would make the governor "go into the ghettos of Watts and Oakland" if he expected to win "any of the 600,000 California Negro votes." Yet other African Americans believed Brown had done as much as he could "publicly" afford to do given the political climate.[84] Though he had expressed some misgivings about Brown's timidity in tackling urban issues, Mervyn Dymally, a black state assemblyman from south central Los Angeles, pledged his support for the governor. He in fact cochaired the "Community Organizations for Brown" (COB), which also served as a liaison between the Democratic Party and minority communities. COB also aimed to thwart "Parkinson's plan to move into areas which have marginal minority populations and gain representatives at the expense of those minorities." To further help rally black support, Byron Rumford and fellow Bay-area state assemblyman Willie Brown agreed to serve on the governor's executive campaign committee.[85] By November, the governor had fairly well firmed up his support among African Americans.

Though fewer than one in ten black voters backed Reagan, he garnered almost 25 percent of the traditionally Democratic Mexican American vote. The Republican candidate paid numerous visits to Hispanic communities in southern California, where "Ya Basta" ("We've had it"), a pro-Reagan group started by local business leaders, helped generate enthusiastic backing.[86] In addition, some Mexican Americans were disillusioned by Brown's failure to appoint more Hispanics to prominent positions in state government and by his decision in April not to discuss the problems of striking migrant grape pickers with their leader, Cesar Chavez. The Brown camp also received reports that voters in the "Mexican precincts" in Los Angeles "shared in the anti-Negro sentiment" due to the "Negroes' seeming monopoly of the anti-poverty programs. . . ."[87]

Despite the consensus among Brown's advisors on the need for a major organizational effort in Mexican American communities, they were uncertain about which of the many competing community groups they should work with to win support. To circumvent this dilemma, one Brown advisor suggested that Mexican president Gustavo Díaz Ordaz should be invited for a "non-political" visit, so the governor could get some political mileage out of a tour through the Southland with him. In the end, however, the Brown campaign had problems on so many fronts that it did not have adequate time or resources to cultivate support in Mexican American neighborhoods outside of traditional get-out-the-vote efforts.[88] Moreover, the renewed attack on the Rumford Act did not necessarily swing Mexican American voters behind Brown because the housing issue had essentially become identified with African Americans regardless of the potential discriminatory impact of the act's repeal on other minority groups.[89]

Though concerned about the inroads Republicans had made with specific minorities, Brown and his staff ultimately focused on how to win back white Democrats who had abandoned the governor in alarming numbers. To that end, in early October Brown appointed a bipartisan commission to draft recommendations for amendments to the Rumford Act. In establishing the commission, the governor appeared to be waffling on the fair housing issue, or, worse yet, pandering to the anti-Rumford forces. He therefore aggravated his already strained relationship with party liberals, and poll numbers gave no indication that Brown's moderated stance on the housing matter made any significant difference in voter preferences in the gubernatorial contest.[90]

Two weeks before the election, the governor decided to bring the white backlash, the "great unspoken issue" of the campaign, "out on the table. . . ." In the wake of early fall riots in largely African American neighborhoods in Oakland and San Francisco, he charged that Reagan "is riding the backlash and . . . subtly contributing to it."[91] Brown proved correct on both points, but to no avail. Reagan did rouse resentments by repeatedly castigating the governor for failing to deal effectively with "racial disturbances," while claiming that it "has never been my intention . . . to capitalize on such tragedy for political purpose."[92] Reagan's exploitation of white fears and animosities should have been transparent to even the nominally astute voter, but his manipulation of the issue of black violence was not nearly as important to the majority of whites as the issue itself. In bringing the backlash matter "out in the open," Brown seemed to be calling for some sort of moral introspection on the part of the electorate. The qualms and resentments that

Reagan helped stir, however, eclipsed whatever moral and ethical concerns most white voters may have had on the matters of race and campaign tactics, especially in southern California. As one white woman in suburban Los Angeles bitterly remarked, the black riots reflected "a complete disrespect for law and order—that's what people are waking up to in this election."[93]

In addition, Brown's accusatory tone on the backlash issue could not help but invoke memories of his charge in 1964 that those who favored Proposition 14 were bigots and fascists—a charge Reagan and others frequently recalled with great indignation. Avoiding any direct references to the Rumford Act, Brown made clear he was now referring to "a relatively few people—the white supremacist and black power people—that [sic] are trying to turn race against race. . . ." Most Californians, however, did not want to hear about the causes of racial enmity; they wanted remedies to the criminal manifestations of this hostility instead. In this regard, Brown had little choice but to try to match his opponent's tough talk on crime, because liberal remedies aimed at ameliorating the social conditions that purportedly spurred criminal behavior appeared to have been largely ineffective. But for a governor who had very publicly agonized over allowing the brutal rapist Caryl Chessman to die in the gas chamber in 1960, a "tough-on-crime" image did not seem to fit him or his record.

Though a pillar of law and order on a rhetorical level, Reagan's affability and political inexperience did not necessarily grant him the image of a governor who would spare no quarter in dealing with miscreants. In the course of stressing Reagan's "good guy" attributes, a major Democratic fundraiser appropriately called him "the Shirley Temple of the male set."[94] Indeed, the well-heeled actor hardly emanated Goldwater's rough rider masculinity, which is one of the reasons he received few Hollywood roles as a Western gunslinger, despite his desire for such castings.[95] Yet Reagan managed to bring an air of the Old West and frontier justice to his campaign, Hollywood style, by often having fellow actor Chuck Connors introduce him to audiences. Best known for his long-running television role as Lucas McCain, the virtuous cowboy with a steady but ever-ready finger on a hair-trigger .44–40 rifle in *The Rifleman,* Connors proved so popular with audiences that some people suggested that he should consider a career in politics.[96] John Wayne, the cinematic epitome of the rugged Westerner and close friend of the candidate, strongly supported Reagan, but was not as involved or prominently associated with Reagan's campaign as he had been with Goldwater's two years earlier.

Brown and his handlers had initially used Reagan's acting career as a backdrop in assailing his political inexperience, but in the last month of the campaign in particular, they increasingly ridiculed their opponent as a political novice who would be an "acting governor." The Republican candidate's lack of experience in public service did concern a considerable number of voters. These apprehensions, however, were largely offset by the widespread belief that the governor had been in office too long, a notion exploited by the image and rhetoric of Reagan, the citizen politician.[97] Having put various negative spins on Reagan's inexperience and B-movie background, the Brown camp released a half-hour television documentary in late October entitled "A Man Versus the Actor." In the documentary, the governor visited a nursery school where he stopped to chat with two young black girls. "You know that an actor shot Abraham Lincoln," he tells them. When first questioned by reporters about the governor's highly controversial remark, Reagan, with a cue from aide Lyn Nofziger, feigned disbelief that the blunder-prone Brown could have actually made such a statement. After the candidate had left the pool of reporters, an impressed Nofziger congratulated him for his deft performance: "Well, you finally won an academy award."[98]

In many ways Reagan's performance throughout the campaign warranted such praise, for he easily met the challenges of the inaugural phase of his long-term quest for what Lou Cannon has called "the role of a lifetime"—the presidency.[99] Rewarded for his citizen politician role by receiving strong support from a broad spectrum of voters, Reagan defeated the governor by a margin almost as great as Brown's in his 1958 landslide over Knowland, and in so doing led California Republicans back to Sacramento after languishing eight years in the political wilderness. In addition to turning back virtually all Democratic attacks on his brand of conservatism and on him personally, he did a commendable job in acquainting himself with state issues and the machinery of state government. Brown backers who had attempted to stump Reagan on such matters during his campaign press conferences discovered that the actor who never forgot a line likewise rarely forgot his scripted positions on gubernatorial concerns.[100] (That would not be the case after he became governor.) Now he was preparing to turn those positions into state policies. To the dismay of the governor-elect's ardent opponents, but to the delight of many of his supporters, Reagan's victory heralded the triumph of the California Right.

While Reagan's success should be seen as the crowning achievement of the 1960s for conservatives in the Golden State, both Brown and Reagan had fought to lay claim to the middle of the road in the political arena. The governor and his troops therefore made every effort to depict the former Goldwater crusader "as somehow not being of the center."[101] As that center moved more to the right, however, Brown seemed to get caught in the undertow of liberalism's waning current. Moving rather tepidly toward more conservative views during the course of the campaign, the governor, who had long championed "*responsible* liberalism," nevertheless could not escape the negative consequences of the rising disaffection for his prevailing left-of-center image. Reflecting this perception, the *Los Angeles Times,* whose shift from an entrenched to a tempered conservatism paralleled the odyssey of the California Right, stated that Brown "has drifted away from the sensible moderation he once embraced. . . ."[102] Actually, public opinion, the political barometer of this "sensible moderation," had drifted away from him until it was too late for him to react expediently and effectively.

Brown and his campaign managers, of course, hinged their reelection strategy not on shoring up the governor's image but on tearing down Reagan's through the extremism bogy. That issue, as this study has attempted to show, had worked well in earlier campaigns in various ways, but had worn thin by 1966. Democratic accusations that Reagan and like-minded Republicans harbored extreme views on the role of government and, to a lesser and usually more subtle extent, on racial matters, bored or offended many voters rather than alarmed them. Moreover, sharp criticism of the Brown campaign's tactics could be found well outside Republican circles. Lamenting the "failure of [Brown's] liberal nerve," *Ramparts* magazine, an influential left-wing publication based in Berkeley, declared that the Democratic attacks on Republican extremism had withered into a collection of "tired clichés." Such charges were "exciting, once," the periodical's editors opined. "But that was a long time ago."[103]

The Brown camp's foibles and the "old hat" factor aside, the extremism issue fizzled in 1966 because California moved to the right, prodded by events and Reagan's message, unique abilities, and appeal. Clearly Spencer–Roberts, BASICO, and the Kitchen Cabinet all had a significant hand in defusing the looming extremist problem as well as others. It is at the very least questionable, however, whether another right-wing candidate, such as Joe Shell or Max Rafferty, could have won the governorship, even with such a formidable campaign organization, weak opponent, and propitious political climate. Learning from earlier electoral disasters, Reagan's initial political backers believed that he alone possessed the requisite attributes as a candidate that would enable him to transcend his liabilities and remove the stigma of extremism from conservative Republican philosophy—first in California and then throughout the nation. Indeed, Reagan's political career attests to the sagacity, if not the certitude, of that judgment.

Eight

Conclusion

Sworn into office on January 5, 1967, Governor Ronald Reagan pledged to "cut and squeeze and trim" the state budget and limit government in accordance with the will of "the people."[1] Nevertheless, while he continued to use conservative populist rhetoric throughout his gubernatorial years, his actions often differed from his oratory, though the latter helped mask his deviations from conservative principles. During his first year he did slash government spending as he had resolutely promised, in addition to leading the successful effort to oust University of California president Clark Kerr, whom conservatives had long seen as sympathetic to campus demonstrators. On a number of other significant matters, however, Reagan frustrated many of his right-wing constituents, especially in regard to taming the leviathan of big government.

Despite the governor's desire to curtail state spending, he discovered that due to California's rapid growth and to the fixed costs of most programs, many of which were mandated by law, the state budget would have to increase substantially. Reagan's refusal to challenge these ultimately inevitable budget hikes and attendant large tax increases angered fiscal conservatives in particular and alienated groups such as the UROC. He also dismayed many supporters who anchored themselves to right-wing social issues when he signed the Beilenson bill, which enacted the most liberal abortion law in any state up to that time. The governor displayed moderate tendencies on some environmental concerns as well, which constituted a departure from the prodevelopment stance he had taken during the campaign and in his controversial opposition to the establishment of Redwoods National Park.[2]

Another major disappointment for conservatives came during the legislative battle over the repeal of the Rumford Act. Reagan did not endorse the repeal bill, which was carried by John Schmitz, until it had been amended beyond recognition and became unacceptable to a majority of legislators, particularly conservatives. Though he did little else for minorities during his governorship, Reagan's deliberate actions regarding the repeal assured its defeat. He later claimed to have reversed his position on the Rumford Act after meeting with "members of the minority community" with whom he had little contact during his campaign. "When I realized the symbolism of [the act]. . . and how much it meant morale-wise to [blacks] . . . , I frankly said no" to the repeal. However, it seems that his ulterior motive was to appease Republican moderates to help in his pursuit of the 1968 GOP presidential nomination.[3] Reagan had little regard for the symbolic and legal import of civil rights laws once he became president. The federal judiciary, led by Reagan appointees, and his administration assailed civil rights statutes and regulations established during the 1960s and proved woefully lax in their enforcement efforts.[4]

Indeed, a major legacy of the conservative movement of the 1960s can be found in the diminution and rejection of governmental authority to remedy race-related social inequities and in the political wedge issues created for Republicans. Goldwater's stand against the federal "tyranny" imposed by civil rights laws won him five states in the solidly Democratic deep South in 1964. Two years later Reagan, in his avuncular way, demonstrated that the politics of race could be highly effective in attacking "big government" outside the South. In 1968, Richard Nixon crafted a race-baiting strategy in which he opposed busing for school desegregation and made frequent use of divisive code phrases such as "states' rights" and "law and order" to make further Republican inroads in the South and other parts of the country as well. As president, Nixon, in a devious tactical twist, supported a policy of "preferential treatment" for minorities in employment practices and a strong affirmative-action agenda with the goal of increasing tension between blacks and organized labor within the Democratic Party.[5] More recently, California governor Pete Wilson exploited opposition to public education and welfare benefits for "illegal" immigrants—particularly Latinos ("they keep coming")—in his 1994 reelection campaign and attacked affirmative action in his short-lived pursuit of the 1996 Republican presidential nomination.[6]

Regardless of their own motivations, together Goldwater and Reagan in the mid-1960s provided a lasting cloak of conservative legitimacy for positions on social issues that often served, on one level or another, discriminatory interests. In essence, they gave preference to the tyranny of institutionalized bigotry over the alleged despotism of the state. Neither of these two men ever seemed to grasp this inherent paradox in their defense of freedom because their celebration of freedom and civic virtue created an element of denial in their perceptions of racism and its history in American society.

In keeping with Hollywood Westerns celebrating the "conquest" of the frontier, such denials put a gloss on the racist notions behind the exterminatory attacks by Anglos on Native Americans in California (and elsewhere in the West), where white perceptions of "inferior" races became deeply embedded in the sociopolitical culture. Though Native Americans suffered more than any other racial group, Chinese and Japanese immigrants experienced overt and sometimes vicious bigotry, which white politicians both fomented and exploited. Politicians catered to the anti-Asian prejudices of the state's white labor groups—especially in northern California—from the 1860s to the 1910s, and later helped maintain xenophobic attitudes in burgeoning and largely segregated white communities.[7] Within the context of California history, therefore, the campaign for Proposition 14 and Reagan's subsequent exploitation of this incarnation of the white backlash followed a trend; but because Reagan's campaign was not overtly racist yet reflected widely held white resentments, he effectively laid claim to the political center on racial concerns as a candidate.

In assessing Reagan's place in the history of California's electoral politics, the fact that he overcame the obstacles opponents posed regarding his extremist image makes him unique. No other candidate who had been so strongly identified with the "radical" wing of either party had been able to win a major partisan political office in the state. The Brown camp's efforts to paint Reagan with the extremist stripe was similar in kind to the Merriam campaign's attacks on Upton Sinclair in 1934. Of course, Merriam's powerful backers, who relentlessly castigated Sinclair as an advocate of free love, revolution, and communism, succeeded in their mission, whereas Brown and his advisors did not. Nevertheless, right-wing extremism would remain a recurrent problem for the Republican Party after 1966, but not as it had been during and immediately after the Goldwater ascendancy.

Though Reagan and his handlers all but erased the extremist label from his campaign, his election did not mark a lasting voter realignment in the state. After Reagan's triumph, some political scientists contended that his victory established a "mass base" for the Republican right.[8] The election of 1970, however, challenged this assertion. Reagan did win reelection that year (by a smaller margin than in 1966), but the Democrats, after losing their ten-year hold of the legislature in 1968, regained majorities in both chambers in 1970, which showed that Reagan did not have coattails. Perhaps the strongest evidence that the large number of Democratic defectors in 1966 were not entirely sold on Republican candidates came in George Murphy's loss to Democrat John Tunney, and in Max Rafferty's defeat by a black challenger, Wilson Riles, in the race for Superintendent of Public Instruction. (Rafferty's decline began in 1968, when he lost to Democrat Alan Cranston in the U.S. Senate race after it had been revealed that Rafferty had shot off a toe to avoid service in World War II.) Moreover, by the early 1970s, even Orange County residents were tempering their conservative views, due in part, it appears, to the organizational efforts of more moderate Republicans.[9]

Reagan, therefore, cannot be credited with bringing about a critical voter realignment or any other political or economic phenomenon on the state level comparable to the "Reagan Revolution" during his presidency. He nonetheless contributed greatly to the legitimation of conservatism by moderating the tone of right-wing rhetoric in the wake of the Goldwater debacle, but without abandoning the senator's principles. Moreover, Governor Reagan's capacity for moderation and compromise helped make conservatism more placable, to the point of bringing conservatism into the mainstream of political discourse in California and across the country. For an ideology and a movement that for many years had languished in the margins of political acceptability, the mainstream was an unfamiliar but welcome realm.

The long journey back to respectability actually began immediately after the conservatism of the "Old Order" fell into disrepute during the Great Depression. Right-wing policies, nevertheless, proved hard to resurrect. During the 1930s, the Liberty League tried to sustain the Republican right by assailing the welfare state and its progenitor, "that man," Franklin Roosevelt. These attacks, however, withered as they came up against the discrediting memories of the Herbert Hoover years and the overwhelming popularity of FDR. Conservatives did find fertile ground for their virulent anticommunism in the decade after World War II, but assaults on the welfare state were not embraced by an electorate that had no desire to roll back the clock to laissez-faire policies redolent of the 1920s. Despite this inhospitable public mood, conservatives of fierce conviction persisted in their efforts to undermine the "socialistic" aspects of federal and state governments. Upset by the Eisenhower administration's foreign policy and tacit approval of the welfare state, the Republican right in the late 1950s, with mounting support from its intellectual vanguard, challenged the "hero" and his brand of Republicanism. This challenge inaugurated the movement that eventually found its greatest political strength in California.

The crushing defeat of William Knowland and other right-wing candidates in 1958 seemed to support Daniel Bell's much-debated proclamation two years later that the "ideological age has ended." This epoch came to a close due to "the acceptance of the Welfare State," which was firmly rooted in a prosperous and diverse economy and in the pluralistic politics championed by vital center liberals. Declaring that "the old [Marxist] ideologies have lost their 'truth' . . . and power to persuade," Bell contended that the "older [laissez-faire] 'counter-beliefs' have lost their intellectual force as well."[10] The Goldwater crusade and the New Left proved Bell wrong on both counts, as the age of "consensus"—to the extent it ever existed—collapsed in the 1960s. The "counter-beliefs" in unreconstructed terms of the Old Order were indeed dead. But as sociologist Jerome Himmelstein has argued, the "new conservatives" revitalized their political and intellectual tradition, and transformed the Republican right into a powerful movement. That transformation was facilitated by political opportunities created by the failures and exhaustion of liberalism, and by the inability of the American left to provide viable alternatives.[11]

The conservative movement also benefited from victories within its own marginal ranks. Richard Nixon's lossess in 1960 and 1962, for example, were critical blows to Modern Republicanism and its chief spokesperson, who in turn became more conservative in the latter half of the 1960s.[12] Nixon's defeat in 1962 allowed Goldwater to take center stage in the GOP, but the Arizonan then became a sacrificial lamb to the memory of JFK. The latter's torch had been passed to Lyndon Johnson, who proceeded to inform voters that many of Kennedy's goals would go unfulfilled if the reactionary Arizona cowboy became president. Though the Johnson camp ran an effective campaign against the foredoomed Goldwater, the ideological implosion within the Republican Party, which heightened the extremism issue, guaranteed a Johnson landslide. Ultimately, the single biggest factor in the collapse of Goldwater's candidacy was the senator himself and his litany of ill-conceived remarks, which exacerbated rather than diminished concerns about Republican extremism. Reflecting the long-standing doubts that many conservative intellectual supporters had about the Arizonan, Buckley privately stated that he had devoted "roughly half of my columns to running interference for Barry Goldwater and cleaning up after him." Buckley and other conservative intellectuals understood, however, that the Goldwater crusade had provided the impetus for a right-wing consensus and established an electoral base on which the movement could build.[13]

Though not immediately evident, in a number of ways the senator's defeat marked the end of the conservative battle against the ghost of Roosevelt and the New Deal. The creation of new bureaucracies during the Johnson years prompted conservatives to finally abandon their attempt to roll back the welfare state and instead focus on thwarting its burgeoning new growth. Besides, the resounding rejection of Goldwater meant that his long-established opposition to compulsory Social Security (his later unequivocal support notwithstanding), farm subsidies, and other lasting New Deal economic programs were well outside the mainstream of public opinion. Reflecting a new focus, Reagan still effectively assailed the "tyranny" of big government in 1966, but he and other conservatives aimed more at stirring the emergent culture wars by exploiting newly potent racial issues and the "subversion" of traditional morality.

In Reagan, of course, right-wing Republicans found a candidate with that long-sought-after balance between electability and ideological commitment, the prototype of the new conservative populist, well suited for a quest for the White House. As one historian has stated in regard to this remarkable equilibrium, Reagan was "a thundering conservative without being thunderous."[14] He often used blunt and alarming language to delineate the forces of good and evil in his speeches; yet references to the "poet Belloc" or the "great French philosopher Alexis de Tocqueville," gave his oratories an element of erudition that combined with his mellifluent style to make him a compelling figure to a wide audience. To many of the more savvy ideologues who supported Reagan, it mattered little that the pithy quotes and citations were an intellectual facade for his rudimentary understanding of issues and ideology. As Henry Salvatori stated shortly after Reagan became president, "[w]e knew then [during his gubernatorial campaign] as we know now, that he doesn't have any depth. But boy was he good on his feet."[15] The latter proved true when Reagan had a scripted speech or response, but his lack of depth often showed in impromptu exchanges with the press. As Lou Cannon noted in 1974, "reporters at televised press conferences were constantly surprised at how often he answered questions with a disarmingly candid 'I don't know.' " Nevertheless, Buckley chided those conservatives who questioned the intellectual capacity of the Republican presidential nominee in 1980. Championing Reagan as a devout disciple of America's civil religion, he declared that the nominee was "a man of amiability and discipline, who is simple enough to cherish no other ideals than those of the Founding Fathers."[16]

Between the years of Reagan's governorship and his presidency, the "New Right," in a sort of second coming, took formal shape. The leaders of this movement possessed a zealous penchant for political activism that allowed them to become the dominant tactical, if not ideological, force in conservative politics. Arguably the strongest group within the New Right, the religious right, under the direction of leaders like Jerry Falwell, helped rally opposition to abortion and the "permissive" liberal culture through direct-mail solicitations, demonstrations and lobbying efforts.[17] In addition to the endeavors of the religious conservatives, the New Right, as Michael Kazin has noted, "joined together businesspeople who chafed at federal regulations with former working-class Democrats outraged at cultural permissiveness and court-ordered busing."[18] This diverse alliance against the "liberal establishment," however, began to take shape for Republicans during Reagan's 1966 campaign, but did not become a relatively consistent and cohesive voting bloc until late in the succeeding decade and into the 1980s.

The social conservatism of blue collar workers was evident in the presidential elections of 1968 and 1972, but many of these disaffected workers in 1968 voted for the populist Democrat turned independent candidate, George Wallace, rather than Richard Nixon. The segregationist Wallace manipulated deep-seated white working-class resentments during 1968, especially on racial matters. Nevertheless, he was not as overtly racist during that presidential campaign as he had been when elected governor of Alabama in 1962, when he made his infamous declaration: "Segregation now! Segregation tomorrow! Segregation forever!" But given that proclamation (among others), his racist reputation preceded him, a factor that made him markedly different from both Reagan and Goldwater. Reagan did exploit the race issue in his 1966 campaign, but subtly, as has been shown, and with mitigating pronouncements on his steadfast opposition to racism and segregation. Furthermore, Wallace generally backed the liberal economic programs stemming from the New Deal that Reagan tended to excoriate (at least in spirit), though both men proved generally supportive of the rank and file in organized labor, a core constituency in the New Deal coalition.[19] Finally, Wallace was almost demagogic in his style. His rhetoric, thunderous in both tone and substance, and his essentially independent status and vocal extremist supporters, made him a marginal yet important player in national politics: Wallace could never seriously hope to win the presidency, but he had a lasting impact on the nature of the country's political discourse.

Contributing significantly to the fragmentation of the Democratic electoral coalition forged during the New Deal, Wallace attracted legions of disaffected blue-collar Democrats who would later vote for Reagan for president and for other conservative candidates.[20] Yet Wallace's influence in this regard can be overstated, and Reagan's understated. In his biography of Wallace, Dan Carter noted that he "thrust himself forward as the authentic defender of the 'common man'" with a raw energy that Reagan lacked: "even when Reagan voiced the most outrageous policies, his soothing, even avuncular style undercut the harshness of his message."[21] Carter is quite right; but the appeal of Reagan's "soothing" message was in those very feel-good encapsulations of the politics of resentment, which enabled him to capitalize on those resentments with a greater number of voters than the abrasive Wallace could ever hope to win over.

Tapping the resentments of California taxpayers in 1978, the backers of Proposition 13, led by Howard Jarvis, sought a rollback of property taxes and consequently sparked a tax revolt that swept through much of the country. Proposition 13 passed with almost two-thirds of the vote from an electorate that favored welfare benefit cuts by a margin of almost three to one.

Opponents of the initiative included blacks, public employees, and a host of liberal interest groups. Therefore the tax revolt, as journalists Thomas Byrne Edsall and Mary Edsall have noted, "provided . . . a new means for conservatives to identify and define [and demonize] an 'establishment' attempting to thwart the populist will of the electorate. . . ." The passage of Proposition 13 was perhaps the most significant conservative victory in California, and arguably elsewhere, between 1966 and 1980.[22]

Working-class voters, along with multitudes of other Americans from groups that had been part of the New Deal coalition, helped bring about the ultimate triumph of the California Right in 1980: the election of Reagan to the presidency. Similar to Pat Brown and his advisors, President Jimmy Carter and his campaign staff underestimated the pervasive appeal of Reagan's congenial conservatism. Once in the White House, however, the president disappointed many conservatives, much as he had done during his gubernatorial years. The disappointments came primarily in regard to social concerns, as he declined to actively pursue such matters as tougher abortion laws and the reinstitution of school prayer.[23] Nevertheless, Reagan stepped-up his attacks on the tyrannical Soviet "evil empire" and breathed new life into the conservative commitment to triumph over communism. Moreover, his supply-side fiscal policy ("Reaganomics") pleased his right-wing backers, especially the wealthy, who prospered even further due to major tax cuts. Among the beneficiaries of these cuts, of course, were the businessmen in California who had initially supported the citizen politician and continued to do so in the 1980s. Replacing Thomas Jefferson's portrait in the East Room of the White House with one of Calvin Coolidge, Reagan symbolically inferred that the true meaning of his victory could be found in "Silent Cal's" only memorable dictum: "The business of America is business."

It is perhaps appropriate that *Mr. Smith Goes to Washington,* the Hollywood version of a citizen politician who prevails over the wayward political establishment, took on a certain reality in Reagan's own political rise. Inspired no doubt by silver-screen stories like that of Mr. Smith, candidate Reagan was essentially a Hollywood product as well, right down to his script and directors. After his gubernatorial years, the telegenic Reagan capitalized on his still-potent citizen politician image by campaigning for the presidency as a non-Eastern outsider, much as Goldwater had done in 1964. These two towering conservatives, in addition to other conservatives, utilized the freedom-versus-tyranny theme as the defining rubric of right-wing attacks on the liberal order through much of the 1960s. With social issues providing the crucial impetus for electoral successes in the latter half of that decade, the Republican right by 1966 had brought about the initial post-Eisenhower retreat of the "bleeding heart" advocates of big government. The Democratic Party, in an often internecine struggle, has sought to shake that pejorative image of liberalism ever since, as much as the Republicans have promoted it.

Yet, as the century comes to a close, the conservative movement is beset with its own image problems and disagreements, stemming largely from the conservative legacy of the 1960s. In an article titled "What Ails Conservatism," William Kristol, the editor of the conservative periodical the *Weekly Standard,* and colleague David Brooks, maintained that a "conservatism that organizes citizens' resentments rather than informing their hopes will always fall short of fundamental victory." Other conservatives have recently warned against "mindless opposition to the state" and of the deleterious consequences of an ideological all-or-nothing mentality. Moreover, the conservative journalist and intellectual George F. Will has noted that the right can no longer consider the word "freedom" as its shibboleth, due to "an insufficiency of virtue revealed by the uses Americans make of their . . . freedom from the restraints of government or social stigmas."[24]

As conservatives labor to reconcile electoral goals with philosophical principles and collective objectives, perhaps they too are discovering that the well of operable ideas is drying up, short of another transformation of the American right—or at least short of another Ronald Reagan, who mastered the politics of divide and conquer, but at the same time informed the hopes of many Americans.

Notes

Abbreviations Used in Notes

CRA Collection   California Republican Assembly Collection
CSA   California State Archives
CSUFFC   California State University, Fullerton, Freedom Center
CSUFOH   California State University, Fullerton, Oral History
RNPP Papers   Richard Nixon Pre-Presidential Papers
UCBBL   University of California, Berkeley, Bancroft Library
UCBOH   University of California, Berkeley, Oral History
UCLAOH   University of California, Los Angeles, Oral History
UCLASC   University of California, Los Angeles, Special Collections

Notes to Introduction

1. The groundbreaking 1955 essays that fostered the status anxiety thesis are Richard Hofstadter's "The Pseudo-Conservative Revolt," and Seymour Martin Lipset's "The Sources of the 'Radical Right,' " in Daniel Bell, ed., *The New American Right*. This book was reissued in 1963 in an "expanded and updated" form, with the new and clearly pejorative title, *The Radical Right* (Bell quoted in his essay "The Dispossessed," p. 2). Still the starting point for discussions on American conservatism, the book(s) contain essays by other prominent "consensus" scholars who were in general agreement with Hofstadter and Lipset on the impact of status anxiety and on the threat the right wing posed to the centrist politics of liberal pluralism. The status anxiety theory and related paradigms drew upon sociologist Theodore Adorno's influential 1950 book, *The Authoritarian Personality*. In another noteworthy study released the same year as *The New American Right*, historian Clinton Rossiter took a "non-pejorative" view of the right in *Conservatism in America*. In a revised 1962 edition, Rossiter seemed upset that some of his liberal colleagues considered him to be on the right politically. This led him to assert that "in politics [I am] well to the right of [United Auto Workers' president] Walter Reuther and well to the left of Senator [Barry] Goldwater." In other words, he essentially chose to reassure his confused colleagues that he was in the "vital center" along with them when it came to his politics. Rossiter, *Conservatism in America: The Thankless Persuasion*, p. ix.

2. Hofstadter, *The Paranoid Style in American Politics*, pp. 3, 29, 110.

3. On the demise of the GOP's liberal wing, see Nicol C. Rae, *The Decline and Fall of the Liberal Republicans*. The term "movement" in this study refers essen-

tially to right-wing Republicans who shared common political values and goals, who organized on the grassroots level and utilized the party's political apparatus as well as other vehicles to advance candidates and causes. Unless otherwise noted, the term "conservative" is synonymous with "right" and "right wing" and refers to Republicans fiercely opposed to communism *and* to the "welfare state" initiated by President Franklin Roosevelt. GOP "moderates" generally accepted the changes brought about by the welfare state and were willing to consider new programs, but often argued for more state and local control and kept a careful eye on spending and taxes. Generally aligned with party moderates, Republican "liberals," by far the party's smallest faction, believed that government needed to pursue and enact legislative remedies for social ills, though not, as a rule, to the extent of liberal Democrats.

4. For insightful comment on the origins and reformulations of the status anxiety thesis and on Hofstadter's paranoid style theory, see William Hixson Jr., *Search for the American Right Wing,* pp. 12–16, 100–112, 198–209. Perhaps the most noteworthy early challenge to the status anxiety thesis is in Michael Rogin's 1967 study, *The Intellectuals and McCarthy.* In a well-argued presentation, Rogin contends that the liberal intellectuals promoting that thesis were themselves ridden with status concerns and that McCarthyites feared communism more than anything else (ibid., p. 20). Despite the criticism leveled by Rogin and others, Lipset in 1970 continued to apply the status anxiety thesis in his and Earl Raab's study of extremism. See Lipset and Raab, *The Politics of Unreason.*

5. Michael Kazin, "The Grass Roots Right: New Histories of U.S. Conservatism in the Twentieth Century," *American Historical Review* 97 (February 1992): 136–155 (quote from p. 140). In this insightful review essay Kazin explains how numerous recent works—but not all—on the American right have moved away from the "extremist" interpretations of earlier scholarship. For an equally perspicacious examination of the shortcomings of historical scholarship on American conservatism, see Alan Brinkley, "The Problem of American Conservatism," *American Historical Review* 99 (April 1994): 409–429. Brinkley also offers enlightening comments on the deeply rooted post–World War II cultural conflict between conservatives—who, despite their traditional "private values," have adapted to the "modern public world"—and liberals and their "progressive modernism." Finding themselves, for the most part, in the "liberal progressive" category, historians, as Brinkley details, have not adequately examined or fully understood American conservatism (ibid., pp. 427–429).

6. There are three books of note that provide extensive analyses of the pivotal Goldwater victory in the California Primary: Theodore White, *The Making of the President 1964,* pp. 138–158; John Kessel, *The Goldwater Coalition,* pp. 80–89; and Robert Novak, *The Agony of the GOP,* chapter 21. For detailed analyses of the impact of the 1964 presidential campaign and election on the Republican Party and American politics, see Mary Brennan, *Turning Right in the Sixties;* and David Reinhard, *The Republican Right Since 1945,* chapter 9.

7. For detailed descriptions of some of the larger contemporary American extremist movements and organizations on the right, see Lipset and Raab, *The Politics of Unreason,* chapters 6–13; and Arnold Forster and Benjamin Epstein, *Danger on the Right.* For an extensive listing of southern California extremist groups and their literature, visit the Special Collections Library at the University of California, Los Angeles (UCLASC), and the Freedom Center at California State University, Fullerton (CSUFFC).

8. Of the multitude of biographies and other studies of Reagan's political career, the author found the following books to be the most valuable for this particular work: Bill Boyarsky, *The Rise of Ronald Reagan;* Lou Cannon, *Ronnie and Jesse,* and *Reagan;* David Broder and Stephen Hess, *The Republican Establishment,* chapter 8; Michael Rogin, *Ronald Reagan, the Movie,* chapter 1; and Garry Wills, *Reagan's America.*

9. In regard to Nixon's isolationist tendencies, as a congressman he voted against both aid to Korea (before the Korean War) and the extension of the Reciprocal Trade Agreements Act, and to reduce Marshall Plan and Atlantic Pact funds and aid to China. See Harry W. Flannery, "Red Smear in California," *Commonweal,* December 8, 1950, p. 224. On such views of the Old Guard in 1950, see Reinhard, *The Republican Right,* pp. 71–74.

10. This distinction is drawn in part from Lisa McGirr, "Suburban Warriors: The Grass-Roots Conservative Movement in the 1960s" (Ph.D. diss., Columbia University, 1995), p. 10.

11. This study provides extensive commentary on the rhetoric of California conservatives, with the goal of ascertaining how that rhetoric animated the movement. While postmodern analysis of political discourse can be revealing and enlightening in some instances, more often language is given far too much weight in the consideration of political agendas and the pursuit of political ends and control. For example, historian David Green, in *The Shaping of Political Consciousness: The Language of Politics in America from McKinley to Reagan,* contends that "[o]nly through language . . . can human understanding be manipulated and people brought to cooperate in their own subjugation," p. ix. He views political discourse essentially as a struggle to control the definition of political labels (e.g., conservative and liberal) and ultimately as *the* vehicle for social domination. Reflective of other wide-ranging studies of "cultural hegemony," Green sees the American electorate as having been repeatedly hoodwinked into submission by the party or faction that established the dominant interpretation of those labels. But where Green sees language as subjugating, one could just as easily see it as the ongoing discourse essential to maintaining pluralistic polities, a discourse in which efforts to persuade verbally are permitted, alongside the right to resist and counter those efforts. Green's linguistic determinism glosses over the fact that the struggle for control over political language is just one of numerous contests between competing interests seeking political power. Finally, while Green offers some interesting and provocative observations on American politics, he and others subscribing to this hegemonic model make correlations between language and behavior that can only be sustained theoretically. For an equally thought-provoking investigation of the power and malleability of important words in American political discourse, but minus Green's notion of a hidden but oppressive linguistic agency, see Daniel Rodgers, *Contested Truths: Keywords in American Politics Since Independence.* Other studies in this vein that the author found particularly useful include: Murray Edelman, *The Symbolic Uses of Politics;* and Raymond Williams, *Keywords: A Vocabulary of Culture and Society.* For an interesting perspective closer to Green's on the subjugating powers of language, see Sacvan Bercovitch, *The American Jeremiad,* which focuses on the hegemonic rhetoric of the "political sermon" in early American Puritan communities.

12. On this shift in general, see Rodgers, *Contested Truths,* pp. 217–223.

13. The one exception to this statement would be actor George Murphy's successful 1964 campaign for the U.S. Senate. While clearly a conservative, Murphy was not as strident in his rhetoric or as inflexible in his policies as Goldwater.

14. Kathleen Hall Jamieson, *Packaging the Presidency*, pp. 198–205.

15. Vernon Cristina, "A Northern Californian Views Conservative Policies and Politics," (UCBOH, 1983), p. 20. Having supported Knowland, Shell, and Goldwater, Cristina had seen enough "losers" to recognize Reagan's potential, p. 21.

16. James Patterson, *America's Struggle Against Poverty*, p. xii.

17. Richard Hofstadter, *Social Darwinism in American Life*, p. 11.

18. T.J. Jackson Lears, "Gutter Populist," *The New Republic*, January 9 and 16, 1995, p. 39. Lears makes clear that pseudo-populism can be found on the left as well, among "politically correct cultural studies programs," for example, p. 39.

19. My observations on the impact of the issue of race in the electoral politics of this period parallel and, in part, are drawn from Thomas Edsall and Mary Edsall, *Chain Reaction*, especially chapters 2 and 3. The Edsalls, however, barely touch on Reagan's 1966 campaign, and instead focus on the racially charged political culture in the years 1964 and 1968, and on Goldwater and Nixon, respectively.

20. On Wallace's race- and class-based populism, see Kazin, *The Populist Persuasion*, chapter 9. For a comprehensive assessment of Wallace's impact on American politics, see Dan Carter, *The Politics of Rage;* of further interest is Stephan Lesher, *George Wallace*.

21. George Nash, *The Conservative Intellectual Movement*, pp. 123–125. Nash provides a good in-depth examination of the intellectual milieu of postwar conservatism, but skirts politics. The *National Review* had many notable contributors during the period highlighted here. In addition to perusing the pages of the magazine, those interested in the views of prominent contributors should begin by looking at two collections of essays: William F. Buckley Jr., ed., *Did You Ever See a Dream Walking?;* and Frank Meyer, ed., *What Is Conservatism?*

22. Buckley quoted in John Judis, *William F. Buckley, Jr.*, p. 119. Aware of Eisenhower's pervasive popularity and low-key charisma, Buckley stated in a 1958 debate on Eisenhower's policies that "I have no doubt that if Mr. Eisenhower were to appear here tonight and speak to us for five minutes, he would have us eating out of his hand, myself included. . . ." This statement, and Buckley's entire opening argument in the debate, appeared in "The Tranquil World of Dwight D. Eisenhower," *National Review*, January 18, 1958, pp. 57–59.

23. Haynes Johnson, *Sleepwalking Through History*, p. 72.

24. See, for example, George Nash, *The Conservative Intellectual Movement*, pp. 247–248.

25. These candidates were Westerners: Reagan, Goldwater, and Nixon—that is, the "new" Nixon of 1968. The Southerner was the segregationist Democrat turned Independent, Wallace.

26. For an insightful discussion of the "sun belt phenomenon," see Kevin Phillips, *The Emerging Republican Majority*, pp. 437–442. Phillips, a political scientist, served as a campaign strategist for Nixon in 1968.

27. Carey McWilliams, *Southern California Country*, p. 179.

28. Lipset has perhaps been the most ardent proponent of this theory in both his early and later works. See "Three Decades of the Radical Right: Coughlinites, McCarthyites and Birchers," in Bell, ed., *The Radical Right;* and (with Raab), *The*

Politics of Unreason, pp. 302–306. Acknowledging McWilliam's influence, Kevin Phillips also pointed to the dynamics of immigration and rapid growth as a major factor in the rise of conservatism in southern California. See Phillips, *The Emerging Republican Majority,* pp. 443–452.

29. Raymond Wolfinger and Fred Greenstein, "Comparing Political Regions: The Case of California," *American Political Science Review* 63 (March 1969): 74–85. The qualified statement on the significance of different backgrounds in political behavior stems from the two authors' admission that on this matter the statistical data are ambiguous and inconclusive. Statistical ambiguities aside, there is ample evidence that while "heartland" immigrants to California made adaptations to the host culture, they maintained significant degrees of regional pride and/or conservative sociopolitical ideas common to individuals from "mid-America." See, for instance, McWilliam's discussion of "state societies" in *Southern California Country,* chapter 9. Denise S. Spooner's study of migrants to southern California from Iowa in the two decades following World War II found that many of these individuals "defined community in terms of likeness to themselves," and tended to be conservative "on matters of race and political ideology." "The Political Consequences of Experiences of Community: Iowa Immigrants and Republican Conservatism in Southern California" (Ph.D. diss., University of Pennsylvania, 1992), p. ix. See also James Gregory's description of "Okie culture" and "plain-folk Americanism" in *American Exodus,* chapter 5.

30. Michael Rogin and John Shover, *Political Change in California,* pp. 184–185, 189. For an excellent critique of Rogin's essay, see Hixson, *Search for the American Right Wing,* pp. 154–162. Of related interest is James Q. Wilson's "A Guide to Reagan Country: The Political Culture of Southern California," *Commentary,* May 1967, pp. 37–45. Though written before Rogin's essay, Wilson's article constitutes a polemic against the primary assertions made by Rogin. While Wilson implicitly granted some validity to McWilliam's thesis, he stated that southern California conservatism derived mainly from a "conventional and bourgeois sense of property . . . [and] intensely middle class values," p. 41. Wilson's explanation actually identifies some of the same conservative motivational factors as Rogin; but where Rogin essentially saw these factors as producing a right-wing pathology, Wilson, more correctly in light of subsequent scholarship, saw normative political behavior. For another rebuttal to Rogin's "hallucinatory politics," see Jackson K. Putnam, "Political Change in California: A Review Essay," *Southern California Quarterly* 53 (December 1971): 551–554.

31. McGirr, "Suburban Warriors," pp. 74–75.

32. Wesley Marx, "Sparta in the Southland," *Frontier,* April 1962, pp. 6–8. Project Alert was the largest organized anticommunist effort in the Southland's history. Retired military officers, including former chiefs of staff, joined with local business leaders at a large, week-long gathering in December 1961. They shrilly warned of public apathy toward communism and inadequate defense measures on the part of the Kennedy administration, and urged project participants to "[t]ell Mr. Khrushchev that he isn't bluffing us into surrender." As cited in "The Conservative Anticommunist Crusade in Southern California and the Military-Industrial Nexus, 1961–1964." Paper by and in possession of the author, presented at the American Historical Association Convention, Chicago, 1995. Project Alert documents can be found at the CSUFFC.

33. Quoted in Roger Lotchin, *Fortress California*, p. 202.

34. Ibid.

35. Negotiated defense contracts were not unique to industries in southern California, but no other region could compare to the Southland in terms of having its economy underpinned by such contracts. See James L. Clayton, "Defense Spending: Key to California's Growth," *Western Political Quarterly* 15 (June 1962): 280–293.

36. For an excellent description of the transformation "from warfare to welfare" in California defense industries, see Lotchin, *Fortress California*.

Notes to Chapter 1

1. On California politics during the latter half of the nineteenth century, see William Deverell, *Railroad Crossing;* Michael Rogin and John Shover, *Political Change in California,* chapter 1; and R. Hal Williams, *The Democratic Party and California Politics.*

2. On California progressivism, see William Deverell, ed., *California Progressivism Revisited;* George Mowry, *The California Progressives;* Spencer Olin, *California's Prodigal Sons;* and Jackson K. Putnam, "The Persistence of Progressivism in the 1920s: The Case of California," *Pacific Historical Review* 35 (November 1966): 395–411. On the tendency toward progressive and pragmatic governance, see J.K. Putnam, "The Pattern of Modern California Politics," *Pacific Historical Review* 61 (February 1992): 23–52. Broader California political histories of note that cover the cross-filing era include Royce Delmatier, et al., *The Rumble of California Politics;* H. Brett Melendy and Benjamin F. Gilbert, *The Governors of California;* J.K. Putnam, *Modern California Politics;* and Rogin and Shover, *Political Change in California.* Studies of California politics by journalists include Gladwin Hill, *Dancing Bear;* Carey McWilliams, *California: The Great Exception;* Herbert Phillips, *Big Wayward Girl.* Other pertinent works include Winston Crouch, et al., *California Government and Politics;* Joseph Harris, *California Politics;* Richard Harvey, *The Dynamics of California Government and Politics;* and Bernard Hyink and David Provost, *Politics and Government in California.*

3. See Putnam, "The Persistence of Progressivism in the 1920s: The Case of California," pp. 395–411.

4. This conservative coalition included Los Angeles insurance magnate Asa Call, *Los Angeles Times* columnist Kyle Palmer, and newspaper mogul William Randolph Hearst. See Greg Mitchell, *The Campaign of the Century,* pp. 570–573. See also Charles Larsen, "The EPIC Campaign of 1934," *Pacific Historical Review* 27 (May 1958): 127–147; and George Rising, "An Epic Endeavor: Upton Sinclair's 1934 Gubernatorial Campaign," *Southern California Quarterly* 79 (Spring 1997): 101–124.

5. On Culbert Olsen's campaign and governorship, see Robert Burke, *Olsen's New Deal for California.*

6. Among the numerous studies of Warren as governor, notable works include Richard Harvey, *Earl Warren: Governor of California;* Lloyd Roy Henderson, *Earl Warren and California Politics;* Leo Katcher, *Earl Warren: A Political Biography;* and G. Edward White, *Earl Warren: A Public Life.* See also Warren, *The Memoirs of Earl Warren.*

7. Quoted in Henderson, *Earl Warren and California Politics,* pp. 135–136; and Katcher, *Earl Warren,* p. 165.

8. Robert Ash, "Alameda Labor Council During the Warren Years" (UCBOH, 1970), p. 7.

9. Quoted in the *Oakland Tribune,* February 20, 1944, p. 1.

10. Earl Warren to Herbert Brownell Jr., November 6, 1945, Earl Warren Papers, F3640: 568–572, CSA.

11. "Address by Earl Lee Kelly," January 31, 1946, Warren Papers, F3640: 568–572, CSA.

12. Thomas Dewey, "Corporate State Not an American System," *Vital Speeches of the Day,* October 15, 1944, pp. 14–15.

13. Katcher, *Earl Warren,* pp. 183–184.

14. Henderson, *Earl Warren and California Politics,* pp. 241–242; and Katcher, *Earl Warren,* p. 196.

15. "Text of Radio Address by Governor Warren over Mutual Network," March 18, 1946, Warren Papers, F3640: 568–572, CSA.

16. Alan Brinkley, "The Idea of the State," in Steven Fraser and Gary Gerstle, eds., *The Rise and Fall of the New Deal Order,* pp. 109–111.

17. Quoted in Katcher, *Earl Warren,* p. 198; as for the others sharing Werdel's opinion, see Janet Stevenson, *The Undiminished Man,* pp. 41–42. On Kenny's opposition to the internment camps, see Stevenson, pp. 43–51; on Warren's support, see Katcher, *Earl Warren,* pp. 137–151.

18. Stevenson, *The Undiminished Man,* p. 56; also see Robert W. Kenny, "California Attorney General and the 1946 Gubernatorial Campaign" (UCBOH, 1975), pp. 43–49.

19. Katcher, *Earl Warren,* pp. 197–198.

20. Kenny campaign press release, April 22, 1946, Warren Papers, F3640: 568–572, CSA.

21. Henderson, *Earl Warren and California Politics,* pp. 252–255. Kenny did find support among AFL officials in the San Francisco Bay area, but not enough to offset the Teamsters' control of the Federation from Los Angeles, p. 252; and "AFL Committee" (San Francisco, n.d.), Warren Papers, F3640: 568–572, CSA. On Kenny's CIO support, see Stevenson, *The Undiminished Man,* pp. 55–56.

22. Kenny quoted in Warren campaign press release (n.d.), Warren Papers, F3640: 568–572, CSA; Palmer in Katcher, *Earl Warren,* pp. 199–200.

23. Katcher, *Earl Warrren,* pp. 34–35.

24. Ibid., pp. 211–212.

25. Warren, "What Is Liberalism?" *New York Times Magazine,* April 18, 1948, p. 10.

26. Quoted in John Diggins, *The Proud Decades,* p. 105.

27. The term "vital center" came from the title of a 1949 book by historian Arthur Schlesinger Jr. and referred specifically to the American intellectuals who believed that New Deal reforms had to be defended from the "unreasoned" attacks by both the radical right and radical left. See Schlesinger Jr., *The Vital Center.*

28. Ed Shattuck and fellow Republican activist Bernard Brennan organized this support in southern California and planned to help in similar efforts in the rest of the state and throughout the nation. Edward Shattuck to Earl Warren, April 15, 1948, Warren Papers, F3640: 614–635, CSA.

29. David Reinhard, *The Republican Right,* pp. 49–50.

30. On Warren's reluctance to run for vice president, see Warren, *Memoirs,* pp. 240–241.

31. Quoted in G.E. White, *Earl Warren,* p. 134.

32. Biddle, Earle, Schneidman, Inc., "Basic Easter[n] Public Relations Campaign for Governor Warren," (n.d.), Warren Papers, F3640: 614–635, CSA.

33. Quoted in G.E. White, *Earl Warren,* p. 135.

34. Edward Barrett Jr., *The Tenney Committee,* p. 335.

35. *San Francisco Chronicle* editorial cited in Richard Donovan, "Jack Tenney: A Post-Mortem," *Frontier,* November 15, 1949, p. 8; and Tenney, *The Tenney Committee: The American Record,* p. i.

36. See Germain Bulcke, "A Longshoreman's Observations" (UCBOH, 1969), pp. 25–27.

37. Barrett, *The Tenney Committee,* pp. 320–325; and McWilliams, "Mr. Tenney's Horrible Awakening," *The Nation,* July 23, 1949, pp. 80–81.

38. Tenney was elected to the State Senate in 1950, but never wielded power there as he did in the Assembly through his committee. In 1954, his reelection bid failed.

39. G.E. White, *Earl Warren,* pp. 115–116; and Clark Kerr, "University of California Crises" (UCBOH, 1976), pp. i, 5. See also David Gardner, *The California Oath Controversy.*

40. G.E. White, *Earl Warren,* p. 117.

41. Quoted in White, *Earl Warren,* p. 119.

42. Ibid., pp. 120–121.

43. Warren, *Memoirs,* pp. 218, 220.

44. "A Trend Is Running Toward an Enlightened Conservatism," *Life,* July 3, 1950, p. 18.

45. Reinhard, *The Republican Right,* p. 65.

46. Paul Bullock, *Jerry Voorhis,* pp. 248–249.

47. Quoted in Roger Morris, *Richard Milhous Nixon,* p. 499.

48. Pink Sheet, Warren Papers, F3640: 579–597, CSA. Douglas did vote with Marcantonio on domestic issues, but Marcantonio usually voted with GOP isolationists such as Robert Taft, Kenneth Wherry and, frequently, Nixon, on foreign policy matters. See Harry W. Flannery, "Red Smear in California," *Commonweal,* December 8, 1950, p. 224; and R. Morris, *Richard Milhous Nixon,* p. 581.

49. R. Morris, *Richard Milhous Nixon,* pp. 581–589.

50. Evelle J. Younger to all members of the RCCLAC, July 20, 1950, Warren Papers, F3640: 579–597, CSA; *Alert,* August 17, 1950 (No. 134), p. 531, ibid.

51. Quoted in R. Morris, *Richard Milhous Nixon,* p. 526.

52. Richard C. Fildew to Fellow Republican, September 21, 1949, Sherrill Halbert Papers, CRA Collection, box 47, UCLASC. The reference to Hoover may have alluded to Truman's decision to name Hoover as the head of a commission investigating wasteful government spending.

53. Quoted in Katcher, *Earl Warren,* p. 246.

54. Warren, *Memoirs,* p. 248; and Katcher, *Earl Warren,* pp. 243–247. Warren received help during his battle with Samish over the Crime Commission when *Collier's* magazine published two articles that exposed Samish's power and arrogance. See Lester Velie, "The Secret Boss of California," *Collier's,* August 13 and

August 20, 1949; also see Arthur Samish and Bob Thomas, *The Life and Good Times of Art Samish.*

55. Katcher, *Earl Warren,* p. 229; and Robert C. Brownell, "Can Roosevelt Win?" *Frontier,* November 3, 1950, p. 5.

56. Democrat quoted in Katcher, *Earl Warren,* p. 248; and Gibbons, *Alert,* (No. 134) August 17, 1950, Warren Papers, F3640: 579–597, CSA.

57. "Interview Between Earl Warren and Interviewing Committee of the California Labor League," April 16, 1950, Warren Papers, F3640: 579–597, CSA. Labor contended that right-to-work laws facilitated union-busting. On Roosevelt's union support, see Langdon Post, "Jimmy Roosevelt's Northern California Campaign" (UCBOH, 1972), pp. 23–24; on the continuing support for Warren from union members, see, for example, Ash, "Alameda Labor Council," p. 44; and U.S. Simmonds, "A Carpenter's Comments" (UCBOH, 1969), pp. 12–17.

58. Warren on McCarthy quoted in Katcher, *Earl Warren,* p. 251. On the Rankin Report file, see NAS (it is unclear who this might have been) to VS (probably Warren aide Verne Scoggins), April 8, 1950, regarding the "Communist connections" of "two persons who signed James Roosevelt's Democratic nomination papers." Warren Papers, F3640: 598–613, CSA.

59. "STOP ROOSEVELT" rally brochure (Embassy Auditorium, Nov. 1 and Nov. 2), Warren Papers, F3640: 579–597, CSA; and Katcher, *Earl Warren,* p. 257.

60. Joe Alex Morris, "Another Roosevelt Makes His Pitch," *The Saturday Evening Post,* October 7, 1950, p. 56.

61. R. Morris, *Richard Milhous Nixon,* pp. 608–610.

62. George H. Sibley to Worth Brown, September 26, 1951, Worth Brown Papers, CRA Collection, box 33, UCLASC.

63. Katcher, *Earl Warren,* p. 265.

64. See Carey McWilliams, "Government by Whitaker and Baxter," *The Nation,* April 14 and April 21, 1951; and Elmer L. Henderson, M.D. (President, AMA), "Medical Progress versus Political Medicine," June 27, 1950, Clem Whitaker and Leone Baxter Papers, box 158, CSA. On Warren's early efforts to enact his health insurance plan, see J.W. Cline, "California Medical Association Crusade Against Compulsory State Health Insurance" (UCBOH, 1971).

65. Warren to Taft, November 14, 1951, Warren Papers, F3640: 17933, CSA. (A handwritten notation on the letter indicates it may never have been sent); Warren (as told to Milton Silverman), "Why I'm Fighting for My Health Plan," *Look,* May 6, 1952, p. 105; and Warren (interviewed by Donald I. Rogers), "Governor Warren on Socialized Medicine and Welfare," *The American Mercury,* April 1952, pp. 87–88.

66. Tenney quoted in the *Oakland Tribune,* November 13, 1951, p. 12; and "Draft MacArthur for President of the U.S.," Sherrill Halbert Papers, CRA Collection, box 60, UCLASC.

67. First Werdel quote in "Werdel Free GOP Delegation"; second quote in J.A. Smith to Earl Warren, March 4, 1952, both in the Warren Papers, F3640: 17933, CSA. For Werdel's reflections on his candidacy, see Katcher, *Earl Warren,* pp. 275–276. For Warren's response to Werdel's allegations, see ibid., p. 279.

68. James Welsh to Warren, "California Independent Delegation Committee [for Werdel]," March 4, 1952, Warren Papers, F3640: 17933, CSA.

69. Warren quoted in Katcher, *Earl Warren,* p. 279; and J.A. Smith to Warren, March 4, 1952, Warren Papers, F3640: 17933, CSA.

70. "Werdel Free GOP Delegation," Warren Papers, F3640: 17933; and Katcher, *Earl Warren,* p. 284.

71. "California Goldwater For President Committee" and "Goldwater California Advisory Committee" lists, Worth Brown Papers, CRA Collection, box 33, UCLASC; "Friends of Ronald Reagan," in Ronald Reagan, "On Becoming Governor" (UCBOH, 1979), p. 4a; and Carl Greenberg, "Ronald Reagan's 'Kitchen Cabinet,'" *Los Angeles Times WEST Magazine,* April 23, 1967, pp. 24–25.

72. *New York Times,* June 3, 1952, p. 19; and October 16, 1956, p. 1.

73. Declining to run for president himself, Smith instructed the party faithful to nominate MacArthur, which they did. Reminiscing in the mid-1960s, Tenney stated, "[t]o have been deemed worthy of such association [with MacArthur] was a tribute I would cherish all my life." The MacArthur–Tenney ticket, which MacArthur never even acknowledged, polled fewer than 1,800 votes. Tenney, *Jack B. Tenney: California Legislator,* (UCLAOH, 1969), p. 1830; and Glen Jeansonne, *Gerald L.K. Smith,* p. 162. In 1954, Tenney released the anti-Semitic tract *Zion's Trojan Horse: A Tenney Report on World Zionism.*

74. Quoted in R. Morris, *Richard Milhous Nixon,* p. 734. On the "great train robbery," see Morris, pp. 704–710.

75. Kathleen Hall Jamieson, *Packaging the Presidency,* pp. 56, 68; and "fund" quoted in Jamieson, p. 69.

76. R. Morris, *Richard Milhous Nixon,* pp. 837–838.

77. The appearance of inactivity did not necessarily reflect reality in Eisenhower's performance as president. See Fred Greenstein, *The Hidden-Hand Presidency.*

78. First quote in Stephen Ambrose, *Eisenhower: The Soldier,* p. 538; second in Ambrose, *Eisenhower: The President,* pp. 128–129; and G.E. White, *Earl Warren,* pp. 146–151. Ambrose stated that despite Eisenhower's "many difficulties with Warren over the next seven years, he remained convinced he had made the right choice." Ambrose, *Eisenhower: The President,* p. 129. After his presidency, however, Eisenhower, in an oft-cited response to a question about "mistakes" he had made as president, noted that two of those mistakes were now serving on the Supreme Court—Warren and fellow Eisenhower appointee, William Brennan.

79. Quoted in Stanley P. Isaacs, "Knight over California: Will He Succeed Himself?" *The Nation,* May 29, 1954, pp. 461, 464–465.

80. Knight address to the CIO–California Industrial Union, November 7, 1953, and C.J. Haggerty to Sirs and Brothers (endorsement of Knight), April 30, 1954, both in Whitaker and Baxter Papers, box 23, CSA. Also see Harry Finks, "California Labor and Goodwin Knight" (UCBOH, 1977–1979), pp. 5–11.

81. Press Release, "Free Enterprise: Being Part of an Address by Goodwin J. Knight," Knight for Governor Committee, (n.d), Whitaker and Baxter Papers, box 24, CSA.

82. Edmund Brown, Sr., "Years of Growth" (UCBOH, 1977–1981), p. 190. Melendy and Gilbert, *The Governors of California,* pp. 431–432.

83. "Democrats for Knight" campaign material, and "Knight Is Right for California" advertisement, both in Whitaker and Baxter Papers, box 23, CSA. Though Knight followed Warren's nonpartisan style, on the campaign trail he did not want to "make any bows" to Warren "nor ride along with his programs particularly." See Leone Baxter to Hicks Coney, April 23, 1954, ibid., box 24, CSA.

84. Melendy and Gilbert, *The Governors of California,* p. 432.

85. Quoted in Reinhard, *The Republican Right,* pp. 124–125; see also David Oshinsky, *A Conspiracy So Immense,* pp. 473–494.

86. "Remarks of the President," Denver, Colorado, September 10, 1955, and "The Eisenhower Conservative," in "Straight from the Shoulder," November 1955, both by the RNC, Thomas Carvey Papers, box 3, UCLASC.

87. John Judis, *William F. Buckley, Jr.,* pp. 128–133.

88. Quoted in Judis, *William F. Buckley, Jr.,* pp. 145–146. According to Judis, Buckley did not cast a vote for president in 1956, p. 146.

89. Reinhard, *The Republican Right,* pp. 131–133. Knight reportedly was interested in being Eisenhower's running mate in place of Nixon, but there is no indication that he actively pursued this position or participated in the effort to oust Nixon. See Thomas Caldecott, "Perspectives on the Republican Party and the Legislature" (UCBOH, 1979), pp. 17–18.

90. John R. Schmidhauser, "Eisenhower Republicans," *The Reporter,* September 20, 1956, p. 27.

91. See Larson, *A Republican Looks at His Party.*

Notes to Chapter 2

1. Quoted in "Republicans: The Look Backward," *Time,* April 22, 1957, p. 25.

2. For a description and analysis of the division between Republicans in 1958, see David Reinhard, *The Republican Right,* chapter 8.

3. Robert E. McDavid to Robert H. Finch, November, 18, 1958, Robert Fenton Craig Papers, box 14, UCLASC.

4. Knowland, like Nixon, had presidential ambitions. Knowland believed he would be in a better position to seek the presidency as governor (which may have been Knight's main reason for desiring to seek reelection as well). Nixon apparently supported Knowland's bid because he knew that the senator, even if elected, would make many Republican enemies in California in challenging Knight, thereby lessening the chances that Knowland could control the California delegation at the 1960 Republican Convention. Nixon also knew there was a distinct chance Knowland would lose, which would eliminate the latter's presidential challenge altogether. On the roles of Nixon and Palmer, see David Halberstam, *The Powers That Be,* pp. 263–265; Robert Gottlieb and Irene Wolt, *Thinking Big,* pp. 281–265; and Stephen Ambrose, *Nixon,* pp. 487–488. See also the *Wall Street Journal,* September 17, 1958, p. 12.

5. See Totton Anderson, "The 1958 California Election," *Western Political Quarterly* 12 (March 1959): 276–300; Royce Delmatier, et al., *The Rumble of California Politics,* 337–353; Gottlieb and Wolt, *Thinking Big,* pp. 281–285; Halberstam, *The Powers That Be,* 261–265; Gladwin Hill, *Dancing Bear,* chapters 11 and 12; Herbert L. Phillips, *Big Wayward Girl,* chapter 26.

6. See especially the following interviews: Earl Behrens, "Gubernatorial Campaigns and Party Issues" (UCBOH, 1977), pp. 16–19; Marjorie Benedict, "Developing a Place for Women in the Republican Party" (UCBOH, 1983), pp. 132–135; Richard Bergholz, "Reporting on California Government and Politics" (UCBOH, 1979), pp. 31–33; George Christopher, "Mayor of San Francisco and Republican Party Candidate" (UCBOH, 1977–78), pp. 46–49; Vernon Cristina, "A Northern

Californian Views Conservative Policies and Politics" (UCBOH, 1983), pp. 22–25; Lucile Hosmer, "A Conservative Republican in the Mainstream of Party Politics" (UCBOH, 1983); Emelyn Knowland Jewett, "My Father's Political Philosophy" (UCBOH, 1979), pp. 7–11; Estelle Knowland Johnson, "My Father as Senator" (UCBOH, 1979) pp. 5–13; Sydney Kossen, "Covering Goodwin Knight and the Legislature" (UCBOH, 1979), pp. 31–35; Paul Manolis, "A Friend and Aide Reminisces" (UCBOH, 1979), pp. 3–11; and Ed Mills interview, "The 'Kitchen Cabinet' " (CSUFOH, 1981), pp. 62–63, 67.

7. The author acknowledges that other studies have focused on different or broader concerns than this one. In regard to the 1958 California election, attention has centered on the "Big Switch" and the obvious split within the Republican Party and, to a lesser extent, on the right-to-work initiative as a divisive and losing issue. A selected list of works in this category are those by Delmatier, Hill, and Phillips (cited in note 5), as well as a study with a statistical emphasis by Michael Rogin and John Shover, *Political Change in California,* pp. 169–179. Works of note with a focus beyond California but cursorily recognizing the significance of the state's 1958 election include: Reinhard, *The Republican Right Since 1945,* pp. 142–143, 145, 147; Theodore H. White, *The Making of the President 1964,* pp. 116–117; and Garry Wills, *Reagan's America,* pp. 344–45. Oddly, John Kessel's *Goldwater Coalition* makes no mention of the 1958 race, an omission all the more curious given that Knowland chaired the Goldwater campaign in California.

8. Such attacks began in 1950 when Brown ran for attorney general. See, for example, "Memo—To All State & County Central Committee Members," from the Republican State Central Committee, September 11, 1950, Earl Warren Papers, F3640: 579–597, CSA.

9. William Knowland, "Labor Should Be Free in Our Republic," *The American Mercury,* March 1958, pp. 5–7.

10. Quoted in William Clark, "The Leader of the Beat Generation," *Frontier,* October 1958, p. 16.

11. *Wall Street Journal,* March 5, 1957, p. 12.

12. Eisenhower quoted in Stephen Ambrose, *Eisenhower: The President,* p. 118.

13. Eisenhower and Knowland quoted in the *New York Times,* August 26, 1958, p. 26.

14. For a discussion of the progressive gubernatorial style, see Jackson Putnam, "The Pattern of Modern California Politics," *Pacific Historical Review* 61 (1992): 23–52.

15. Mills interview, "The 'Kitchen Cabinet,' " p. 62. Richfield Oil and other California oil companies encouraged their employees to be active in the Knowland and right-to-work campaigns. See Robert Gaston, interview by Eric C. Larson (CSUFOH, 1974), p. 1; and Hosmer, "A Conservative Republican," p. 117.

16. *Los Angeles Times,* November 18, 1957, p. 2.

17. Robert Fenton Craig to Howard Ahmanson, August 30, 1957, Craig Papers, box 14, UCLASC.

18. Frances Larsen and Donald D. Doyle to Fellow Republicans, September 13, 1957, ibid.

19. As for Knowland's ambition, Vernon Cristina, a close associate of the senator and head of his campaign in Santa Clara County, stated that Knowland "was truly dedicated to the conservative cause . . . [but] was motivated by power. I think

that's all [he] ever really recognized and wanted." Cristina later became one of the elite members of Ronald Reagan's "Kitchen Cabinet." See Cristina, "A Northern Californian Views Conservative Policies," p. 24. The Los Angeles County Republican chairman Robert Finch, an Eisenhower moderate, stated that Knowland was "determined to come back and boost his presidential aspirations by running for governor and pushing 'Goodie' Knight out. . . ." Bitter over the senator's candidacy, Finch lamented that "when Knowland came charging in and introduced [the] right-to-work [issue] . . . it really hurt us with a lot of the new constituencies we were trying to develop in the party." Finch, "A View from the Lieutenant Governor's Office" (CSUFOH, 1981), pp. 8–9.

20. Brown quoted in the *Los Angeles Times,* October 4, 1957, p. 6; and November 6, 1957, p. B4.

21. Hill, *Dancing Bear,* p. 146. Richard Nixon, in his unsuccessful run for governor in 1962, appears to have suffered from this same "myopia," though not to the extent of Knowland.

22. Edmund G. Brown, Sr., "Years of Growth" (UCBOH, 1977–81), p. 233; and Anderson, "The 1958 California Election," pp. 289–291.

23. John A. McCone to Craig, April 24, 1958, Craig Papers, box 15, UCLASC. San Francisco, in stark contrast to Los Angeles, had been a strong union city since the early 1900s. The most comprehensive examination of the rise of labor unions in San Francisco is Michael Kazin's *Barons of Labor.* See also Carey McWilliams, *California: The Great Exception,* chapter 8. On the labor movement in Los Angeles, see Grace Heilman Stimson, *The Rise of the Labor Movement in Los Angeles.*

24. Raymond Moley, "The Choice in California," *Newsweek,* April 14, 1958, p. 124. Moley's article criticizing northern California businessmen was enclosed with the fundraising letter circulated by campaign chairman McCone (cited in note 23).

25. Anderson, "The 1958 Election in California," p. 285.

26. *Los Angeles Times,* June 5, 1958, p. B4.

27. Ibid., September 18, 1957, p. B4 and October 29, 1958, p. 1. See also Gottleib and Wolt, *Thinking Big,* pp. 282–283.

28. This observation applies to campaign coverage from August 29, 1958, when Knowland officially launched his general election campaign, to the election on November 4. The *Los Angeles Times* was fairer to Brown in both the amount and tone of its news coverage.

29. Quoted in the Santa Ana *Register,* October 26, 1958, p. A7.

30. Quoted in ibid., October 18, 1958, p. A10.

31. For a brief yet eloquent and cogent interpretation (via Henry Adams) of the Founders' intent regarding the control of capitalism, see John Diggins, *The Lost Soul of American Politics: Virtue, Self-Interest,* pp. 265–267.

32. *Los Angeles Times,* September 25, 1958, p. 23. Fred Dutton, one of Brown's chief aides, recalled that while the UAW was "very active . . . , [w]e were trying to establish that we were not a patsy to the union bosses. . . ." Brown, therefore, "publicly chided [Reuther] on something," though Dutton did not remember the particular issue. Frederick G. Dutton, "Democratic Campaigns and Controversies" (UCBOH, 1977–78), p. 125.

33. Goldwater quoted in Jean Gould and Lorena Hickok, *Walter Reuther,* p. 321. For details of the Senate investigation, see ibid., pp. 319–324.

34. Ads referring to the "New Slavery" (in which the last quote in the paragraph

appeared) and asking "What Is Reuther Up To?" ran in the Pacific Coast Edition of the *Wall Street Journal,* the *Los Angeles Times,* and the Santa Ana *Register.* The ad campaigns for and against Proposition 18 were conducted separately from those for the candidates. This fact notwithstanding, Knowland and the right-to-work initiative were electoral Siamese twins.

35. "Who's Really Behind Prop. 18?" (ad), *Los Angeles Times,* October 24, 1958, p. A13.

36. Roger Kent to John F. Kennedy, May 15, 1958, Pat Brown Papers, Box 45, UCBBL; and Kennedy to Thomas B. Carvey, August 30, 1958, Thomas Carvey Papers, Box 7, UCLASC.

37. Moley quoted in the *San Diego Union,* October 2, 1958, p. a4.

38. Taft received 40 percent of the labor vote in 1950, while Knowland got only 15 percent in 1958. For a narrative of Taft's campaign and an assessment of the reasons for his victory, see James T. Patterson, *Mr. Republican,* pp. 456–473.

39. John J. Synon, "Knowland at the Crossroads," *Human Events,* June 16, 1958, p. 1 (article section).

40. Eisenhower quoted in the *New York Times,* October 21, 1958, p. 24.

41. The full text of Eisenhower's speech can be found in the *New York Times,* October 21, 1958, p. 24.

42. Ibid., October 22, 1958, p. 1.

43. Alcorn quoted in the *Los Angeles Times,* September 24, 1958, p. 16; and Mitchell in the *Los Angeles Times,* October 27, 1958, p. 18.

44. Anderson, "The 1958 California Election," pp. 289–290.

45. Knight quoted in William J. Keller, "What Governor Knight Thinks of His Party," *Frontier,* September 1958, pp. 5, 12.

46. Along with General Electric, Lockheed and Boeing contributed funds to the right-to-work campaign. Other large contributors among California-based companies included the *Los Angeles Times,* the Southern California Edison Company, and the Merchants and Manufacturers Association of Los Angeles. Anderson, "The 1958 California Election," p. 291.

47. *New York Times,* September 21, 1958, p. 52.

48. Cordiner quoted in the Santa Ana *Register,* October 19, 1958, p. A2.

49. Reagan gubernatorial campaign literature, CRA Collection, box 2, UCLASC.

50. Bill Boyarsky, *The Rise of Ronald Reagan,* p. 100.

51. For an incisive analysis of The Speech, see Wills, *Reagan's America,* pp. 332–343. See also Mary Stuckey, *Getting into the Game.* As for Reagan's speeches themselves, see "Encroaching Control: Keep Government Poor and Remain Free," *Vital Speeches of the Day,* September 1, 1961, pp. 677–681; "A Time for Choosing," *Human Events,* November 28, 1964, pp. 1–3; "A Moment of Truth: Our Rendezvous with Destiny," *Vital Speeches of the Day,* September 1, 1965, pp. 681–686.

52. Santa Ana *Register,* September 12, 1966, p. A3.

53. See Mills and Holmes Tuttle interviews, "The 'Kitchen Cabinet,' " pp. 62–63, 123. Echoing Mills, James Halley, a conservative member of the Republican State Central Committee member in the mid-1960s, stated that the early Goldwater men and women got their start in the Knowland campaign. Halley's statement is cited by Malca Chall (interviewer) in Hosmer, "A Conservative Republican," p.

119. Virtually everyone from Knowland's northern California staff from the 1958 campaign enlisted in the Goldwater crusade. See Hosmer interview, p. 120.

54. Santa Ana *Register,* October 27, 1958, p. 7.

55. Christopher, "Mayor of San Francisco," p. 47. Reagan quoted in the Santa Ana *Register,* September 13, 1966, p. 11.

56. Charles Beaman and Michael Jones, "Turmoil and Change" (CSUFOH, 1980), pp. 24–25. In this compilation of interviews, see also Don Smith, "A Journalistic Assessment" (CSUFOH, 1980), pp. 90–91.

57. Circulation of these pamphlets exceeded 20,000 by the early 1960s. Walter Knott, "The Enterprises of Walter Knott" (UCLAOH, 1965) pp. 112–113.

58. Hosmer, "A Conservative Republican," pp. 117–120. Benedict, "Developing a Place for Women," pp. 132–135. Despite their opposition to the right-to-work platform, the women in the Federation's northern division (CFRWND) were committed in principle to conservative Republicanism. See CFRWND, "The Principles of Americanism," William Knowland Papers, box 109, UCBBL. On the importance of the Women's Federation in Republican campaigns in California, see also Weinberger, "The California Assembly," pp. 47–48.

59. Kamp pamphlet cited in the *New York Times,* September 14, 1958, p. 1. For more on the smear campaigns that both Republicans and Democrats engaged in, see Anderson, "The 1958 California Election," pp. 292–298.

60. Helen and William Knowland quoted in the *San Francisco Chronicle,* October 24, 1958, p. 1.

61. Santa Ana *Register,* October 15, 1958, p. A3.

62. Craig Papers, box 15, UCLASC. Distributed by the "Republican Association of California," this campaign piece originally appeared in the conservative periodical *Human Events,* September 29, 1958. While mainly concerned with Reuther, Helen Knowland also expressed a fear of the Teamsters' leader Jimmy Hoffa, who wanted "to get control of the lifeline [transportation] of our economic structure . . . and any means goes!"

63. *San Francisco Chronicle,* November 7, 1958, p. 30.

64. William F. Buckley Jr., "The Tranquil World of Dwight D. Eisenhower," *National Review,* January 18, 1958, p. 58.

65. *Phoenix Gazette,* October 17, 1958, p. 1.

66. William Buchanan and Eugene C. Lee, "The 1960 Election in California," *Western Political Quarterly* 14 (March 1961): 316. Howard Jarvis, head of the California Republican Assembly in Los Angeles County in 1959 and 1960, recalled that shortly after Goldwater's reelection he had made arrangements to bring the senator to Los Angeles to speak at a fundraiser. He was forced to cancel this arrangement, however, when party moderates, led by Robert Finch, pressured him to do so. Jarvis believed that the conservative movement grew out of the divisiveness of the election of 1958. Howard Jarvis, interview by Eric C. Larson (CSUFOH, 1974), pp. 27–28. Gaylord Parkinson, the influential head of the Republican State Central Committee from 1962 through 1966, concurred with Jarvis's assessment. Parkinson contended that while the movement saw its "first fruition" with Goldwater's victory in the 1964 primary, "it was a conservative movement long before that. . . ." Parkinson, "California Republican Party Official" (UCBBL, 1978), p. 12.

67. Robert Welch, *The Blue Book,* p. 96.

68. Arnold Forster and Benjamin Epstein, *Danger on the Right,* p. 51.

69. "The Committee for Home Protection" literature, Knowland Papers, box 158, UCBBL; Joseph B. Robison, "Ghettos, Property Rights and Myths," *Frontier,* June 1964, p. 6; and the *New York Times,* May 10, 1964, p. 59.

70. Barry Goldwater, *The Conscience of a Conservative* (New York: McFadden edition, August 1964), p. 1; the "freedom" quote, essentially the book's thesis, is printed in bold letters on the back cover.

71. Stuckey, *Getting into the Game,* p. 11.

Notes to Chapter 3

1. For a good overview of Orange County politics and Republican trends, see "A Century of Politics in Orange County," *Los Angeles Times,* March 21, 1976, Special Section, Orange County Edition. On the transformation of Orange County from rural to urban, see Rob Kling, Spencer Olin Jr., and Mark Poster, eds., *Postsuburban California.* See also Pamela Hallan-Gibson, *The Golden Promise.* Of related interest, and more germane to this study, are Duff Griffith, "Before the Deluge: An Oral History"; Lisa McGirr, "Suburban Warriors: The Grass-Roots Conservative Movement in the 1960s" (Ph.D. diss., Columbia University, 1995); Denise Spooner, "The Political Consequences of Experiences of Community: Iowa Immigrants and Republican Conservatism in Southern California, 1946–1964" (Ph.D. diss., University of Pennsylvania, 1992); and Kevin Phillips, *The Emerging Republican Majority,* pp. 435–452.

2. Kling, Olin, and Poster, "The Emergence of Postsuburbia: An Introduction," *Postsuburban California,* pp. 1–2.

3. Sheldon Zalaznick, "The Double Life of Orange County," *Fortune,* October 1968, p. 184.

4. Pereira quoted in ibid., p. 186; Knott in "California: A Little Piece of America," *Newsweek,* November 14, 1966, p. 33. On the importance of property in southern California in general, see James Q. Wilson, "A Guide to Reagan Country: The Political Culture of Southern California," *Commentary,* May 1967, pp. 37–45.

5. For a good overview of the sanctity of property among suburbanites, see Kenneth Jackson, *The Crabgrass Frontier.*

6. Quoted in "Raymond Cyrus Hoiles," a brief biography and summary of his political and social philosophy on the occasion of Hoiles's seventy-fifth birthday, by Bob Segal Sr., Santa Ana *Register,* Special Insert, November 24, 1953, p. 9.

7. This observation stems from the author's perusal of editorials by Hoiles from 1958 through 1966. One might assume that among the "masters" Hoiles referred to were classical liberals such as Adam Smith, John Stuart Mill, or David Ricardo, but their names were never encountered. There were, however, frequent invocations of the Founding Fathers, as well as recurrent biblical references.

8. Albert Nock, *Our Enemy, the State.* On Nock's influence on modern conservatism, see George Nash, *The Conservative Intellectual Movement,* pp. 14–18; and John Judis, *William F. Buckley, Jr.,* pp. 44–46.

9. Segal, "Raymond Cyrus Hoiles," p. 15.

10. Quoted in Curt Gentry, *The Last Days,* 231.

11. Ibid.

12. Griffith, "Before the Deluge," p. 32.

13. Zalaznick, "The Double Life of Orange County," pp. 185–186.

14. Ibid., p. 141.

15. Patt Morrison, "L.A. vs. O.C.," *Los Angeles Times Magazine,* June 17, 1990, p. 13; and Mike Davis, *City of Quartz,* pp. 161–164.

16. Howard Seelye and Don Smith, "Arch-Conservatives and a 'Kooky' Image" (in "A Century of Politics in Orange County"), *Los Angeles Times,* March 21, 1976, p. 9. Though Knott was a great fundraiser, he personally did not contribute substantial amounts of money to political campaigns. On Knott's contributions, see Griffith, "Before the Deluge," interview with Randall Smith (aide to John Schmitz), p. 19.

17. *Los Angeles Times,* February 22, 1970, p. 7C; and Knott, "The Enterprises of Walter Knott" (UCLAOH, 1965), p. ii.

18. Knott had used the Freedom Center's expenses for employee education programs as a tax deduction until 1962, when the Internal Revenue Service deemed the deductions illegal and required him to pay over $60,000 in back taxes. He avoided future tax problems by donating the Center to the nonprofit ultraconservative Americanism Educational League, thus making his contributions to the center legally deductible. Gentry, *The Last Days,* p. 230. Knott was on the board of trustees of the League, along with his chief aide, Dr. William E. Fort Jr., who made movies and recordings on Americanism, many of which featured Knott and his homespun patriotic aphorisms. Other prominent trustees included Nixon challenger Joe Shell and Loyd Wright, a prominent Los Angeles attorney. "Americanism Educational League Board of Trustees" (1965), Knox Mellon Collection (John Birch Society materials), box 33, UCLASC. The replica of Independence Hall opened on July 4, 1966. The Hall was heralded as a "must see" experience in the *CRA Newsletter,* August 1966, p. 6, CRA Collection, box 2, UCLASC. Thus replication became reification in a patriotic shrine far removed from the original, but seemingly no less inspiring.

19. Quoted in the *Los Angeles Times,* February 22, 1970, p. 7C.

20. Ibid., p. 6C; and Dennis Carpenter, interview by author, tape recording, Sacramento, CA, October 16, 1997.

21. The Knott biography is cited in Gentry, *The Last Days,* p. 228. A not-so-flattering portrayal of Knott appeared in 1961 as the character of Walter Tighe in Harold Bienvenu's satirical novel, *The Patriot.* Depicted as a cretinous "dupe" for the John Birch Society, Tighe was also the grandfather of a lesbian with the name of Knott's wife. When friends urged Knott to sue for libel or seek to keep the book out of circulation, Knott declined. He stated that Bienvenu, an education professor at California State College, Los Angeles, "just doesn't understand this country's heritage. . . . He just doesn't know enough to realize he doesn't know everything." Quoted in the *Los Angeles Times,* February 22, 1970, p. 6C.

22. Knott, "The Enterprises of Walter Knott," pp. 120–122.

23. JBS founder Robert Welch led the attacks on Eisenhower in his sensational manuscript, titled *The Politician,* in which he declared that the president and his brother Milton were "conscious" communist agents. This indictment of the Eisenhowers was in Welch's original manuscript but was toned down when the book was published in 1963. Nixon is not linked to communist activities like Eisenhower, but, according to Welch, he was a back-stabber sorely lacking in dedication to the conservative cause and was not "committed to anything other than the career of Richard Nixon." Welch, *The Blue Book,* pp. 110–113.

24. *Los Angeles Times,* February 22, 1970, p. 7C.

25. Apparently believing they could hurt Reagan by closely linking him to Knott, some Democrats asserted in 1966 that Knott was chairman of Reagan's Southern California Finance Committee when in fact Cy Rubel, the former president of Union Oil, held that position. Knott, while admitting strong support for Reagan, adamantly denied that he was even the chairman in Orange County; but as one of the initial "Friends of Ronald Reagan," he was a principal fundraiser. On Knott's statement, see the Santa Ana *Register,* September 12, 1966, p. A3. For a list of the members of Reagan's Southern California Finance Committee, see Ronald Reagan, "On Becoming Governor" (UCBOH, 1979), p. 4A.

26. The amendment was first introduced in 1952. See Arnold Forster and Benjamin Epstein, *Danger on the Right,* pp. 164–171.

27. Quoted in "California: A Little Piece of America," p. 37.

28. Quoted in Seelye and Smith, "Arch-Conservatives and 'Kooky' Image," p. 12R.

29. Ibid.

30. McGirr, "Suburban Warriors," p. 122.

31. Quoted in Charles Beaman and Michael Jones, "Turmoil and Change," interview with Gordon X. Richmond, p. 18.

32. Howard Seelye and Don Smith, "Triumvirate Taught Lesson in Teamwork," *Los Angeles Times,* March 21, 1976, p. 5R. Only one legislative proposal that they introduced failed to pass in the legislature. Charles Beaman and Michael Jones, "Turmoil and Change," p. 17.

33. Beaman and Jones, "Turmoil and Change," interview with Bruce Sumner, pp. 51–52.

34. Seelye and Smith, "Arch-Conservatives and 'Kooky' Image," p. 5R.

35. Beaman and Jones, "Turmoil and Change," Sumner interview, pp. 77–78; and Carpenter, author's interview.

36. Beaman and Jones, "Turmoil and Change," Sumner interview, pp. 75–78. Other factors that contributed to Sumner's loss included the lack of media coverage of the race, which allowed the Goldwater volunteers to have a greater impact. In addition, moderate and liberal votes were split between several candidates, while Schmitz garnered the conservative votes. Beaman and Jones, "Turmoil and Change," p. 19. (Appendix D provides a detailed analysis of this campaign.) A good case can be made for Schmitz being pulled along by Goldwater's coattails and the fervent support for Proposition 14. Goldwater crushed Rockefeller in Orange County by a two-to-one margin, while Proposition 14 passed in the general election with 78 percent of the vote—14 percentage points greater than the statewide vote.

37. Quoted in the *Los Angeles Times,* November 5, 1964, p. 10.

38. While JBS chapters maintained a high profile in southern California, the society never disclosed a full list of members from the region or complete details of all its activities. In a certain sense, therefore, the JBS did take on an air of secrecy, despite the organization's anxious admonitions about the clandestine nature of its conspiratorial foes. The best overview of the Society is in Seymour Lipset and Earl Raab, *The Politics of Unreason,* chapter 7. On the JBS in California, see Barbara Stone, "The John Birch Society of California" (Ph.D. diss., University of Southern California, 1968).

39. Seymour Lipset and Earl Raab, *The Politics of Unreason,* p. 305. On views

of the JBS in California, see Lipset, "Three Decades of the Radical Right," in Daniel Bell, ed., *The Radical Right.*

40. California Senate, *The Twelfth Report of the Senate Factfinding Committee on Un-American Activities,* 1963, pp. 58–62. For a detailed analysis of this investigation, see Robert L. Pritchard, "California Un-American Activities Investigations: Subversion on the Right," *California History* 69 (December 1970): 309–327; on the career of California's Un-American Activities Committee, see M.J. Heale, "Red Scare Politics: California's Campaign Against Un-American Activities, 1940–1970," *Journal of American Studies* 20 (Summer 1986): 5–32.

41. *Pasadena Star-News,* June 17, 1963, p. 12; *Los Angeles Herald-Examiner,* June 17, 1963, p. 17; and letter to "Rolling Hills Neighbor from Murray C. Beebe, Jr.," March 21, 1961, Thomas Carvey Papers, box 3, UCLASC. The *Los Angeles Times* series referred to by Beebe began on March 5, 1961. See Robert Gottlieb and Irene Wolt, *Thinking Big,* pp. 335–339.

42. Stone, "The John Birch Society of California," p. 25; Hallan-Gibson, *The Golden Promise,* p. 244.

43. Quoted in Seelye and Smith, "Arch-Conservatives and a 'Kooky' Image," p. 9R; and Carpenter, author's interview.

44. Quoted in "Cuba Under the Lens: No Missiles But . . . ," *Newsweek,* February 18, 1963, p. 20. Goldwater recalled being very concerned about what the missile crisis might have revealed about America's willingness to use nuclear weapons: "If it came to a question of national survival, would we have the will to use them?" In addition, "my interest in world politics was [now] increasing." Goldwater, *With No Apologies,* p. 149. In addition, books such as *Strike in the West: The Complete Story of the Cuban Missile Crisis,* by conservatives James Daniel and John Hubbell, asserted that not all the missiles were removed by the Soviets (see the above-mentioned *Newsweek* article on this as well), and accused the Kennedy administration of deceiving the public, a charge repeated by hard-line conservative periodicals such as the *National Review* (e.g., June 4, 1963, pp. 438–439.)

45. Goldwater, *Why Not Victory?* p. 19. The book expanded on the argument Goldwater made about the "Soviet Menace" in his earlier bestseller, *The Conscience of a Conservative.* Goldwater contended that to "contain" communism was not enough, that the United States had to employ a strategy to "win" the Cold War, or many Americans freedoms would perish in accommodating the Soviets, *Why Not Victory?* pp. 19–21.

46. Goldwater, *The Conscience of a Conservative,* pp. 89, 108.

47. Welch, *The Blue Book,* p. 109.

48. Ibid., pp. 33–34, 44. Welch stated that presidents Woodrow Wilson and Franklin Roosevelt were the main culprits in America's decline, because during the two world wars they had put the country "in the same bed" with Europe, which "was already yielding to the collectivist cancer," p. 44.

49. Quoted in the *Los Angeles Times,* November 5, 1964, p. 10.

50. For Hofstadter's comments on Welch in this regard, see *The Paranoid Style,* pp. 27–30, 37.

51. Griffith, "Before the Deluge," interview with John Schmitz, pp. 11–12.

52. Quoted in the *Los Angeles Times,* November 5, 1964, p. 10. On the JBS and other right-wing attacks on the CFR, see Robert Schulzinger, *The Wise Men of Foreign Relations,* pp. 243–254.

53. Griffith, "Before the Deluge," interview with James Toft, pp. 2–4.

54. In support of this assertion, Toft cited two works published in 1970: Gary Allen's *None Dare Call It Conspiracy* (Rossmoor, CA: Concord, 1970); and W. Cleon Skouson's *The Naked Capitalist* (Salt Lake City: *The Reviewer*, 1970). Griffith, "Before the Deluge," Toft interview, pp. 13–14. Expounding on the rationale for the money interest–communist connection, Allen, an editor of the JBS publication *American Opinion*, declared that "the super-capitalists became super-socialists, realizing that only a World government under their control can give them the power necessary to achieve their goal. . . . The financiers and cartelists do not expect to be injured by the socialists so long as they can manipulate them, using them for their own purposes." "The C.F.R. Conspiracy to Rule the World," *American Opinion*, April 1969, p. 56.

55. Griffith, "Before the Deluge," Toft interview, pp. 4, 14–15, 20. McCarthy quoted in Hofstadter, *The Paranoid Style*, p. 7.

56. *San Francisco Chronicle*, October, 28, 1966, p. 10.

57. Founding the evangelical Crusade in 1953, Schwarz moved the organization from Iowa to southern California in 1956. Having "conscientiously studied communism as a pathologist studies disease," Schwarz left the more outlandish diatribes to the JBS by the early 1960s. He continued to warn, however, that the communists were seeking to "demoralize" the United States and test the "American moral fiber," as they had during the Cuban missile crisis. "They are confident," he declared, "that one of these future tests will reveal an inadequate will." *Christian Anti-Communism Crusade Newsletter*, March 1964, pp. 4, 7. Knox Mellon Collection, box 17, UCLASC. Less controversial than the JBS, Schwarz's Crusade proved quite popular with right-wing Hollywood celebrities and other prominent individuals, as well as with certain well-known companies. (For example, Richfield Oil sponsored the Crusade's TV shows.) The best description of the Crusade is in Forster and Epstein, *Danger on the Right*, chapter 3.

58. Griffith, "Before the Deluge," interview with Sam Campbell, pp. 3–4; interview with Marvin Olsen, p. 14; and Carpenter, author's interview.

59. Griffith, "Before the Deluge," interview with Claude Bunzel, p. 13; and Knott quoted in the *Los Angeles Times*, February 22, 1970, p. 1C.

60. Quoted in the *Los Angeles Times*, p. 6C.

61. The text of Kuchel's speech is in the *Congressional Quarterly* 21 (May 10, 1963): 717–721. Kuchel's quotes are from pp. 717 and 721. The quotes from Utt and Rousselot are from pp. 721 and 715, respectively. A somewhat shorter version of Kuchel's speech appeared in article form in " 'A PLOT!! To OVERTHROW America!!!' " *New York Times Magazine*, July 21, 1963, pp. 6+.

62. Hofstadter, *The Paranoid Style*, pp. 6–67.

63. Ibid., p. 106; and Kazin, "The Grass-Roots Right: New Histories of U.S. Conservatism in the Twentieth Century," *American Historical Review* 97 (February 1992): 137.

64. For a broader look at Hofstadter's interpretation of populism, see his groundbreaking 1955 book *The Age of Reform: From Bryan to FDR*, chapters 1 and 2.

65. Published shortly after *The Paranoid Style*, Bailyn's book posited that after 1763, many American colonists became convinced that in both England and America agents were conspiring against liberty, "and it was this above all else that in the end propelled them into Revolution." Bernard Bailyn, *The Ideological Origins of*

the American Revolution, p. 95. On the "paranoid" aspects of these fears, see, for example, Lance Banning, "Republican Ideology and the Triumph of the Constitution, 1789–1793," *William and Mary Quarterly* 31 (April 1974): 167–188; and James Hutson, "The American Revolution: The Triumph of a Delusion?" in Erich Angermann et al., eds., *New Wine in Old Skins*, pp. 179–194.

66. Gordon Wood, "Conspiracy and the Paranoid Style: Causality and Deceit in the Eighteenth Century," *William and Mary Quarterly* 39 (July 1982): 403–405.

67. Ibid., p. 441. Even Hofstadter stopped short of Wood's assessment of the paranoid style in contemporary (and other) times as providing evidence of "psychological disturbance." "It is the use of paranoid modes of expression," Hofstadter remarked, "by more or less normal people that makes the phenomenon significant." *The Paranoid Style*, p. 4.

68. See *The Gallup Poll: Public Opinion 1935–1971*, vol. 2, pp. 1199, 1201.

69. Eric Goldman, *The Crucial Decade*, p. 122. On the "Great Conspiracy" see chapter 7. Also see, David Oshinsky, *A Conspiracy So Immense*, chapter 6.

70. In a 1990 study that incorporated a view of Cold War anticommunism as largely rational, historian M.J. Heale stated: "Hardheaded calculations and coherent ideological perspectives were closer to the heart of red scare politics than was mindless hysteria." *American Anticommunism*, p. xiv. As for the tendency of historians to emphasize the "hysterical" aspects of American anticommunism, John Gaddis has noted in a reassessment of Cold War fears that "because some charges of Soviet espionage were exaggerated, [historians] assumed all too easily that all of them had been, that the spies were simply figments of right-wing imaginations." Similar to Wood, at least in the following regard, Gaddis attributed this propensity to the "lingering effects of McCarthyism. . . ." "The Tragedy of Cold War History," *Diplomatic History* 17 (Winter 1993): 8.

71. Stephen Whitfield, *The Culture of the Cold War*, p. 4.

72. Allen J. Matusow, *The Unraveling of America*, p. 377. The American right viewed détente as an accommodation to the communists, which would facilitate the spread of Marxism through covert means.

73. Hofstadter, *The Paranoid Style*, p. 3.

74. Reagan, "Encroaching Control: Keep Government Poor and Remain Free," *Vital Speeches of the Day*, September 1, 1961, p. 679.

75. A good description of some of the more outlandish activities and beliefs of individuals and organizations on the extreme right in southern California in the 1960s is in Gentry, *The Last Days*, pp. 223–233.

Notes to Chapter 4

1. Richard Nixon, *RN: The Memoirs of Richard Nixon*, vol. 1, p. 295.

2. In early 1962, 40 percent of Californians believed that Nixon would use the governorship as a stepping stone to the 1964 Republican presidential nomination. Poll cited in Totton Anderson and Eugene Lee, "The 1962 Election in California," *Western Political Quarterly* 16 (June 1963): 399. Other polls indicated even higher percentages of voters who believed Nixon would run in 1964. Nixon, *RN*, p. 300. The best accounts of Nixon's run for governor are Anderson and Lee, "The 1962 Election in California," pp. 396–420; Stephen Ambrose, *Nixon*, vol. 1, pp. 642–674; and Herbert Parmet, *Richard Nixon and His America*, pp. 411–

436. Other good but less detailed accounts are in Fawn Brodie, *Richard Nixon,* pp. 450–463; Gladwin Hill, *Dancing Bear,* pp. 172–178; Herbert G. Klein, *Making It Perfectly Clear,* pp. 54–64; Herbert Phillips, *Big Wayward Girl,* pp. 203–213; and Jules Witcover, *The Resurrection of Richard Nixon,* pp. 26–32.

3. Quoted in Robert Gottlieb and Irene Wolt, *Thinking Big,* p. 278.

4. The California Poll surveys on Nixon's popularity are cited in William Buchanan and Eugene Lee, "The 1960 Election in California," *Western Political Quarterly* 14 (March 1961): 315. As the authors stated, it "appear[ed] that Nixon could maintain popular support only so long as he could display his image in some spectacular manner," as in his famous "Kitchen Debate" with Nikita Khrushchev. Kennedy's popularity proved steadier, pp. 314–15.

5. Loyd Wright to Patrick J. Hillings, April 13, 1960, Nixon Pre-Presidential Papers (hereafter referred to as RNPP Papers), box 834, National Archives and Records Administration, Pacific Southwest Region, Laguna Niguel, California.

6. Robert Welch, *The Blue Book,* p. 113; Goldwater quoted in the *New York Times,* July 28, 1960, p. 23.

7. Buchanan and Lee, "The 1960 Election in California," p. 310.

8. Brown had ordered a sixty-day stay of execution for Chessman. The governor had hoped to persuade the legislature to abolish the death penalty, but grossly miscalculated. Public outrage over Brown's actions caused his political stock to tumble for a time, but the issue was largely behind him by 1962. The matter appears to have hurt him more in 1966 in his race against Reagan. See Earl Behrens, "The Squire of San Francisco Political Reporters" (UCBOH, 1977), p. 20.

9. Buchanan and Lee, "The 1960 Election in California," pp. 312–317.

10. Caspar Weinberger, "The California Assembly, Republican State Central Committee, and Elections" (UCBOH, 1978–1979), p. 65. Though Nixon claimed to have little desire to run for governor, Weinberger stated, "I found out later that anybody who advised him *not* to run he barely spoke to again" p. 65.

11. William Steif, "Nixon's Uphill Campaign: The Republicans Are His First Problem," *The New Republic,* February 26, 1962, p. 18.

12. Shortly after Nixon's return from Washington he told Shell that he had no intention of running for governor. Barbara Stone (Shell's daughter), interview by author, tape recording, Whittier, CA, August 3, 1992.

13. Shell campaign literature, RNPP Papers, box 640.

14. Stone, author's interview.

15. Quoted in the *Los Angeles Examiner,* November 12, 1961, p. B1.

16. Reinforcing the "stepping stone" notion was the release of Nixon's *Six Crises* in March 1962. Focusing on national and international issues, the book strengthened Nixon's image as a national figure, but also exhibited his distance from California politics. Furthermore, as aide Robert Finch recalled, as the titular head of his party, Nixon "could remain mute on national issues, and look silly, or he could speak out. It was a very sticky wicket." Quoted in Witcover, *The Resurrection of Richard Nixon,* p. 30.

17. Quoted in the Santa Ana *Register,* May 30, 1962, p. A5.

18. Vernon Cristina, "A Northern Californian Views Republican Politics" (UCBOH, 1983), p. 7. CYR member quoted in Eric Larson, "The Issue of Birchism in the 1962 Gubernatorial Primary" (Master's thesis, California State University, Fullerton, 1975), p. 165.

19. Shell campaign literature, RNPP Papers, box 640.

20. Hill, *Dancing Bear*, p. 174.

21. *Los Angeles Examiner,* February 12, 1962, p. B1.

22. "Public Opinion Survey for Joe Shell," conducted by the John B. Knight Co., April 1962, pp. vi–vii, courtesy of Barbara Stone. A February 1962 California Poll indicated that a candidate accepting support from the JBS would lose seven times as many votes as he would gain. Cited in Anderson and Lee, "The 1962 Election in California," p. 401.

23. Nixon, *RN*, p. 298.

24. Nixon quoted in the *Los Angeles Times,* March 4, 1962, p. 1; and Nixon, *RN,* p. 298.

25. Quoted in the *Los Angeles Times,* March 5, 1962, p. 11.

26. Nixon, *RN,* 298.

27. All quotes and comments from the *Los Angeles Times,* March 3, 1962, pp. 1, 10.

28. Ambrose, *Nixon,* p. 658.

29. Eric Larson, "The Issue of Birchism," pp. 190, 202.

30. Quoted in the *Los Angeles Times,* March 4, 1962, pp. 1, 13.

31. Wright campaign literature, RNPP Papers, box 834. Murray Chotiner served as Wright's campaign manager.

32. First quote is in the *Los Angeles Times,* March 7, 1962, p. 3; second quote is in Jarvis campaign literature, RNPP Papers, box 380.

33. Quoted in the *Los Angeles Times,* March 5, 1962, p. 1.

34. Nixon's wealthier backers included Californians Jack Drown, a lawyer and longtime acquaintance; Justin Dart, owner of the Rexall Drugstore chain; Los Angles tire and rubber manufacturer Leonard Firestone; and Nixon's wealthy friend from Florida, Bebe Rebozo; Ambrose, *Nixon,* pp. 656–657. Later Reagan "Kitchen Cabinet" members and campaign financiers Henry Salvatori and Holmes Tuttle were behind Shell initially but came to back Nixon due to the latter's perceived electability. It is unclear whether they were substantial contributors to Nixon's campaign. Cy Rubel stayed with Shell through the primary, serving as finance chairman of his campaign. See Salvatori and Tuttle interviews, "The 'Kitchen Cabinet' " (CSUFOH, 1981) pp. 9, 116–117.

35. William L. Roper, "Nixon May Be the Man," *Frontier,* March 1961, p. 9; and Stone, author's interview. On Rubel's involvement with Shell, see Salvatori and Tuttle interviews, "The 'Kitchen Cabinet,' " p. 117; on Russell see Rus Walton, "Turning Political Ideas into Government Programs" (UCBOH, 1983), p. 11.

36. Shell campaign literature, RNPP Papers, box 640.

37. *Los Angeles Times,* March 7, 1962, p. 3. The early financial support for the right-wing infiltration into the CYR and other GOP volunteer organizations, which began in earnest in 1960, came mainly from Joseph Crail, president of the Coast Federal Savings Bank in Los Angeles. Crail also actively backed Fred Schwarz's anticommunist crusade and similar operations. See Larson, "The Issue of Birchism," pp. 66–70.

38. Santa Ana *Register,* May 27, 1962, p. B20.

39. Jarvis quoted in Ambrose, *Nixon,* p. 656; and Wright in the *Los Angeles Times,* March 3, 1962, p. 3.

40. Ambrose, *Nixon,* p. 657.

41. Quoted in the *San Diego Union,* May 24, 1962, p. A4.

42. Santa Ana *Register,* May 17, 1962, p. A6; and William Bagley, "Some Complexities of Social Progress and Fiscal Reform" (UCBOH, 1981), p. 4.

43. Quoted in the Santa Ana *Register,* May 2, 1962, p. C14.

44. Nixon to Worth Brown, March 8, 1962, Worth Brown Papers, CRA Collection, box 32, UCLASC.

45. Quoted in the *Los Angeles Times,* March 3, 1962, p. 2.

46. *San Diego Union,* May 20, 1962, p. C6.

47. *Los Angeles Examiner,* November 12, 1961, p. B1.

48. Santa Ana *Register,* June 6, 1962, p. A16.

49. Shell declined to be interviewed by the author; this information is from Stone, author's interview. Though there was apparently no evidence to corroborate Shell's suspicion, Ms. Stone did state that Nixon's longtime associate and aide, Herb Klein, told her father years later that Shell was on President Nixon's "enemies list."

50. Quoted in the *New York Times,* June 20, 1962, p. 59. Charles Jones had sought Shell's assurance on April 8, well before the primary election, that he would support Nixon if the latter proved victorious, but apparently to no avail. Also see Salvatori interview, "The 'Kitchen Cabinet,' " p. 9.

51. Brown "Special Campaign Bulletin" (no date), Thomas Carvey Papers, box 9, UCLASC. The CDC was founded in 1953 in a belated response by state Democrats to the CRA.

52. Nixon and Burns quoted in the *Sacramento Bee,* September 14, 1962, p. A12.

53. Ambrose, *Nixon,* p. 659; and Fulton Lewis, "Pat Brown's Extremists," Carvey Papers, box 21, UCLASC.

54. *Oakland Tribune,* October 22, 1962, p. B3; and Brown quoted in the *Sacramento Bee,* September 24, 1962, p. A6.

55. CDC "Special Campaign Bulletin: Anything to Win," October 23, 1962, Carvey Papers, box 9, UCLASC; and Nixon, *RN,* p. 74.

56. Quoted in the *Sacramento Bee,* May 25, 1962, p. A11.

57. Anti–Francis Amendment literature, Carvey Papers, box 23, UCLASC.

58. *Los Angeles Times,* April 1, 1962, p. 6C; and Santa Ana *Register,* November 4, 1962, p. B12.

59. Quoted in Elizabeth Poe, "The Francis Police State Amendment," *Frontier,* October 1962, p. 11.

60. California Poll cited in the *Los Angeles Times,* October 5, 1962, p. 11.

61. Not surprisingly, this regional electoral distinction was fairly consistent from 1958 through 1966 when it came to voting for right-wing initiatives and candidates. See Michael Rogin and John Shover, *Political Change in California,* pp. 169–177.

62. *San Francisco Chronicle,* October 12, 1962, p. 10.

63. *Sacramento Bee,* September 2, 1962, p. B2.

64. Ibid., November 2, 1962, p. A6. The "Dynasty of Communism" booklet contained an altered photo of Brown bowing to Khrushchev, with the statement that "Brown is a red appeaser." Carvey Papers, box 10, UCLASC.

65. Weinberger, "The California Assembly," p. 54; Donald Bradley, "Managing Democratic Campaigns" (UCBOH, 1977–1979), p. 134.

66. Quoted in the *Sacramento Bee,* November 2, 1962, p. D10.

67. After the election both Nixon and Haldeman admitted that campaign staffers had mailed out anti-Brown literature from the "Democrats from California," a phony committee. On this effort and other unethical tactics, see Ambrose, *Nixon,* pp. 660–661; and Brodie, *Richard Nixon,* 457. Nixon quoted in Evan Thomas and Lucy Shackelford, "And Now, Tricky Dick," *Newsweek,* November 3, 1997, p. 54.

68. Anderson and Lee, "The 1962 Election in California," p. 409. See also Totton Anderson, "Extremism in California Politics," *Western Political Quarterly* 16 (June 1963): 371–372.

69. H.R. Haldeman to Fair Political Practices Committee, August 10, 1962, RNPP Papers, box 311; and John Ehrlichman, *Witness to Power,* p. 31.

70. Shell Campaign Literature, RNPP Papers, box 690.

71. Quoted in the *Los Angeles Times,* November 4, 1962, p. 2.

72. Quoted in the *San Francisco Chronicle,* October 2, 1962, p. 2.

73. Quoted in ibid.

74. Nixon, *RN,* pp. 299–301.

75. Ibid., p. 301; and Klein, *Making It Perfectly Clear,* p. 61.

76. *San Francisco Chronicle,* October 12, 1962, p. 10.

77. Quoted in the *San Diego Union,* October 10, 1962, p. A8.

78. Quoted in ibid.

79. Quoted in the *Los Angeles Times,* October 25, 1962, p. 22.

80. Quoted in ibid., October 24, 1962, p. 4.

81. Ibid., October 28, 1962, p. 8C; Anderson and Lee, "The 1962 Election in California," p. 410.

82. Quoted in the *Los Angeles Times,* October 28, 1962, p. 8C.

83. Ibid. p. 3.

84. Quoted in the *San Diego Union,* November 2, 1962, p. A4.

85. Quoted in ibid., October 26, 1962, p. A4.

86. "Statement of Joe Shell," August 24, 1962, Richard Nixon Library (from Nixon campaign literature, not filed as of July 1993), Yorba Linda, CA; and Ed Mills interview, "The 'Kitchen Cabinet,' " p. 65.

87. "California Voters' Draft Of Joseph C. Shell for Governor," Nixon Library.

88. Larson, "The Issue of Birchism," pp. 262–264.

89. Quoted in ibid., p. 262.

90. Bradley, "Managing Democratic Campaigns," p. 134.

91. Nixon, *RN,* p. 301. Also see Brodie, *Richard Nixon,* p. 460.

92. Quoted in the *Los Angeles Times,* November 1, 1962, p. 1.

93. Klein, *Making It Perfectly Clear,* p. 62.

94. Hill, *Dancing Bear,* p. 176.

95. Among those who believed Nixon lost primarily due to a lack of Democratic support are Anderson and Lee, "The 1962 Election in California," pp. 414–416; and Hill, *Dancing Bear,* p. 176. Ambrose implied as much in *Nixon,* p. 665. On the other hand, Larson contended that the Republican right was largely responsible for Nixon's loss. "The Issue of Birchism," pp. 262–265. Weinberger also believed that the "Shell people" cost Nixon the election. See Jim Wood, "California Republicans: Are the Birchers Taking Over?" *The Reporter,* May 1964, p. 25. This opinion was echoed by Weinberger's successor as chairman of the Republican State Central Committee, Gaylord Parkinson, "California Republican Party Official" (UCBOH, 1978) p. 12.

96. Nixon, *RN,* p. 301.

97. On Otis Chandler's changes at the *Times,* see Gottlieb and Wolt, *Thinking Big,* pp. 322–339; and David Halberstam, *The Powers That Be,* pp. 284–289. For a reporter's perspective on the *Times* and Nixon in 1962, see Richard Bergholz, "Reporting on California Government and Politics" (UCBOH, 1979), pp. 47–48. Ironically, in 1958, Greenberg, then a reporter for the *Los Angeles Examiner,* discreetly provided campaign advice to Brown through one of the governor's aides and offered to be an informal advisor throughout the campaign. William V. O'Connor to Pat Brown, January 22, 1958, Pat Brown Papers, box 45, UCBBL.

98. See Ambrose, *Nixon,* p. 664; and Klein, *Making It Perfectly Clear,* p. 63.

99. Chandler quoted in the *Los Angeles Times,* November 8, 1962, p. 1; and Nixon in Thomas and Shackelford, p. 54.

100. *Los Angeles Times,* November 9, 1962, p. 3.

Notes to Chapter 5

1. Rus Walton, "Turning Political Ideas into Government Programs" (UCBOH, 1983), pp. 6–7, 11.

2. Ibid.; "UROC Statement of Principles," William Knowland Papers, box 158, UCBBL.

3. "Son of the Birch," *Newsweek,* March 4, 1963, pp. 27–28.

4. Walton, "Political Ideas," pp. 6, 8.

5. Rafferty's speech, "The Passing of a Patriot," from which all quotes were taken, was published in *Reader's Digest,* October 1961, pp. 107–110.

6. Ibid., pp. 107–110. Expounding on his views of American education, Rafferty wrote two books during the period of interest here: *Suffer, Little Children,* and *What They Are Doing to Your Children.* For a critique of Rafferty's beliefs, see William O'Neill, *Readin, Ritin, and Rafferty!*

7. Gene Marine, "New Hope of the Far Right," *The Nation,* January 27, 1964, p. 90.

8. Richardson quoted in "California: An Educational Election," *Time,* November 16, 1962, p. 42; Rafferty in *San Diego Union,* November 4, 1962, p. A6.

9. *San Diego Union,* November 4, 1962, p. A6.

10. Quoted in Alice Richards, "Nativism and Politics: Just Plain Folks Wanted Wyatt Earp—and They Got Him," *Frontier,* September 1964, p. 16. For a fine essay on the myth of the West in American culture, see Richard White, *"It's Your Misfortune and None of My Own,"* pp. 613–631.

11. William Rickenbacker, "60,000,000 Westerners Can't Be Wrong," *National Review,* October 23, 1962, pp. 322, 325. Rickenbacker hailed Westerns as representing the essence of "the American Dream ... of righteousness, the flowering of personal virtue, ... the selfless battle against Evil, the simple moral code," p. 322.

12. Quoted in Emanuel Levy, *John Wayne,* p. 314; and Garry Wills, *John Wayne's America,* p. 201.

13. The platform agreement between Nixon and Rockefeller became known as the "Compact of Fifth Avenue." See Theodore White, *The Making of the President 1960,* pp. 196–205. Goldwater quoted in ibid., p. 112.

14. See F. Clifton White, *Suite 3505;* and Mary Brennan, *Turning Right in the Sixties,* chapters 1–5.

15. Robert Goldberg, *Barry Goldwater,* p. 187.

16. Schlafly, *A Choice Not An Echo,* p. 115. Another book popular with Goldwaterites in the 1964 campaign was John Stormer's *None Dare Call It Treason.* This tract dealt with the "impending doom" for America due to the "20 years of retreat [in foreign policy] in the face of the communist enemy." (Quote on back cover.)

17. Hofstadter (and Adorno quoted in), *The Paranoid Style in American Politics,* pp. 44, 95.

18. Quoted in the *Los Angeles Times,* February 25, 1964, p. 1.

19. Knowing they did not have the votes for Rockefeller, moderates sought to forgo an endorsement of either candidate. Conservatives, however, managed to overturn the bylaw requiring a two-thirds majority vote, which they did not have, so they could give Goldwater the endorsement with a straight majority vote. *Los Angeles Times,* March 16, 1964, p. 1; and *CRA Enterprise* (Garden Grove, CA), May 1964, p. 1, Worth Brown Papers, CRA Collection, box 32, UCLASC.

20. Nelligan quoted in the *Los Angeles Times,* March 16, 1964, p. 16; the "FAB Society," William Bagley, interview by author, tape recording, Sacramento, CA, October 29, 1997; Goldwater, press release on extremism, Knox Mellon Collection, box 29, UCLASC.

21. Martin quoted in Novak, *The Agony of the G.O.P.,* p. 387; the second Martin quote is from Rowland Evans and Robert Novak, "The Big Crisis for Goldwater," *The Saturday Evening Post,* May 29, 1964, p. 16; the *New York Times,* May 31, 1964, p. 8.

22. Lipset and Raab, *The Politics of Unreason,* p. 305. A January 1962 poll indicated that 10 percent of California Republicans had a positive attitude toward the JBS, 21 percent were neutral, 36 percent were against it, and 33 percent had no opinion. The majority of pro-Birch and neutral Republicans were from southern California. See Lipset, "Three Decades of the Radical Right," in Daniel Bell, ed., *The Radical Right,* pp. 429–431. The favorable and neutral ratings for the JBS in the Southland may have gone up over the next two years due to the anxiety over the Cuban missile crisis, as well as to the favorable findings of the California Un-American Activities Committee in 1963 in regard to the Society's purpose and actions. It also appears that Goldwater's candidacy had an impact on the significant increase in the organization's ranks in California in 1964. On this growth see Barbara Stone, "The John Birch Society in California" (Ph.D. diss., University of Southern California, 1968), p. 25.

23. Goldwater quoted in Goldberg, *Barry Goldwater,* p. 160; Buckley and Kirk in Goldberg, p. 159. On Buckley's views of Goldwater's presidential candidacy, see John Judis, *William F. Buckley, Jr.,* pp. 319–334.

24. Barbara Stone, "The John Birch Society in California," 24–25; Barbara Stone, interview by author, tape recording, Whittier, CA, August 3, 1992.

25. All references to California Republican voter concerns are from a California Poll cited in John Kessel, *The Goldwater Coalition,* p. 81. The views of southern California conservatives on these and other important topics during the Goldwater ascendancy can be found in Lisa McGirr, "Suburban Warriors: The Grass-Roots Conservative Movement in the 1960s" (Ph.D. diss., Columbia University, 1995), chapters 2 and 3; and Denise Spooner, "The Political Consequences of Experiences of Community: Iowa Migrants and Republican Conservatism in Southern California, 1946–1964" (Ph.D. diss., University of Pennsylvania, 1992), chapter 4.

26. Stone, author's interview.

27. *Los Angeles Times,* June 1, 1964, various campaign ads.

28. Goldwater, *Conscience of a Conservative,* p. 75.

29. F.C. White, *Suite 3505,* p. 334.

30. Patricia Limerick, *The Legacy of Conquest,* p. 88. For an analysis of the New Deal in California, see Richard Lowitt, *The New Deal and the West,* pp. 189–202.

31. Garry Wills, *Reagan's America,* pp. 67–76.

32. Phillips, *The Emerging Republican Majority,* p. 449.

33. *San Diego Union,* May 31, 1964, p. 1.

34. Goldwater, *Conscience of a Conservative,* back cover (August 1964, paperback ed.). Goldwater was well off financially himself, but his wealth paled in comparison to the Rockefeller fortune.

35. Quoted in Gilbert A. Harrison, "Way Out West," *The New Republic,* November 23, 1963, p. 19.

36. All campaign ads and literature came from the Worth Brown Papers, CRA Collection, box 32, UCLASC.

37. Wills, *Reagan's America,* p. 233.

38. Both Reagans quoted in the *Goldwater for President Campaign Newsletter,* March 16, 1964, Knox Mellon Collection, box 29, UCLASC; Goldwater Gals "instruction" also in the above. The Gals were young volunteers who appeared at rallies and parades, sometimes riding in uncovered wagons.

39. *Goldwater for President Campaign Newsletter,* March 16 and May 14, 1964, ibid.

40. T. White, *The Making of the President 1964,* p. 148.

41. Salvatori to Worth Brown, April 15, 1964, Worth Brown Papers, CRA Collection, box 32, UCLASC; Salvatori to Frederick Bale, April 6, 1964, Knox Mellon Collection, box 29, UCLASC. On Salvatori's role as finance chairman, see Salvatori interview, "The 'Kitchen Cabinet'" (CSUFOH, 1981), pp. 4–5. Another eventual member of the Kitchen Cabinet, San Francisco businessman Jaquelin Hume, was Goldwater's northern California finance chairman. He later recalled, "I was always jealous of the south's ability to raise money, and came to the conclusion that we could raise about a third as much here as they could in southern California." Hume, "Basic Economics and the Body Politic" (UCBOH, 1982), p. 12.

42. *Wall Street Journal,* May 27, 1964, p. 18.

43. Dick Darling, "Republican Activism" (UCLAOH, 1982), pp. 8–9.

44. T. White, *The Making of the President 1964,* p. 151.

45. Rockefeller quoted in the *San Diego Union,* May 27, 1964, p. A6; *New York Times,* May 31, 1964, p. 2E; Goldwater's response is in the Santa Ana *Register,* May 27, 1964, p. 5.

46. "Rockefeller" flyer, Knox Mellon Collection, box 29, UCLASC; and T. White, *The Making of the President 1964,* p. 153.

47. Quoted in the *Los Angeles Times,* June 2, 1964, p. 1.

48. Burdick, "Trailing a Curious Political Animal," *New York Times Magazine,* May 31, 1964, p. 38.

49. *Washington Post,* June 3, 1964, p. 1.

50. Quoted in the *Los Angeles Times,* May 31, 1964, sect. 1, p. A. Rockefeller and Goldwater both criticized the Johnson administration's handling of the Vietnam conflict. It was not much of an issue between the two in the campaign.

51. Novak, *The Agony of the GOP,* p. 414.

52. *Los Angeles Times,* June 1, 1964, various ads.

53. "The Man on the Bandwagon," *Time,* June 12, 1964, p. 32.

54. Kessel reported that Goldwater won only four counties, while Novak stated that he won only three. However, the 1964 "Statement of Vote" issued by the California Secretary of State showed that Goldwater won thirteen counties in the primary.

55. *San Diego Union,* June 4, 1964, p. 1.

56. "The Man on the Bandwagon," p. 33. Gardiner Johnson, a Goldwater campaign aide in California, stated that all workers received a membership card (signed by William Knowland, chairman of the crusade) certifying "I am a Goldwater volunteer," which "built up sort of an *esprit de corps.*" Gardiner Johnson, "Oral History interview with Gardiner Johnson" (UCBOH, 1983), p. 210.

57. For example, see Bill Stout, "How Goldwater Won in California," *The Reporter,* July 2, 1964, p. 18.

58. According to the California Poll, racial problems ranked fifth among the issues of major concern to Republicans likely to vote, Kessel, *The Goldwater Coalition,* p. 81. Also see Edward Carmines and James Stimson, *Issue Evolution,* pp. 44–47.

59. Gardiner Johnson quoted in Schlafly, *A Choice Not An Echo* (1964 post-primary ed.), p. 4; and Stephen Shadegg, *What Happened to Goldwater?* p. 266.

60. *San Francisco Chronicle,* June 4, 1964, p. 40.

61. "From Behind in the Stretch," *Time,* May 29, 1964, p. 20.

62. "The Man on the Bandwagon," p. 33. On the motivations and critical importance of Goldwater volunteers, see Jud Leetham's assessment in T. White, *The Making of the President 1964,* pp. 156–158.

63. Conrad Joyner, "Whose Republican Party?" *The New Republic,* June 13, 1964, p. 10; and the *Los Angeles Times,* June 4, 1964, p. 2.

64. Quoted in David Reinhard, *The Republican Right,* p. 189.

65. Scranton's and the succeeding quote in ibid., p. 190.

66. Quoted in Bill Becker, "Death Wish of the Republicans," *Frontier,* July 1964, p. 8.

67. Worth Brown to Paul Manolis, June 9, 1964, Worth Brown Papers, CRA Collection, box 32, UCLASC; and Caspar Weinberger, "The California Assembly, Republican State Central Committee, and Elections" (UCBOH, 1978–79), p. 57.

68. Quoted in the *Los Angeles Times,* July 13, 1964, p. 3.

69. A JBS spokesman at the convention stated that 100 of the 1,300 convention delegates were Birchers, but there is no corroboration of this assertion. Reinhard, *The Republican Right,* p. 194. William Knowland stated that none of the California delegates were members of the JBS, though that seems highly unlikely. *New York Times,* July 17, 1964, p. 12.

70. Cannon, *Reagan,* p. 102.

71. Reinhard, *The Republican Right,* p. 199.

72. Quoted in the *Los Angeles Times,* September 9, 1964, p. 1.

73. Ibid., p. 25.

74. For example, on the zealously independent Goldwater "citizens' committees," see Worth Brown to William Knowland, July 23, 1964, Worth Brown Papers, CRA Collection, box 32, UCLASC.

75. Weinberger, "The California Assembly," p. 82. On the many organizational and strategical woes afflicting the Goldwater campaign in general, see Brennan, *Turning Right in the Sixties,* chapter 5.

76. *New York Times,* October 18, 1964, p. 56.

77. See Salvatori and Ed Mills interviews, "The 'Kitchen Cabinet,'" pp. 12, 66.

78. T. White, *The Making of the President 1964,* p. 118.

79. Salvatori and Holmes Tuttle interviews, "The 'Kitchen Cabinet,'" pp. 14, 114; Walton, "Political Ideas," pp. 11–14; and Cannon, *Reagan,* pp. 98–99. Gardiner Johnson claimed that an Orange County group, led by John B. Kilroy of Newport Beach, was behind the effort to film the Reagan speech and put it on national television. Kilroy (of "Kilroy was here" fame during World War II, according to Johnson) may have been involved in the production and distribution of the film, but neither he nor the Orange County group was mentioned by Salvatori or Tuttle, or by Rus Walton, Goldwater's public relations director in California. See Johnson, "Oral History interview," pp. 212–215.

80. Shadegg, *What Happened to Goldwater?* pp. 251–252.

81. Quoted in "A Time for Choosing," *Human Events,* November 28, 1964, pp. 8–9.

82. It is unclear how much money Reagan's speech helped bring in. Gardiner Johnson contended that it raised $3.5 million, but others have cited smaller, but still significant figures. Whatever the actual amount, after the election, surplus funds were distributed to various Republican organizations. See Johnson, "Oral History interview," p. 215; and Mills interview, "The 'Kitchen Cabinet,'" p. 66.

83. Quoted in Cannon, *Reagan,* p. 102.

84. Quoted Jamieson, *Packaging the Presidency,* p. 204.

Notes to Chapter 6

1. The most comprehensive examination of Reagan's politics in Hollywood and HUAC testimony is in Stephen Vaughn, *Ronald Reagan in Hollywood,* see especially pp. 145–170; and Garry Wills, *Reagan's America,* chapters 26 and 27.

2. Murphy received about 700,000 Democratic votes in his victory over Salinger. Gladwin Hill, *Dancing Bear,* p. 189. Monson quoted in Herbert Gold, "Nobody's Mad at Murphy," *New York Times Magazine,* December 13, 1964, p. 48. Kuchel later withdrew his support for Murphy when the latter refused to repudiate the JBS. *New York Times,* August 2, 1966, p. 32.

3. See Totton Anderson and Eugene Lee, "The 1964 Election in California," *Western Political Quarterly* 18 (June 1965): 452–455.

4. On Salinger and the CDC, see Don Bradley, "Managing Democratic Campaigns" (UCBOH, 1977–1979), pp. 157–168; and Pierre Salinger, "A Journalist as Democratic Campaigner" (UCBOH, 1979), pp. 45–51.

5. *Los Angeles Times,* November 3, 1964, p. 15. In addition to his endorsement, Disney made a significant financial contribution to his longtime friend's campaign. (Disney later contributed to Reagan's campaign as one of the Friends of Ronald Reagan.) Richard Schickel, *The Disney Version,* pp. 157–158. Murphy received strong backing from his employer, the Technicolor Corporation, for which he served as a public relations executive. The company's board chairman, Patrick Frawley, supported many right-wing causes. Gold, "Nobody's Mad at Murphy," p. 48.

6. Robert Finch, "A View from the Lt. Governor's Office" (CSUFOH, 1981), p. 10.

7. Quoted in "Who Is the Good Guy"? *Time,* October 16, 1964, p. 36.

8. Quoted in ibid., p. 36; and Gold, "Nobody's Mad at Murphy," p. 48.

9. Quoted in "Who Is the Good Guy?" p. 37; and Salinger, "A Journalist as Democratic Campaigner," p. 46.

10. Gold, "Nobody's Mad at Murphy," p. 48.

11. Shana Alexander, "My Technicolor Senator," *Life,* December 4, 1964, p. 30.

12. See W. Byron Rumford, "Legislator for Fair Employment, Fair Housing and Public Health" (UCBOH, 1970–1971), pp. 119–133; and the *New York Times,* May 10, 1964, p. 59.

13. CRA resolution in *New York Times,* September 7, 1964, p. 6; Frizzelle quoted in "Proposition 14," *Time,* September 23, 1964, p. 23; Gaston in Joseph Lewis, "California: A Wild Card in the Deck," *The Reporter,* October 22, 1964, p. 32; and "The Committee For Home Protection" literature, William Knowland Papers, box 158, UCBBL.

14. Betty Farris (UROC Unit 129) to U.S. Senate & Americans, March 12, 1964, Knowland Papers, box 158, UCBBL.

15. "Committee for Home Protection," Knowland Papers, box 158, UCBBL; and Lewis, "A Wild Card in the Deck," p. 32.

16. A California Poll found that 59.3 percent of blacks were initially for the proposition, but opposition grew as knowledge of the measure's actual meaning spread through the black community. Lewis, "A Wild Card in the Deck," p. 29. It seems that few voters were confused by the initiative by the time of the election. Raymond Wolfinger and Fred Greenstein, "The Repeal of Fair Housing in California: An Analysis of Referendum Voting," *American Political Science Review* 62 (September 1968): 755–757. Blacks ended up voting against the proposition by a nine to one margin. Anderson and Lee, "The 1964 Election in California," p. 471. On the misunderstanding of Proposition 14 among minorities, see Judy Royer Carter, "Pat Brown" (UCBOH, 1977), p. 4.

17. J.R. Carter, "Pat Brown," p. 3. Polls revealed that Californians were no more racist than Americans in other parts of the country outside the South, and that the attitudes of whites toward blacks in northern and southern California did not significantly differ. Yet the Bay area vote against the proposition was 10 percent greater than that in metropolitan Los Angeles. Wolfinger and Greenstein attributed this difference to the tendency of southern middle-class and, especially, wealthy voters, to be more in favor of the proposition than their northern counterparts. This disparity appears to have stemmed from regional "leadership group influence," which resulted in the anti-14 campaign being most effective in the liberal north, while militant pro-14 forces generated strong support in the Southland. "The Repeal of Fair Housing," pp. 754, 761–763. In white state assembly districts—whether Republican or Democrat—65 to 75 percent of the voters supported the proposition. Raphael Soneshein, *Politics in Black and White,* p. 69.

18. There was so much dissension between moderates and conservative "nuts" at the convention that the presiding officers, seeking to avoid embarrassment, adjourned the convention without a platform. William T. Bagley, interview by author, tape recording, Sacramento, CA, October 29, 1997.

19. Ibid.; and Thomas Edsall and Mary Edsall, *Chain Reaction.* Wolfinger and

Greenstein could not find compelling evidence that the vote for Proposition 14 in southern California was supported by a disproportionately strong "belief in 'property rights,' " though James Q. Wilson implies that the latter might have been a prominent factor. Wolfinger and Greenstein concluded that "the broader body of literature . . . suggest[s] . . . that white resistance to Negro equality is particularly strong where housing is concerned." See Wolfinger and Greenstein, "Repeal of Fair Housing," pp. 764–767; and Wilson, "A Guide to Reagan Country: The Political Culture of Southern California," *Commentary,* May 1967, pp. 40, 44.

20. My observations here on the white backlash are drawn in part from Michael J. Klarman, "How Brown Changed Race Relations: The Backlash Thesis," *The Journal of American History* 81 (June 1994): 81–118 (especially pp. 92–118).

21. Lewis, "A Wild Card in the Deck," p. 32.

22. Walton, "Turning Political Ideas into Government Programs" (UCBOH, 1983) pp. 14–15; and Kathleen Hall Jamieson, *Packaging the Presidency,* pp. 214–215.

23. Quoted in F. Clifton White, *Suite 3505,* pp. 414–415. The tone of the film proved to be a harbinger of Republican advertising in future campaigns in which candidates stirred and exploited middle-class resentments.

24. Barry Goldwater, *The Conscience of a Conservative,* p. 38.

25. Robert Goldberg, *Barry Goldwater,* p. 218.

26. Dan Carter, *The Politics of Rage,* pp. 221–222.

27. While Democrats had garnered the majority of the black presidential vote during and since the New Deal, the biggest break with Republican presidential nominees came with Goldwater's candidacy and has remained ever since. See Edward Carmines and James Stimson, *Issue Evolution,* p. 46; relatedly, see Edsall and Edsall, *Chain Reaction,* pp. 18–19.

28. Gardiner Johnson, "Oral History interview" (UCBOH, 1983) pp. 234–235, 238. The California Declaration, founding membership list, and the general statement of purpose of the CCA can be found on pp. 234–238.

29. Ronald Reagan, "On Becoming Governor" (UCBOH, 1979), p. 4.

30. Johnson, "Oral History interview," pp. 219–222.

31. Quoted in Ben Bagdikian, "In the Hearts of the Right, Goldwater Lives," *New York Times Magazine,* July 18, 1965, p. 41.

32. Ibid., p. 6.

33. Ibid.

34. The presidents of several California college chapters resigned after the election of the three Birchers. In addition, the National Young Republican Federation (NYRF) sought to revoke the California branch's charter due to its financial conflicts with the NYRF, and due to the latter's charge that the "newly elected officers have publicly stated immature and irresponsible views. . . ." Quoted in the *New York Times,* February, 26, 1966. The reaction of the NYRF to the JBS infiltration in California reflected the mounting adamant rejection of the JBS within the Republican Party. See David Broder and Stephen Hess, *The Republican Establishment,* pp. 260–266.

35. Ascertaining the number of members in the JBS in California at any given time is of course largely speculative. It is clear that Goldwater's candidacy significantly increased the ranks of the Society, but it seems there was no similar growth spurt in the years immediately after his defeat. On the Society's growth in 1964, see Barbara Stone, "The John Birch Society of California" (Ph.D. diss., University of Southern California, 1968), pp. 24–25.

36. Editors, et al., "The John Birch Society and the Conservative Movement," *National Review,* October 19, 1965, pp. 914–929. Quotes (respectively) on pp. 915, 928, 929.

37. Quoted in Bill Boyarsky, *The Rise of Ronald Reagan,* p. 104. Holmes Tuttle and Ed Mills had been part of the group that approached Reagan in 1962. See Mills interview, "The 'Kitchen Cabinet'" (CSUFOH, 1981), pp. 66–67.

38. First quote from "Encroaching Control," *Vital Speeches of the Day,* September 1, 1961, p. 681; second from "A Moment of Truth," *Vital Speeches,* September 1, 1965, p. 686.

39. See Mills, Salvatori, and Tuttle interviews, "The 'Kitchen Cabinet,'" pp. 14, 68, 114–115.

40. Reagan, "On Becoming Governor," p. 4.

41. Vernon Cristina, "A Northern Californian Views Conservative Policies and Politics" (UCBOH, 1983), p. 21; Walton, "Political Ideas," pp. 16–17.

42. Tuttle interview, "The 'Kitchen Cabinet,'" pp. 116–117. It appears that Shell never met with Reagan during the campaign. Reagan, however, did meet with Shell's wife, Barbara, for lunch, where she presented her views (and presumably her husband's) on "many vital subjects." Reagan to Barbara Shell, August 23, 1966, Ronald Reagan Papers, box 13, Hoover Institute on War, Revolution and Peace, Stanford University, Stanford, CA.

43. *New York Times,* February 12, 1965, p. 23.

44. Lou Cannon, *Ronnie and Jesse,* pp. 73–74; and Bagley, author's interview.

45. Quoted in Cannon, *Ronnie and Jesse,* p. 76.

46. "Friends" letter, Reagan Papers, box 20.

47. Cannon, *Ronnie and Jesse,* p. 75.

48. Quoted in Stewart Alsop, "Can Goldwater Win in '64?" *The Saturday Evening Post,* August 24, 1963, p. 21.

49. Cannon, *Reagan,* p. 98; Leetham quoted in Jessica Mitford, "The Rest of Ronald Reagan," *Ramparts,* November 1965, p. 35.

50. Quotes from the *Los Angeles Times,* January 5, 1966, p. 35. Parkinson's eleventh commandment was: "Thou shalt not speak ill of any fellow Republican."

51. "Biography of Ronald Reagan: A Truly Qualified Citizen Politician," campaign literature, CRA Collection, box 2, UCLASC.

52. Reagan, "On Becoming Governor," pp. 9–10.

53. Stanley Plog, "More Than Just an Actor" (UCLAOH, 1981), pp. 4–6, 12; and McBirnie to Reagan, November 30, 1965, Reagan Papers, box 23.

54. Pat Brown to Elmer C. Woodmansee, March 17, 1966, Pat Brown Papers, box 921, UCBBL.

55. *New York Times,* February 21, 1966, p. 19.

56. Quoted in Boyarsky, *The Rise of Ronald Reagan,* pp. 148–149. Christopher tried in vain to make more of an issue of this matter, offering, for example, to donate $5,000 to any charity Reagan designated if "your contention could be verified." Christopher to Reagan, May 4, 1966, Thomas Kuchel Papers, box 477, UCBBL.

57. Ronald Reagan and Richard Hubler, *Where's the Rest of Me?* p. 8.

58. Quoted in Vaughn, *Ronald Reagan in Hollywood,* p. 171.

59. Ibid., pp. 175–181.

60. Joseph Roddy, "Ronnie to the Rescue," *Look,* November 1, 1966, p. 54.

61. Reagan quoted in the *Los Angeles Times,* June 2, 1966, p. 3. Wills, "Mr. Magoo Remembers," *The New York Review of Books,* December 20, 1990, p. 3. Wills used the Mr. Magoo analogy mainly to describe Reagan's perpetually cheerful demeanor, whereas I am applying it more to his myopic worldview.

62. Quoted in the *New York Times,* September 5, 1965, p. 42.

63. Reagan to Rousselot, September 24, 1965, Reagan Papers, box 11; and "Statement of Ronald Reagan Regarding the John Birch Society," no date (but probably early 1966), Reagan Papers, box 25.

64. Quoted in the *San Francisco Examiner,* April 3, 1966, p. 1.

65. *San Francisco Chronicle,* April 4, 1966. p. 9.

66. Quoted in the *San Francisco Examiner,* April 3, 1966, p. 15.

67. Spencer, "Developing a Campaign Management Organization" (UCBOH, 1979) p. 31; and Dutton, "Democratic Campaigns and Controversies" (UCBOH, 1977–1978), p. 145.

68. Walton, "Political Ideas," p. 19.

69. Crosby quoted in *Los Angeles Times,* May 2, 1966, p. 34; dissenter in the *New York Times,* May 2, 1966, p. 21.

70. Quoted in the *New York Times,* May 2, 1964, p. 21; and Walton, "Political Ideas," p. 19. It is unclear whether Joe Shell had any major role in the UROC at this point. Given his negative comments on the JBS and Reagan, however, it seems unlikely that he would have exerted much influence over the new leaders of the organization.

71. *Los Angeles Times,* May 2, 1966, p. 3.

72. For a discussion of these polls, see Totton Anderson and Eugene Lee, "The 1966 Election in California," *Western Political Quarterly* 20 (June 1967): 539; and William Bagley to Ronald Reagan, April 15, 1966, Reagan Papers, box 23.

73. William Bagley to Ronald Reagan, April 15, 1966, Reagan Papers, box 23; and quoted in Mitford, "The Rest of Ronald Reagan," p. 35.

74. William Bagley, "Some Complexities of Social Progress and Fiscal Reform" (UCBOH, 1981) pp. 2, 14; and Bagley, author's interview.

75. Bagley, author's interview.

76. Cannon, *Ronnie and Jesse,* p. 78.

77. *Los Angeles Times,* June 3, 1966, p. 3.

78. Anderson and Lee, "The 1966 Election in California," p. 538.

79. Dutton, "Democratic Campaigns," p. 142.

80. Quotes from the *Los Angeles Times,* May 11, 1966, p. 20; and *CRA Newsletter,* June 1966, CRA Collection, box 2, UCLASC.

81. *New York Times,* August 7, 1966, p. 30; and Reagan campaign news release (from a speech in Riverside), October 13, 1966, Reagan Papers, box 25.

82. Quoted in Curt Gentry, *The Last Days,* pp. 201, 207.

83. *New York Times,* June 1, 1966, p. 38.

84. Quoted in the *Los Angeles Times,* June 3, 1966, p. 3.

85. Ibid.

86. Reagan and Hubler, *Where's the Rest of Me?* pp. 139, 141; and Murphy comment in Broder and Hess, *The Republican Establishment,* p. 251.

87. Reagan and Hubler, *Where's the Rest of Me?* p. 162.

88. See John Judis, *William F. Buckley, Jr.,* pp. 146–147; and George Nash, *The Conservative Intellectual Movement,* pp. 148–153.

89. Buckley, "How Is Ronald Reagan Doing?" *National Review,* January 11, 1966, p. 17.

90. *New York Times,* June 5, 1966, p. 84.

91. Reagan and Brown quoted in the *Los Angeles Times,* June 8, 1966, p. 3.

Notes to Chapter 7

1. First quote in the Santa Ana *Register,* October 19, 1966, p. A5; second quote in Reagan, "On Becoming Governor" (UCBOH, 1979), p. 23. Reagan's Creative Society entailed no actual programs until he became governor. Instead he made numerous proclamations on his intention to curtail bureaucracy and taxes. Reagan's "The Creative Society" address, which he delivered at his 1967 inauguration, is in Reagan, *The Creative Society,* pp. 1–11.

2. *New York Times,* June 14, 1966, p. 28.

3. Ibid. The percentage of conservatives in the state Republican Party cited in Lucien Haas to Gladwin Hill, April 7, 1966, Pat Brown Papers, box 927, UCBBL.

4. *New York Times,* June 5, 1966, p. 83.

5. Parkinson to Kuchel, May 31, 1966, Reagan Papers, box 20, Hoover Institute on War, Revolution and Peace, Stanford University, Stanford, CA.

6. Quoted in the *New York Times,* June 5, 1966, p. 83.

7. Reagan to McCone, October 3, 1966, Reagan Papers, box 35.

8. Reagan claimed, "[a]t no time did I ever engage actively in campaigning in [Wright's] behalf. . . ." (ibid.). He did, however, provide the sole signature at the bottom of Wright's fundraising letter. Reagan to Fellow Californian (no date), Wright campaign literature, Richard Nixon Pre-Presidential Papers, box 834, National Archives and Records Administration, Pacific Southwest Region, Laguna Niguel, California.

9. Among the three right-wing Kuchel opponents indicted (and later convicted) for circulating the false affidavit was John F. Fergus, a public relations executive for Frawley's Eversharp-Schick Safety Razor Company. Frawley testified before a grand jury in the Kuchel case, stating that he had hired Fergus in 1962 to "make speeches on free enterprise and against communism." Though never directly linked to the Kuchel smear, Frawley made sizable contributions to many groups that fit the senator's qualifications for "fright peddler" organizations, such as the Americanism Educational League, the Committee for the Monroe Doctrine, and the American Security Council. *New York Times,* June 28, 1965, p. 22.

10. Reagan to McCone, October 3, 1966, Reagan Papers, box 35. On Frawley's fundraising, see Reagan, "On Becoming Governor," p. 23.

11. Memorandum for the Senator from Leon E. Panetta, June 22, 1966, Thomas Kuchel Papers, box 477, UCBBL; Memorandum for the Senator from John E. Merriam, June 22, 1966, Kuchel Papers, box 477; and Kuchel to Ronald Reagan, July 8, 1961, Kuchel Papers, box 270.

12. Quoted in Herbert Phillips, *Big Wayward Girl,* p. 279.

13. *Los Angeles Times,* June 8, 1966, p. 3; and Editors, "Golly Gee, California Is a Strange State," *Ramparts,* October 1966, p. 15.

14. Winslow Christian to Fred Jordan, June 20, 1966; and Cruz Reynoso to Winslow Christian, June 22, 1966, both in Pat Brown Papers, box 921, UCBBL.

15. *Los Angeles Times,* October 27, 1966, p. 3.

16. *New York Times,* June 30, 1966, p. 26.

17. Hale Champion, "Communication and Problem-Solving" (UCBOH, 1978), p. 72.

18. Quoted in Joseph Roddy, "Ronnie to the Rescue," *Look,* November 1, 1966, p. 54.

19. Reagan to Goldwater, January 13, 1966, Reagan Papers, box 23.

20. Goldwater to Reagan, June 2, 1966, ibid.

21. Reagan to Goldwater, June 11, 1966, ibid.

22. On the Gipper and other Reagan images, see Michael Rogin, *Ronald Reagan, the Movie,* pp. 1–43.

23. "Biography of Ronald Reagan: A Truly Qualified Citizen-Politician," CRA Collection, box 2, UCLASC.

24. Quoted in Editors, "Golly Gee," p. 27. (Reagan commented on this emotional meeting in his inaugural address.) On the turmoil at Berkeley, see W.J. Rorabaugh, *Berkeley at War,* pp. 473–494.

25. Quoted in the Santa Ana *Register,* October 21, 1966, p. 3.

26. Quoted in Lou Cannon, *Ronnie and Jesse,* p. 83.

27. Quoted in *The Californian* (published by the Republican State Central Committee), September 1965, p. 28, CRA Collection, box 3, UCLASC.

28. Quoted in the *New York Times,* May 15, 1966, p. 52.

29. Quoted in Phillips, *Big Wayward Girl,* 258.

30. Reagan to John R. Lechner, September 17, 1965, Reagan Papers, box 34; and Reagan to George Murphy, August 19, 1966, Reagan Papers, box 23.

31. Hale Champion to Fred Dutton, et al., July 19, 1966, Pat Brown Papers, box 927, UCBBL.

32. See Fred Dutton, "Democratic Campaigns and Controversies" (UCBOH, 1977–1978), p. 152; and Meredith Burch, "Political Notes" (UCBOH, 1977), pp. 22–23.

33. *New York Times,* August 28, 1966, p. 71; and Roger Kent, "Building the Democratic Party in California" (UCBOH, 1976–1977), pp. 267–270.

34. Quoted in the *New York Times,* August 7, 1966, p. 27.

35. Ibid., p. 1.

36. "Ronald Reagan, Extremist Collaborator: An Exposé," p. 1, Political Literature Collection, CSUFFC. Approximately one month before the "Exposé" was distributed, State Democratic Chairman Robert L. Coate released a "documentary" study of Reagan's connections with the JBS. Unlike the "Exposé," it does not appear to have been widely circulated as campaign literature. See Totton Anderson and Eugene Lee, "The 1966 Election in California," *Western Political Quarterly* (June 1967): 545.

37. "Ronald Reagan, Extremist Collaborator," pp. 2–4, 6, 10–11.

38. Franklyn Nofziger, "Press Secretary for Ronald Reagan" (UCBOH, 1978), p. 14.

39. The publisher of the *Manteca Bulletin* informed Brown that "out here [in the San Joaquin Valley] . . . the John Birch Society is not an ussue *[sic]* and, in fact, is virtually unknown." George Murphy Jr. to Pat Brown, October 21, 1966, Pat Brown Papers, box 921, UCBBL.

40. Jennett to Ronald Reagan, November 22, 1965; and William Roberts to Jennett, December 17, 1965, both in Reagan Papers, box 20.

41. Jennett, "The Story of Ronald Reagan—The Next Governor of California," p. 4, Reagan Papers, box 35. Ronald Reagan and Richard Hubler, *Where's the Rest of Me?* pp. 118, 119.

42. The most detailed account of Reagan's activities in Hollywood during the war, including his role in bomber training films, is in Stephen Vaughn, *Ronald Reagan in Hollywood,* pp. 112–118.

43. Jennett, "The Story of Ronald Reagan," p. 8, Reagan Papers, box 35.

44. Jennett connected Goldwater and Reagan most vividly in an ad for "Reagan stamps," which appeared at the end of his biography of the actor (and also in several issues of *Human Events*). Boldly proclaiming that Reagan was "picking up where Goldwater left off," the ad contended that the stamps, available through the Spirit of '76 House, would help "zoom" Reagan to national prominence, much as Goldwater stamps had aided the Arizonan in 1964. Jennett, "The Story of Ronald Reagan," p. 15, ibid. As for the actor's participation in the senator's presidential campaign, 30 percent of all voters considered that support to be one of Reagan's "weak points," while 43 percent were bothered by his refusal to reject backing from the JBS. California Poll cited in the Santa Ana *Register,* September 6, 1966, p. A14.

45. According to *Los Angeles Times* reporter Carl Greenberg, there were ten members of the Kitchen Cabinet when Reagan became governor. Greenberg, "Ronald Reagan's 'Kitchen Cabinet,' " *Los Angeles Times WEST Magazine,* April 23, 1967, pp. 24–25. Other businessmen, however, appeared (and claimed) to have been part of this group, especially Vernon Cristina and the owner of the Los Angeles–based Dart Industries, Justin Dart. The latter seems to have been involved with Reagan mainly after he became governor and not so much during the campaign. See Justin Dart interview, "The 'Kitchen Cabinet' " (CSUFOH, 1980), pp. 37–49. On the influence of the Kitchen Cabinet during the 1966 campaign and Reagan's governorship, see Joel Kotkin and Paul Grabowics, *California, Inc.,* chapter 3; and "The 'Kitchen Cabinet.' "

46. Tuttle interview, "The 'Kitchen Cabinet,'" p. 119.

47. See "Ronald Reagan, Extremist Collaborator," p. 3. Salvatori founded the Anti-Communist Voters League in the 1950s and was an initial contributor to Fred Schwarz's Christian Anti-Communism Crusade, neither of which was particularly virulent when compared to numerous other anticommunist organizations, such as the JBS. Salvatori's participation as a "member of the faculty" for "Project Alert" could be deemed a controversial activity given the highly inflammatory statements made by some of the project's participants. But the author found no truly fire-eating or ultramilitant utterances attributed to Salvatori in his public or private life.

48. Salvatori donated over $1 million to the University of Southern California to establish an anticommunist research school and gave $1 million to the Claremont Men's College Center for the Study of Individual Freedom. He also made a large contribution to the conservative Hoover Institute at Stanford University. Cannon, *Ronnie and Jesse,* p. 73. On Salvatori's political philosophy, see Salvatori interview, "The 'Kitchen Cabinet,'" pp. 3, 9.

49. See Greenberg, "Ronald Reagan's 'Kitchen Cabinet,'" p. 24; and Hume, "Basic Economics and the Body Politic: Views of a Northern California Reagan Loyalist" (UCBOH, 1982), pp. 14–24.

50. Hume, "Basic Economics," p. 10.

51. On Tuttle's pivotal influence on Reagan, see Neil Reagan, "Private Dimen-

sions and Public Images" (UCLAOH, 1981), p. 35; Jack Wrather, "On Friendship, Politics, and Government" (UCBOH, 1982), p. 6; and Stanley Plog, "More Than Just an Actor" (UCLAOH, 1981), p. 17.

52. Haynes Johnson, *Sleepwalking Through History,* pp. 73–75; and Dart, "The 'Kitchen Cabinet,' " p. 43.

53. Brown to Reagan, Western Union telegram, September 10, 1966, Reagan Papers, box 34.

54. Quoted in the *Los Angeles Times,* September 13, 1966, p. 26.

55. Reagan quotes from "Extremism" script for a sixty-second radio ad, Reagan Papers, box 25.

56. *Orange County Republican* (published by the Orange County Republican Central Committee), September 1966, p. 3, Political Literature Collection, CSUFFC.

57. Quoted in the *New York Times,* August 7, 1966, p. 27.

58. Santa Ana *Register,* October 11, 1966, p. A3.

59. Burch, "Political Notes," pp. 23–24.

60. Anderson and Lee, "The 1966 Election in California," p. 544.

61. Reagan claimed that the decision to team with Finch was made "on my specific demand," because Republican polls showed Finch running well behind the incumbent lieutenant governor, Glen Anderson. Reagan, "On Becoming Governor," p. 17. Ironically, Finch polled more votes than Reagan on election day. On the Reagan–Finch "team," see also Finch, "A View from the Lt. Governor's Office" (CSUFOH, 1981), pp. 23–24.

62. Santa Ana *Register,* October 31, 1966, p. A6.

63. Frawley's Schick corporation was the only corporate sponsor noted in an eleven-page ad insert appearing within the *Los Angeles Times* "Calendar" section on November 6.

64. *Los Angeles Times,* September 12, 1966, p. 3.

65. All quotes from *Los Angeles Times,* ad insert in Calendar, November 6, 1966, pp. 6, 7, 9. The author(s) of the ad specifically assailed graphic literature, but the initiative targeted all pornography in the effort to "prohibit obscene matter."

66. Ibid., p. 3.

67. Quoted in Robert Kirsch, "Proposition 16: What Hath the Smut Rakers Wrought?" *Los Angeles Times,* Calendar, November 6, 1966, p. 24.

68. Tuttle interview, "The 'Kitchen Cabinet,' " p. 130.

69. Creative Society quote in the Santa Ana *Register,* October 19, 1966, p. A5. TV ad quotes in "Ronald Reagan talks about . . . Leadership and Morality, . . . Vietniks, Beatniks, and Filthy Speachers *[sic]*." *Los Angeles Times,* Calendar, November 6, 1966, p. 33.

70. Santa Ana *Register,* October 19, 1966, p. A5.

71. R.E. Lawson to Pat Brown, October 28, 1966, Pat Brown Papers, box 921, UCBBL.

72. Paul Perlin to Pat Brown, August 1, 1966, Pat Brown Papers, box 922.

73. William Becker to Hale Champion, et al., August 12, 1966, Pat Brown Papers, box 921. See also William Becker, "Working for Civil Rights" (UCBOH, 1979), pp. 57–59.

74. Caspar Weinberger stated that Republican polls after the Reagan–Brown contest showed that Reagan won "something in excess of forty percent of the union

labor vote. . . ." Weinberger, "The California Assembly" (UCBOH, 1978–1979), 87. California Poll of union households cited in the *San Francisco Chronicle,* October 12, 1966, p. 10. On "working-class" support for Reagan in 1966, see Matthew Dallek, "Liberalism Overthrown," *American Heritage,* October 1996, p. 56.

75. A nationwide Harris Poll shortly before the election showed that the number of whites who believed that blacks had "tried to move too fast" went from 34 percent in 1964 to 85 percent. Harris and California pollster Don Muchmore both predicted that the backlash would have great impact in California. *Los Angeles Times,* November 6, 1966, p. 2. On Muchmore's poll results, see Champion, "Communications and Problem Solving," pp. 58–60. See also the *San Francisco Chronicle,* October 12, 1966, p. 10.

76. Quoted in the *Los Angeles Times,* October 31, 1966, p. 3.

77. The filmstrips were circulated by Constructive Action, Inc. (not to be confused with Citizens for Constructive Action). The organization claimed to have distributed three million copies of John Stormer's *None Dare Call It Treason* and Schlafly's *A Choice Not an Echo* in 1964, and pledged to distribute "thousands" of filmstrips on Watts, Berkeley, and other controversial issues. Herbert K. Philbrick to Dear Friend (solicitation letter, no date), Reagan Papers, box 19.

78. Reagan to Mary L. Gallivan, October 21, 1966, Reagan Papers, box 34.

79. Santa Ana *Register,* September 6, 1966, p. C16.

80. Roberts, "Professional Campaign Management and the Candidate" (UCBOH, 1979), p. 21. Parkinson, "California Republican Party Official" (UCBOH, 1978), pp. 17–18. Parkinson did take issue with Republicans who encouraged visits to California by avowed segregationists such as Strom Thurmond. *San Diego Union,* May 9, 1966, p. 9.

81. Parkinson, "California Republican Party Official," p. 17.

82. Allen Matusow, *The Unraveling of America,* p. 195. All arguments against perceptions that black families have historically been "pathological" should begin with Herbert Gutman, *The Black Family in Slavery and Freedom;* on the "Moynihan Report," see Gutman, pp. 461–467. Liberal perceptions of the African American "dilemma" were significantly influenced by Stanley Elkins's 1959 book, *Slavery: A Problem in American Institutional and Intellectual Life.*

83. Quoted in "Exclusive interview with Ronald Reagan," *Human Events,* February 19, 1966, p. 10. Reagan's remark about "paternalism" seemingly refers to slavery, a curious reference given that slavery had been over for 100 years.

84. Goodlett quoted in the *New York Times,* March 17, 1966, p. 27; and Rudolph Barker to Pat Brown, September 2, 1966, Pat Brown Papers, box 921, UCBBL.

85. Mervyn M. Dymally to Pat Brown, July 29, 1966; Community Organizations for Brown press release, July 26, 1966; and Brown Campaign Committee press release, March 21, 1966, all in Pat Brown Papers, box 921, UCBBL.

86. Polls cited in Roberts, "Professional Campaign Management," p. 21.

87. Cruz Reynoso to Winslow Christian, and Fred Jordan to Winslow Christian, both June 22, 1966, Pat Brown Papers, box 921.

88. Jordan to Christian, June 22, 1966, ibid.; and Burt Corona to William Becker, October 13, 1966, Pat Brown Papers, box 921.

89. Parkinson, "California Republican Party Official," p. 18. Led by Los Angeles businessman and Republican State Central Committee official David Chow, a significant percentage of Chinese Americans in southern California also supported

Reagan. Chow was also a member of Reagan's Southern California Finance Committee. Reagan, "On Becoming Governor," p. 4a.

90. *New York Times,* October 17, 1966, p. 27.

91. Quoted in the *Los Angeles Times,* October 29, 1966, p. 3.

92. Quoted in the *San Francisco Examiner,* October 9, 1966, sec. 2, p. 2.

93. Quoted in the *San Francisco Chronicle,* October 24, 1966, p. 17.

94. Quoted in Cannon, *Ronnie and Jesse,* p. 79.

95. Rogin, *Ronald Reagan, the Movie,* pp. 38–39.

96. Bill Boyarsky, *The Rise of Ronald Reagan,* p. 136.

97. A California Poll revealed that 71 percent of all voters believed that Reagan's inexperience in government was a "weak" point; but the same poll indicated that 49 percent of voters thought Brown had been in office too long, while 29 percent believed he was "too much of a politician." Santa Ana *Register,* September 6, 1966, p. A14.

98. Nofziger, "Press Secretary for Ronald Reagan," p. 42. Hale Champion later stated that Brown's remark was "not staged" and was intended to be a "joke." Champion, "Communications and Problem Solving," p. 82.

99. Lou Cannon, *President Reagan: The Role of a Lifetime.*

100. Champion recalled that "We had people out there asking [Reagan] . . . tough questions. Only once or twice did we catch him completely unprepared." Champion, "Communications and Problem Solving," p. 83.

101. Ibid., p. 67.

102. *Los Angeles Times,* November 6, 1966, p. 6G.

103. Editors, "Golly Gee," p. 22.

Notes to Chapter 8

1. Reagan, *The Creative Society,* pp. 2, 8.

2. Jackson Putnam, *Modern California Politics,* pp. 60–61; and Garin Burbank, "Speaker Moretti, Governor Reagan, and the Search for Tax Reform in California, *Pacific Historical Review* 61 (May 1992): 193–214. On the right's alienation, see Kent Steffgren, *Here's the Rest of Him;* and Barbara Stone, interview by author, tape recording, Whittier, CA, August 3, 1992.

3. Reagan, "On Becoming Governor" (UCBOH, 1979), p. 15; and William Bagley, interview by author, tape recording, Sacramento, CA, October 29, 1997.

4. See Herman Schwartz, *Packing the Courts: The Conservative Campaign to Rewrite the Constitution.*

5. On the Republican Party's post-Goldwater "Southern Strategy," see Kevin Phillips, *The Emerging Republican Majority,* pp. 203–289; Mary Brennan, *Turning Right in the Sixties,* pp. 125–128; and Thomas Edsall and Mary Edsall, *Chain Reaction,* pp. 74–79. On Nixon's attempt to divide the Democratic Party, see William Berman, *America's Right Turn,* p. 11.

6. See, for example, Robert Scheer, "California Scheming," *The Nation,* April 15, 1996, p. 6+.

7. See Tomás Almaguer, *Racial Fault Lines;* Roger Daniels and Spencer Olin, in *Racism in California;* and Alexander Sexton, *The Indispensable Enemy.*

8. Michael Rogin and John Shover, *Political Change in California,* pp. xv, 175–178.

9. See Karl Lamb, *As Orange Goes,* p. 13; and Melvin Bernstein, "The Orange County Myth: Are Its Politics as Mickey Mouse as Disneyland?" *California Journal,* October 1974, pp. 324–328. For a more recent assessment of this trend, see Jean O. Pasco, "Losing Its Grip," *California Journal,* September 1997, pp. 28–33.

10. Daniel Bell, *The End of Ideology,* p. 373.

11. Himmelstein, *To the Right,* pp. 5–6. Michael Kazin credits "the conservative capture" of populism as the main impetus behind the right's success since the late 1960s. Kazin, *The Populist Persuasion,* chapter 10. Neither Kazin nor Himmelstein, however, sees Reagan's 1966 campaign as a principal catalyst in the revitalization of the conservative movement and tailoring its populist appeal.

12. On the need for Nixon to be conservative in 1968 for the sake of unifying the GOP behind him, see Brennan, *Turning Right in the Sixties,* pp. 121–128.

13. John Judis, *William F. Buckley, Jr.,* pp. 221 (quote), 231. On the right-wing consensus, known as "fusionism," see Frank Meyer, ed., *What Is Conservatism?* pp. 7–20; and George Nash, *The Conservative Intellectual Movement,* pp. 174–181.

14. Robert Dallek, *Ronald Reagan,* p. 34.

15. Quoted in Joel Kotkin and Paul Grabowics, *California, Inc.,* p. 53.

16. Lou Cannon, "The Reagan Years: An Evaluation of the Governor Californians Won't Soon Forget," *California Journal,* November 1974, p. 364; and Buckley quoted in Judis, *William F. Buckley, Jr.,* p. 421. On conservative intellectuals and Reagan, see also David Hoeveler Jr., *Watch on the Right.*

17. Richard Viguerie, the chief tactician of the New Right, began to solicit campaign funds through his innovative direct mail technique in the mid-1960s. Viguerie contended that Max Rafferty, one of his earliest clients, defeated Thomas Kuchel in the Republican primary in 1968 mainly due to direct mail appeals. Richard Viguerie, *The New Right,* pp. 33–34. On the foundations of the New Right, see Sidney Blumenthal, *The Rise of the Counter-Establishment;* and Alan Crawford, *Thunder on the Right.*

18. Michael Kazin, "The Grass-Roots Right: New Histories of U.S. Conservatism in the Twentieth Century," *American Historical Review* 97 (February 1992): 147.

19. According to Caspar Weinberger, Reagan received considerable support from Democratic, working-class voters because "they knew he wasn't going to bust the union[s] . . . [or] have a right-to-work bill." Weinberger, "The California Assembly" (UCBOH, 1978–1979), pp. 86–87.

20. William Hixson, *Search for the American Right-Wing,* pp. 115–123. Also see Jonathan Rieder, "The Rise of the 'Silent Majority,' " in Steve Fraser and Gary Gerstle, eds., *The Rise and Fall of the New Deal Order,* pp. 243–268. Though many prominent conservatives found Wallace's populism repellent, others saw him as an attractive figure, especially in terms of winning over blue collar workers to the conservative cause. Some conservatives envisioned an independent Reagan–Wallace presidential ticket in 1976, until it became clear that Reagan would mount a strong challenge to President Gerald Ford in the Republican primary. Himmelstein, *To the Right,* p. 83.

21. Dan Carter, *Politics of Rage,* pp. 313–314.

22. Edsall and Edsall, *Chain Reaction,* pp. 130–131. Some analysts of the tax revolt have argued that measures restricting the revenue base of local government, thereby reducing local authority and autonomy in favor of the state, cannot be

viewed as truly conservative. See Ronald Heckart and Terry Dean, *Proposition 13 in the 1978 California Primary,* p. 3.

23. E.J. Dionne Jr., *Why Americans Hate Politics,* pp. 289–291.

24. William Kristol and David Brooks, "What Ails Conservatism," *Wall Street Journal,* September 15, 1997, p. A22; and George F. Will, "Three Questions for Conservatives to Gather Around," *The Sacramento Bee,* August 31, 1997, Forum, p. 5. (Will's observation was drawn from a commentary by Walter Berns of the American Enterprise Institute.) See also Jacob Weisberg, "Con Air: What the Right's Fighting About," *Slate* (Microsoft Online), posted October 25, 1997.

Bibliography

Manuscript Collections

Brown, Edmund G. ("Pat") Sr. University California, Berkeley, Bancroft Library.
California Republican Assembly (CRA) Collection. (Including the Worth Brown Papers and the Sherrill Halbert Papers.) University of California, Los Angeles, Special Collections.
Carvey, Thomas B. University of California, Los Angeles, Special Collections.
Craig, Robert Fenton. University of California, Los Angeles, Special Collections.
Knowland, William F. University of California, Berkeley, Bancroft Library.
Knox Mellon Collection. University of California, Los Angeles, Special Collections.
Kuchel, Thomas H. University of California, Berkeley, Bancroft Library.
Nixon, Richard M. Pre-Presidential Papers. National Archives and Records Administration, Pacific Southwest Division, Laguna Niguel, California.
———. Richard Nixon Library, Yorba Linda, California.
Political Literature Collection. California State University, Fullerton, Freedom Center of Political, Social, and Religious Ephemera.
Reagan, Ronald. Hoover Institute on War, Revolution, and Peace, Stanford University, Stanford, California.
Warren, Earl. California State Archives, Sacramento, California.
Whitaker, Clem, and Leone Baxter. California State Archives, Sacramento, California.

Newspapers

Los Angeles Examiner
Phoenix Gazette
Los Angeles Herald-Examiner
Sacramento Bee
Los Angeles Times
San Diego Union
New York Times

San Francisco Chronicle
Oakland Tribune
San Francisco Examiner
Register (Santa Ana, California)
Wall Street Journal
Pasadena Star-News
Washington Post

Oral Histories

Oral History Program, California State University, Fullerton. (Referred to in the notes as CSUFOH.) Claude Bunzel (1976); Sam Campbell (1976); Justin Dart (1980); Robert Finch (1981); Robert Gaston (1974); Howard Jarvis (1974); Edward

Mills (1981); Marvin Olsen (1976); Gordon X. Richmond (1980); Henry Salvatori (1981); John Schmitz (1976); Don Smith (1980); Randall Smith (1980); Bruce Sumner (1980); James Toft (1976); Holmes Tuttle (1981).

Oral History Program, University of California, Los Angeles. (Referred to in the notes as UCLAOH.) Dick Darling (1982); Walter Knott (1965); Stanley Plog (1981); Neil Reagan (1981); Jack Tenney (1969).

Regional Oral History Office, Bancroft Library, University of California, Berkeley. (Referred to in the notes as UCBOH.) Robert Ash (1970); William T. Bagley (1981); William Becker (1979); Earl Behrens (1977); Marjorie H.E. Benedict (1983); Richard Bergholz (1979); Don Bradley (1977–79); Edmund Brown, Sr. (1977–81); Germain Bulcke (1969); Meredith Burch (1977); Thomas Caldecott (1979); Dennis Carpenter (1982); Judy Royer Carter (1977); Hale Champion (1978); George Christopher (1977–78); John W. Cline (1970); Vernon Cristina (1983); Fred Dutton (1977–78); Harry Finks (1977–79); Lucile Hosmer (1983); Jaquelin Hume (1982); Emelyn Knowland Jewett (1979); Estelle Knowland Johnson (1979); Gardiner Johnson (1973); Robert Kenny (1975); Roger Kent (1976–77); Clark Kerr (1969); Sydney Kossen (1979); Paul Manolis (1979); Franklyn Nofziger (1978); Gaylord Parkinson (1978); Langdon Post (1972); Ronald Reagan (1979); William Roberts (1979); W. Byron Rumford (1970–71); Pierre Salinger (1979); U.S. Simmonds (1969); Stuart Spencer (1979); Rus Walton (1983); Caspar Weinberger (1978–79); Jack Wrather (1982); Sam Yorty (1975).

Interviews by the Author. Bagley, William, tape recording, Sacramento, CA, October 29, 1997. Carpenter, Dennis, tape recording, Sacramento, CA, October 16, 1997. Stone, Barbara, tape recording, Whittier, CA, August 3, 1992.

Books, Articles, Dissertations and Theses

Adorno, Theodore W., et al. *The Authoritarian Personality.* New York: Harper, 1950.

Alexander, Shana. "My Technicolor Senator." *Life,* December 4, 1964, p. 30.

Allen, Gary. "The C.F.R. Conspiracy to Rule the World." *American Opinion,* April 1969, p. 56.

Almaguer, Tomás. *Racial Fault Lines: The Historical Origins of White Supremacy in California.* Berkeley: University of California Press, 1994.

Alsop, Stewart. "Can Goldwater Win in '64?" *The Saturday Evening Post,* August 24, 1963, pp. 19+.

Ambrose, Stephen E. *Eisenhower: Soldier, General of the Army, President-Elect, 1890–1952.* New York: Simon and Schuster, 1983.

———. *Eisenhower: The President.* New York: Simon and Schuster, 1984.

———. *Nixon: The Education of a Politician, 1913–1962.* New York: Simon and Schuster, 1987.

Anderson, Totton J. "Extremism in California: The Brown–Knowland and Brown–Nixon Campaigns Compared." *Western Political Quarterly* 16 (June 1963): 371–372.

———. "The 1958 California Election." *Western Political Quarterly* 12 (March 1959): 276–300.

Anderson, Totton J., and Eugene C. Lee. "The 1962 Election in California." *Western Political Quarterly* 16 (June 1963): 396–420.

———. "The 1964 Election in California." *Western Political Quarterly* 18 (June 1965): 445–476.

———. "The 1966 Election in California." *Western Political Quarterly* 20 (June 1967): 535–554.

Angermann, Erich, et al. *New Wine in Old Skins: A Comparative View of Socio-Political Structures and Values Affecting the American Revolution.* Stuttgart, Germany: Klett, 1976.

Bagdikian, Ben H. "In the Hearts of the Right, Goldwater Lives." *New York Times Magazine,* July 18, 1965, pp. 6+.

Bailyn, Bernard. *The Ideological Origins of the American Revolution.* Cambridge: Harvard University Press, 1967.

Banning, Lance. "Republican Ideology and the Triumph of the Constitution, 1789–1793." *William and Mary Quarterly* 31 (April 1974): 167–188.

Barrett, Edward L., Jr. *The Tenney Committee.* Ithaca, NY: Cornell University Press, 1951.

Beaman, Charles C., and Michael Jones. "Turmoil and Change: An Interim Report on the Politics of Orange County, California." Oral History Program, California State University, Fullerton, 1980.

Bean, Walton, and James J. Rawls. *California: An Interpretive History.* 4th ed. New York: McGraw-Hill, 1983.

Becker, Bill. "Death Wish of the Republicans." *Frontier,* July 1964, pp. 5–8.

Bell, Daniel. *The End of Ideology: On the Exhaustion of Political Ideas in the Fifties.* New York: The Free Press, 1960.

———, ed. *The New American Right.* New York: Criterion Books, 1955.

———, ed. *The Radical Right: The New American Right* (expanded and updated). Garden City, NY: Anchor Books, 1964.

Bercovitch, Sacvan. *The American Jeremiad.* Madison: University of Wisconsin Press, 1978.

Berman, William C. *America's Right Turn: From Nixon to Bush.* Baltimore: Johns Hopkins University Press, 1994.

Bernstein, Melvin H. "The Orange County Myth: Are Its Politics as Mickey Mouse as Disneyland?" *California Journal,* October 1974, pp. 324–328.

Bienvenu, Harold. *The Patriot.* New York: St. Martins Press, 1964.

Blumenthal, Sidney. *The Rise of the Counter-Establishment: From Conservative Ideology to Political Power.* New York: Times Books, 1986.

Boyarsky, Bill. *The Rise of Ronald Reagan.* New York: Random House, 1968.

Brennan, Mary C. *Turning Right in the Sixties: The Conservative Capture of the GOP.* Chapel Hill: University of North Carolina Press, 1995.

Brinkley, Alan. "The New Deal and the Idea of the State." In Steve Fraser and Gary Gerstle, eds., *The Rise and Fall of the New Deal Order, 1930–1980,* pp. 85–121.

———. "The Problem of American Conservatism." *American Historical Review* 99 (April 1994): 409–429.

Broder, David S., and Stephen Hess. *The Republican Establishment: The Present and Future of the GOP.* New York: Harper and Row, 1967.

Brodie, Fawn. *Richard Nixon: The Shaping of His Character.* New York: W.W. Norton, 1981.

Brownell, Robert C. "Can Roosevelt Win?" *Frontier,* November 3, 1950, pp. 5–7.

Buchanan, William, and Eugene C. Lee. "The 1960 Election in California." *Western Political Quarterly* 14 (March 1961): 309–326.

Buckley, William F., Jr., ed. *Did You Ever See a Dream Walking?* Indianapolis: Bobbs-Merrill, 1970.

———. "The Tranquil World of Dwight Eisenhower." *National Review,* January 18, 1958, pp. 57–59.

———. "How Is Ronald Reagan Doing?" *National Review,* January 11, 1966, p. 17.

Bullock, Paul. *Jerry Voorhis: The Idealist as Politician.* New York: Vantage Press, 1978.

Burbank, Garin. "Speaker Moretti, Governor Reagan, and the Search for Tax Reform in California." *Pacific Historical Review* 61 (May 1992): 193–214.

Burdick, Eugene. "Trailing a Curious Political Animal." *New York Times Magazine,* May 31, 1964, pp. 10+.

Burke, Robert E. *Olsen's New Deal for California.* Berkeley: University of California Press, 1953.

"California: A Little Piece of America." *Newsweek,* November 14, 1966, pp. 32+.

"California: An Educational Election." *Time,* November 16, 1962, p. 42.

"California: Proposition 14." *Time,* September 23, 1964, p. 32.

"California: Son of the Birch." *Newsweek,* March 4, 1963, pp. 27–28.

"California: Who Is the Good Guy?" *Time,* October 16, 1964, pp. 35–36.

California Senate. *Twelfth Report of the Senate Factfinding Committee on Un-American Activities,* "Report on the John Birch Society," 1963, pp. 1–62.

Cannon, Lou. *President Reagan: The Role of a Lifetime.* New York: Simon and Schuster, 1991.

———. *Reagan.* New York: G.P. Putnam's Sons, 1982.

———. "The Reagan Years: An Evaluation of the Governor Californians Won't Soon Forget." *California Journal,* November 1974, pp. 360–366.

———. *Ronnie and Jesse: A Political Odyssey.* Garden City, NY: Doubleday, 1969.

Carmines, Edward G., and James A. Stimson. *Issue Evolution: Race and the Transformation of American Politics.* Princeton: Princeton University Press, 1989.

Carter, Dan T. *The Politics of Rage: George Wallace, the Origins of the New Conservatism, and the Transformation of American Politics.* New York: Simon and Schuster, 1995.

Chafe, William H. *The Unfinished Journey: America Since World War II.* New York: Oxford University Press, 1986.

Clark, William A. "Leader of the Beat Generation." *Frontier,* October 1958, pp. 5+.

Clayton, James L. "Defense Spending: Key to California's Growth." *Western Political Quarterly* 15 (June 1962): 280–293.

Crawford, Alan. *Thunder on the Right: The 'New Right' and the Politics of Resentment.* New York: Pantheon Books, 1980.

Crouch, Winston W., et al. *California Government and Politics.* 5th ed. Englewood Cliffs, NJ: Prentice-Hall, 1972.

"Cuba Under the Lens: No Missiles But. . . ." *Newsweek,* February 18, 1963, pp. 20–21.

Dallek, Matthew. "Liberalism Overthrown." *American Heritage,* October 1996, pp. 39+.

Dallek, Robert. *Ronald Reagan: The Politics of Symbolism.* Cambridge: Harvard University Press, 1984.

Daniel, James, and John Hubbell. *Strike in the West: The Complete Story of the Cuban Missile Crisis.* New York: Holt, Winston and Reinhart, 1963.

Daniels, Roger, and Spencer C. Olin, Jr. *Racism in California: A Reader in the History of Oppression.* New York: Macmillan, 1972.

Davis, Mike. *City of Quartz: Excavating the Future in Los Angeles.* New York: Vintage, 1992.

Delmatier, Royce, et al. *The Rumble of California Politics, 1848–1970.* New York: Wiley and Sons, 1970.

Deverell, William. *Railroad Crossing: Californians and the Railroad, 1850–1910.* Berkeley: University of California Press, 1994.

―――, ed. *California Progressivism Revisited.* Berkeley: University of California Press, 1994.

Diggins, John P. *The Lost Soul of American Politics: Virtue, Self-Interest, and the Foundations of Liberalism.* Chicago: University of Chicago Press, 1983.

―――. *The Proud Decades: America in War and in Peace, 1941–1960.* New York: W.W. Norton, 1988.

Dionne, E.J., Jr. *Why Americans Hate Politics.* New York: Touchstone, 1992.

Donovan, Richard. "Jack Tenney: A Post-mortem." *Frontier,* November 15, 1949, pp. 7–9.

Edelman, Murray. *The Symbolic Uses of Politics.* Urbana: University of Illinois Press, 1964.

Editors, "A Trend Is Running Toward an Enlightened Conservatism," *Life,* July 3, 1950, p. 18.

Editors, "Golly Gee, California Is a Strange State." *Ramparts,* October 1966, pp. 12–33.

Editors, et al. "The John Birch Society and the Conservative Movement." *National Review,* October 19, 1965, pp. 914–929.

Edsall, Thomas Byrne, and Mary D. Edsall. *Chain Reaction: The Impact of Race, Rights, and Taxes on American Politics.* New York: W.W. Norton, 1992.

Elkins, Stanley. *Slavery: A Problem in American Institutional and Intellectual Life.* Chicago: University of Chicago Press, 1959.

Evans, Rowland, and Robert Novak. "The Big Crisis for Goldwater." *The Saturday Evening Post,* May 29, 1964, pp. 16+.

"Exclusive Interview with Ronald Reagan." *Human Events,* February 19, 1966, pp. 9–10.

Flannery, Harry W. "Red Smear in California." *Commonweal,* December 8, 1950, pp. 223–225.

Forster, Arnold, and Benjamin R. Epstein. *Danger on the Right: The Attitudes, Personnel and Influence of the Radical Right and Extreme Conservatives.* New York: Random House, 1964.

Fraser, Steve, and Gary Gerstle, eds. *The Rise and Fall of the New Deal Coalition, 1930–1980.* Princeton: Princeton University Press, 1989.

"From Behind in the Stretch." *Time,* May 29, 1964, pp. 18–20.

Gaddis, John L. "The Tragedy of Cold War History." *Diplomatic History* 17 (Winter 1993): 1–16.

Gallup Poll: Public Opinion 1935–1971, vol. 2. New York: Random House, 1971.

Gardner, David P. *The California Oath Controversy*. Berkeley: University of California Press, 1967.

Gentry, Curt. *The Last Days of the Late, Great State of California*. New York: G.P. Putnam's Sons, 1968.

Gitlin, Todd. The Sixties: Years of Hope, Days of Rage. New York: Bantam Books, 1987.

Gold, Herbert. "Nobody's Mad at George Murphy." *New York Times Magazine*, December 13, 1964, pp. 42+.

Goldberg, Robert Alan. *Barry Goldwater*. New Haven: Yale University Press, 1995.

Goldman, Eric F. *The Crucial Decade—and After: America, 1945–1960*. New York: Vintage, 1960.

Goldwater, Barry M. *The Conscience of a Conservative*. New York: McFadden, August 1964 ed.

———. *Why Not Victory? A Fresh Look at American Foreign Policy*. New York: McFadden, 1963.

———. *With No Apologies: The Personal and Political Memoirs of United States Senator Barry M. Goldwater*. New York: William Morrow, 1979.

Gottfried, Paul, and Thomas Fleming. *The Conservative Movement*. Boston: Twayne, 1988.

Gottlieb, Robert, and Irene Wolt. *Thinking Big: The Story of the* Los Angeles Times, *Its Publishers, and Their Influence on Southern California*. New York: G.P. Putnam's Sons, 1977.

Gould, Jean, and Lorena Hickok. *Walter Reuther: Labor's Rugged Individualist*. New York: Dodd/Mead, 1972.

Green, David. *The Shaping of Political Consciousness: The Language of Politics in America from McKinley to Reagan*. Ithaca, NY: Cornell University Press, 1987.

Greenberg, Carl. "Ronald Reagan's 'Kitchen Cabinet.' " *Los Angeles Times WEST Magazine*, April 23, 1967, pp. 24–25.

Greenstein, Fred I., *The Hidden-Hand Presidency: Eisenhower as Leader*. New York: Basic Books, 1982.

Gregory, James N. *American Exodus: The Dust Bowl Migration and Okie Culture in California*. New York: Oxford University Press.

Griffith, Duff W. "Before the Deluge: An Oral History Examination of Pre-Watergate Conservative Thought in Orange County." Master's thesis, California State University, Fullerton, 1976.

Gutman, Herbert G. *The Black Family in Slavery and Freedom, 1750–1925*. New York: Pantheon Books, 1975.

Hacker, Andrew. *Two Nations: Black and White, Separate, Hostile, Unequal*. New York: Charles Scribner's Sons, 1992.

Halberstam, David. *The Powers That Be*. New York: Alfred E. Knopf, 1979.

Hallan-Gibson, Pamela. *The Golden Promise: An Illustrated History of Orange County*. Northridge, CA: Windsor, 1986.

Harris, Joseph P. *California Politics*. 4th ed. San Francisco: Chandler, 1967.

Harrison, Gilbert A. "Way Out West." *The New Republic*, November 23, 1963, pp. 17–22.

Harvey, Richard B. *The Dynamics of California Government and Politics*. 2d ed. Monterey, CA: Brook/Cole, 1985.

———. *Earl Warren: Governor of California*. Dubuque, IA: Kendall/Hunt, 1990.

Heale, M.J. *American Anticommunism: Combatting the Enemy Within, 1830–1970.* Baltimore: Johns Hopkins University Press, 1990.

———. "Red Scare Politics: California's Campaign Against Un-American Activities, 1940–1970." *Journal of American Studies* 20 (Summer 1986): 5–32.

Heckart, Ronald J., and Terry J. Dean. *Proposition 13 in the 1978 California Primary: A Post Election Bibliography.* Berkeley: Institute of Governmental Studies, University of California, 1981.

Henderson, Lloyd Roy. "Earl Warren and California Politics." Ph.D. diss., University of California, 1965.

Hill, Gladwin. *Dancing Bear: An Inside Look at California Politics.* Cleveland: World Publishing, 1968.

Himmelstein, Jerome L. *To The Right: The Transformation of American Conservatism.* Berkeley: University of California Press, 1990.

Hixson, William B., Jr. *Search for the American Right Wing: An Analysis of the Social Science Record, 1955–1987.* Princeton: Princeton University Press, 1992.

Hoeveler, J. David. *Watch on the Right: Conservative Intellectuals in the Reagan Era.* Madison: University of Wisconsin Press, 1991.

Hofstadter, Richard. *The Age of Reform: From Bryan to FDR.* New York: Alfred A. Knopf, 1995.

———. *Anti-Intellectualism in American Life.* New York: Vintage, 1962.

———. *The Paranoid Style in American Politics and Other Essays.* Reprint, Chicago: University of Chicago Press, 1979, originally 1965.

———. *Social Darwinism in American Life.* New York: George Braziller, 1944.

Hyink, Bernard, and David Provost. *Politics and Government in California.* 13th ed. New York: Harper Collins, 1996.

Isaacs, Stanley P. "Knight over California: Will He Succeed Himself?" *The Nation,* May 29, 1954, pp. 461+.

Jackson, Kenneth T. *The Crabgrass Frontier: The Suburbanization of the United States.* New York: Oxford University Press, 1985.

Jamieson, Kathleen Hall. *Packaging the Presidency: A History and Criticism of Presidential Campaign Advertising.* New York: Oxford University Press, 1984.

Jeansonne, Glen. *Gerald L.K. Smith: Minister of Hate.* New Haven: Yale University Press, 1988.

Johnson, Haynes. *Sleepwalking Through History: America in the Reagan Years.* New York: Anchor Books, 1992.

Joyner, Conrad. "Whose Republican Party?" *The New Republic,* June 13, 1964, pp. 10–11.

Judis, John B. *William F. Buckley, Jr.: Patron Saint of the Conservatives.* New York: Simon and Schuster, 1988.

Katcher, Leo. *Earl Warren: A Political Biography.* New York: McGraw-Hill, 1967.

Kazin, Michael. *Barons of Labor: The San Francisco Labor Trades and Union Power in San Francisco.* Urbana: University of Illinois Press, 1987.

———. "The Grass-Roots Right: New Histories of U.S. Conservatism in the Twentieth Century." *American Historical Review* 97 (February 1992): 136–155.

———. *The Populist Persuasion: An American History.* New York: Basic Books, 1995.

Keller, William J. "What Governor Knight Thinks of His Party." *Frontier,* September 1958, pp. 5+.

Kessel, John J. *The Goldwater Coalition: Republican Strategies in 1964.* Indianapolis: Bobbs-Merrill, 1968.

Kirsch, Robert R. "Proposition 16: What Hath the Smutrakers Wrought?" *Los Angeles Times,* "Calendar" sec., November 6, 1966, p. 24.

Klarman, Michael J. "How Brown Changed Race Relations: The Backlash Thesis." *The Journal of American History* 81 (June 1994): 81–118.

Klein, Herbert G. *Making It Perfectly Clear.* Garden City, NY: Doubleday, 1980.

Kling, Rob, Spencer C. Olin, Jr., and Mark Poster, eds. *Post Suburban California: The Transformation of Orange County Since World War II.* Berkeley: University of California Press, 1991.

Knowland, William F. "Labor Should Be Free in Our Republic." *The American Mercury,* March 1958, pp. 5–8.

Kotkin, Joel, and Paul Grabowics. *California Inc.* New York: Rawson, Wade, 1982.

Kristol, William, and David Brooks. "What Ails Conservatism." *Wall Street Journal,* September 15, 1997, p. A22.

Lamb, Karl. *As Orange Goes: Twelve California Families and the Future of American Politics.* New York: W.W. Norton, 1974.

Larsen, Charles E. "The Epic Campaign of 1934." *Pacific Historical Review* 27 (May 1958): 127–147.

Larson, Arthur. *A Republican Looks at His Party.* New York: Harper, 1956.

Larson, Eric C. "The Issue of Birchism in the 1962 California Republican Gubernatorial Primary." Master's thesis, California State University, Fullerton, 1975.

Lears, T.J. Jackson. "Gutter Populist." *The New Republic,* January 9 and 16, 1995, pp. 39+.

Lesher, Stephan. *George Wallace: American Populist.* New York: Addison-Wesley, 1994.

Levy, Emanuel. *John Wayne: Prophet of the American Way of Life.* Metuchen, NJ: Scarecrow, 1988.

Lewis, Joseph. "California: A Wild Card in the Deck." *The Reporter,* October 22, 1964, pp. 29–33.

Limerick, Patricia N. *The Legacy of Conquest: The Unbroken Past of the American West.* New York: W.W. Norton, 1987.

Lipset, Seymour Martin. "Three Decades of the Radical Right." In Daniel Bell, ed., *The Radical Right,* pp. 307–371.

———, and Earl Raab. *The Politics of Unreason: Right-Wing Extremism in America, 1790–1977,* 2d ed. Chicago: University of Chicago Press, 1977.

Lotchin, Roger W. *Fortress California 1910–1961: From Warfare to Welfare.* New York: Oxford University Press, 1992.

Lowitt, Richard. *The New Deal in the West.* Bloomington: Indiana University Press, 1984.

McGirr, Lisa. "Suburban Warriors: The Grass-Roots Conservative Movement in the 1960s." Ph.D. diss., Columbia University, 1995.

McWilliams, Carey. *California: The Great Exception.* Reprint. Santa Barbara, CA: Peregrine Smith, 1976, originally 1949.

———. "Government by Whitaker and Baxter." *The Nation,* April 14, 1951, pp. 346–348, and April 21, 1951, pp. 366–369.

———. "Mr. Tenney's Horrible Awakening." *The Nation,* July 23, 1949, pp. 80–82.

————. *Southern California: An Island on the Land.* Reprint. Santa Barbara, CA: Peregrine Smith, 1973, originally 1946.

Marine, Gene. "New Hope of the Far Right." *The Nation,* January 27, 1964, pp. 89–93.

Marx, Wesley. "Sparta in the Southland." *Frontier.* April 1962, pp. 6–8.

Matusow, Allen J. *The Unraveling of America: A History of Liberalism in the 1960s.* New York: Harper and Row, 1984.

Melendy, H. Brett, and Benjamin F. Gilbert. *The Governors of California: Peter H. Burnett to Edmund G. Brown.* Georgetown, CA: Talisman Press, 1965.

Meyer, Frank, ed. *What Is Conservatism?* New York: Holt, Rinehart and Winston, 1964.

Mitchell, Greg. The Campaign of the Century: Upton Sinclair's Race for Governor of California and the Birth of Media Politics. New York: Random House, 1992.

Mitford, Jessica. "The Rest of Ronald Reagan." *Ramparts,* November 1965, pp. 30–36.

Morris, Joe Alex. "Another Roosevelt Makes His Pitch." *The Saturday Evening Post,* October 7, 1950, pp. 22+.

Morris, Roger. *Richard Milhous Nixon: The Rise of an American Politician.* New York: Henry Holt, 1990.

Mowry, George. *The California Progressives.* Berkeley: University of California Press, 1951.

Nash, George H. *The Conservative Intellectual Movement in America Since 1945.* New York: Basic Books, 1976.

Nixon, Richard M. *RN: The Memoirs of Richard Nixon,* vol. 1. New York: Warner Books, 1979.

————. *Six Crises.* Garden City, NY: Doubleday, 1962.

Nock, Albert Jay. *Our Enemy, the State* (New York: W. Morrow, 1935)

Novak, Robert D. *The Agony of the G.O.P.* New York: Macmillan, 1965.

Olin, Spencer C., Jr. *California's Prodigal Sons: Hiram Johnson and the Progressives.* Berkeley: University of California Press, 1968.

O'Neill, William. F. *Readin, Ritin, and Rafferty! A Study of Educational Fundamentalism.* Berkeley: Glendessary Press, 1969.

Oshinsky, David. *A Conspiracy So Immense: The World of Joe McCarthy.* New York: Free Press, 1983.

Parmet Herbert. *Richard Nixon and His America.* Boston: Little, Brown, 1990.

Pasco, Jean O. "Losing Its Grip." *California Journal,* September 1997, pp. 28+.

Patterson, James T. *America's Struggle Against Poverty, 1900–1986.* Cambridge: Harvard University Press, 1986.

————. *Mr. Republican: A Biography of Robert A. Taft.* New York: Houghton Mifflin, 1972.

Pemberton, William E. *Exit with Honor: The Life and Presidency of Ronald Reagan.* Armonk, NY: M.E. Sharpe, 1997.

Phillips, Herbert L. *Big Wayward Girl: An Informal Political History of California.* Garden City, NY: Doubleday, 1968.

Phillips, Kevin P. *The Emerging Republican Majority.* Garden City, NY: Anchor Books, 1970.

Poe, Elizabeth. "The Francis Police State Amendment." *Frontier,* October 12, 1962, pp. 10–12.

Pritchard, Robert L. "California Un-American Activities Investigations: Subversion on the Right." *California History* 69 (December 1970): 309–327.

Putnam, Jackson K. *Modern California Politics.* 3d ed. Sparks, NV: MTL, 1990.
———. "The Pattern of Modern California Politics." *Pacific Historical Review* 61 (February 1992): 23–52.
———. "The Persistence of Progressivism in the 1920s: The Case of California." *Pacific Historical Review* 35 (November 1966): 395–411.
———. "Political Change in California: A Review Essay." *Southern California Quarterly* 53 (December 1971): 345–355.
Rae, Nicol C. *The Decline and Fall of the Liberal Republicans: From 1952 to the Present.* New York: Oxford University Press, 1989.
Rafferty, Max. "The Passing of a Patriot." Reader's Digest, October 1961, pp. 107–110.
———. *Suffer, Little Children.* New York: Signet, 1962.
———. *What They Are Doing to Your Children.* New York: New American Library, 1963.
Reagan, Ronald. *An American Life.* New York: Simon and Schuster, 1990
———. *The Creative Society: Some Comments on Problems Facing America.* New York: Devin-Adair, 1968.
Reagan, Ronald, and Richard G. Hubler. *Where's the Rest of Me?* New York: Duell, Sloan, and Pearce, 1965.
Reinhard, David W. *The Republican Right Since 1945.* Lexington: University of Kentucky Press, 1983.
"Republicans: The Look Backward." *Time,* April 22, 1957, pp. 25–26.
"Republicans: The Man on the Bandwagon." *Time,* June 12, 1964, pp. 32–35.
Richards, Alice. "Nativism and Politics: Just Plain Folks Wanted Wyatt Earp—and They Got Him." *Frontier,* September 1964, pp. 14–16.
Rickenbacker, William F. "60,000,000 Westerners Can't Be Wrong." *National Review,* October 23, 1962, pp. 322–325.
Rieder, Jonathan. "The Rise of the Silent Majority." In Fraser and Gerste, eds., *The Rise and Fall of the New Deal Order, 1930–1980.* Princeton, NJ: Princeton University Press, 1989, pp. 243–268.
Rising, George C. "An Epic Endeavor: Upton Sinclair's 1934 California Gubernatorial Campaign." *Southern California Quarterly* 79 (Spring 1997): 101–124.
Robison, Joseph B. "Ghettos, Property Rights and Myths." Frontier, June 1964, pp. 5–8.
Roddy, Joseph. "Ronnie to the Rescue." *Look,* November 1, 1966, pp. 51–54.
Rodgers, Daniel T. *Contested Truths: Keywords in American Politics Since Independence.* New York: Basic Books, 1987.
Rogin, Michael P. *The Intellectuals and McCarthy: The Radical Specter.* Cambridge: MIT Press, 1967.
———. *Ronald Reagan, the Movie: And Other Episodes in Political Demonology.* Berkeley: University of California Press, 1987.
Rogin, Michael P. and John L. Shover. Political Change in California: Critical Elections and Social Movements, 1890–1966. Westport CT: Greenwood Press, 1970.
Roper, William L. "Nixon May Be the Man." *Frontier,* March 1961, pp. 8–10.
Rorabaugh, W.J. *Berkeley at War: The 1960s.* New York: Oxford University Press, 1989.
Rossiter, Clinton. *Conservatism in America: The Thankless Persuasion.* 2d ed., revised. New York: Random House, 1962.

Samish, Arthur H., and Bob Thomas. *The Secret Boss of California: The Life and Good Times of Art Samish.* New York: Brown, 1971.

Saxton, Alexander. *The Indispensable Enemy: Labor and the Anti-Chinese Movement in California.* Berkeley: University of California Press, 1971.

Schaller, Michael. *Reckoning with Reagan: America and Its President in the 1980s.* New York: Oxford University Press, 1992.

Scheer, Robert. "California Scheming." *The Nation,* April 15, 1996, pp. 6+.

Schickel, Richard. *The Disney Version: The Life, Times, Art and Commerce of Walt Disney.* 3d ed., revised. New York: Touchstone, 1997.

Schlafly, Phyllis. *A Choice Not an Echo.* Alton, IL: Pere Marquette Press, 1964.

Schlesinger, Arthur, Jr. *The Vital Center: The Politics of Freedom.* Boston: Houghton Mifflin, 1949.

Schmidhauser, John R. "Eisenhower Republicans." *The Reporter,* September 20, 1956, p. 27+.

Schulzinger, Robert D. *The Wise Men of Foreign Relations: The History of the Council on Foreign Relations.* New York: Columbia University Press, 1984.

Schuparra, Kurt. "Barry Goldwater and Southern California Conservatism: Ideology, Image and Myth in the 1964 California Republican Presidential Primary." *Southern California Quarterly* 74 (Fall 1992): 277–298.

———. "Freedom vs. Tyranny: The 1958 California Election and the Origins of the State's Conservative Movement." *Pacific Historical Review* 63 (November 1994): 537–560.

Schwartz, Herman. *Packing the Courts: The Conservative Campaign to Rewrite the Constitution.* New York: Charles Scribner's Sons, 1988.

Seelye, Howard, and Don Smith, "A Century of Politics in Orange County." *Los Angeles Times* (special section, Orange County ed.), March 21, 1976.

Segal, Bob. "Raymond Cyrus Hoiles." *Santa Ana Register,* special supplement, November 24, 1953, pp. 1–20.

Shadegg, Stephen. *What Happened to Goldwater? The Inside Story of the 1964 Republican Campaign.* New York: Holt, Rinehart and Winston, 1965.

Sitkoff, Harvard, ed. *Fifty Years Later: The New Deal Evaluated.* New York: Alfred A. Knopf, 1985.

Soneshein, Raphael J. *Politics in Black and White: Race and Power in Los Angeles.* Princeton: Princeton University Press, 1993.

Spooner, Denise S. "The Political Consequences of the Experiences of Community: Iowa Immigrants and Republican Conservatism in Southern California." Ph.D. diss., University of Pennsylvania, 1992.

Steffgren, Kent. *Here's the Rest of Him.* Reno, NV: Foresight Books, 1968.

Steif, William. "Nixon's Uphill Campaign: The Republicans Are His First Problem." *The New Republic,* February 26, 1962, pp. 18–20.

Stevenson, Janet. *The Undiminished Man: A Political Biography of Robert Walker Kenny.* Novato, CA: Chandler and Sharp, 1980.

Stimson, Grace Heilman. *The Rise of the Labor Movement in Los Angeles.* Berkeley: University of California Press, 1955.

Stone, Barbara. "The John Birch Society of California." Ph.D. diss., University of Southern California, 1968.

Stormer, John. *None Dare Call It Treason.* Florissant, MO: Liberty Bell, 1964.

Stout, Bill. "How Goldwater Won in California." *The Reporter,* July 2, 1964, pp. 18+.

Stuckey, Mary E. *Getting into the Game: The Pre-Presidential Rhetoric of Ronald Reagan.* New York: Praeger, 1989.

Synon, John J. "Knowland at the Crossroads." *Human Events.* June 16, 1958, p. 1 (article section).

Tenney, Jack B. *The Tenney Committee: The American Record.* Tujunga, CA: Standard Publications, 1952.

————. *Zion's Trojan Horse: A Tenney Report on World Zionism.* Sacramento: Standard Publications, 1954.

Thomas, Evan, and Lucy Shackelford. "And Now, Tricky Dick." *Newsweek,* November 3, 1997, p. 54.

Vaughn, Stephen. *Ronald Reagan in Hollywood: Movies and Politics.* Cambridge: Cambridge University Press, 1994.

Velie, Lester. "The Secret Boss of California." *Colliers,* August 13 and August 20, 1949.

Viguerie, Richard. *The New Right: We're Ready to Lead.* Falls Church, VA.: The Viguerie Co., 1981.

Warren, Earl. Interview (by Donald I. Rogers), "Governor Warren on Socialized Medicine and Welfare." *The American Mercury,* April 1952, pp. 87–88.

————. *The Memoirs of Earl Warren.* New York: Doubleday, 1977.

————. "What Is Liberalism?" *New York Times Magazine,* April 18, 1948, p. 10.

————. "Why I'm Fighting for My Health Plan." *Look,* May 6, 1952, pp. 105+.

Weisberg, Jacob. "Con Air: What the Right Is Fighting About." *Slate* (Microsoft online), posted October 25, 1997.

Welch, Robert. *The Blue Book of the John Birch Society.* Belmont, MA: Western Islands, 1959.

————. *The Politician.* Belmont, MA: Belmont Publishing, 1963.

White, G. Edward. *Earl Warren: A Public Life.* New York: Oxford University Press, 1982.

White, F. Clinton. *Suite 3505: The Story of the Draft Goldwater Movement.* New Rochelle, NY: Arlington House, 1967.

White, Richard. *"It's Your Misfortune and None of My Own": A New History of the American West.* Norman: University of Oklahoma Press, 1991.

White, Theodore H. *The Making of the President 1960.* New York: Antheum House, 1961.

————. *The Making of the President 1964.* New York: Mentor Books, 1965.

Whitfield, Stephen J. *The Culture of the Cold War.* Baltimore: Johns Hopkins University Press, 1991.

Will, George. F. "Three Questions for Conservatives to Gather Around." *Sacramento Bee,* August 31, 1997, *Forum,* p. 5.

Williams, R. Hal. *The Democratic Party and California Politics, 1880–1896.* Stanford: Stanford University Press, 1973.

Williams, Raymond. *Keywords: A Vocabulary of Culture and Society.* Rev. ed. New York: Oxford University Press, 1985.

Wills, Garry. "Mr. Magoo Remembers." *The New York Review of Books,* December 20, 1990, pp. 3–4.

————. *Nixon Agonistes: The Crisis of the Self-Made Man.* Boston: Houghton Mifflin, 1969.

————. *Reagan's America.* New York: Penguin, 1988.

———. *John Wayne's America: The Politics of Celebrity.* New York: Simon and Schuster, 1997.

Wilson, James Q. "A Guide to Reagan Country: The Political Culture of Southern California." *Commentary,* May 1967, pp. 37–45.

Witcover, Jules. *The Resurrection of Richard Nixon.* New York: G.P. Putnam's Sons, 1970.

Wolfinger, Raymond E., and Fred I. Greenstein. "Comparing Political Regions: The Case of California." *American Political Science Review* 63 (March 1969):74–85.

———. "The Repeal of Fair Housing in California: An Analysis of Referendum Voting." *American Political Science Review* 62 (September 1968): 753–769.

Wood, Gordon S. "Conspiracy and the Paranoid Style: Causality and Deceit in the Eighteenth Century," *William and Mary Quarterly* 39 (July 1982): 401–441.

Wood, Jim. "California Republicans: Are the Birchers Taking Over?" *The Reporter,* May 1964, pp. 24–26.

Zalaznick, Sheldon. "The Double Life of Orange County." *Fortune.* October 1968, pp. 139+.

Speeches

Dewey, Thomas. "Corporate State Not An American System." *Vital Speeches of the Day,* October 15, 1944, pp. 14–15.

Kuchel, Thomas H. "Speech on Extremism." *Congressional Quarterly Almanac 1963,* Washington, D.C.: Congressional Quarterly, pp. 715–721.

Reagan, Ronald. "A Moment of Truth." *Vital Speeches of the Day,* September 1, 1965, pp. 681–686.

———. "A Time for Choosing." *Human Events,* November 28, 1964, pp. 1–3.

———. "Encroaching Control: Keep Government Poor and Remain Free." *Vital Speeches of the Day,* September 1, 1961, pp. 677–681.

Index

Civil rights movement *(continued)*
  and "white backlash," 138–139,
    193*n75*
Coate, Robert L., 190*n36*
Committee of Mothers for Barry
  Goldwater (CMBG), 94–95
Community Organizations for Brown
  (COB), 140
Congress of Industrial Organizations
  (CIO), 6, 8, 31
  and CIO-PAC, 6, 14
Connors, Chuck, 142
Conservatism, 6
  and anticommunism, *see*
    Anticommunism
  and capitalism, xvii, xxi-xxii, 33, 38
  and "culture wars," xvi, 149–150
  definition of (conservative
    movement), 155–156*n3*
  Eisenhower's views on, 22, 24
  and extremism, xii, 40, 57
  and factional views of, xviii, xxii
  and Goldwater, xi, xxii, 28, 41, 84,
    96, 99–100, 108, 113, 152
  and isolationism, xiv, xviii
  and liberal intellectuals, xi-xii, 54,
    155*n1*, 156*n4*
  and Modern Republicanism, xiii,
    xviii, 25, 39
  and "New Right," 150
  populist shift of, xvii-xviii, 123
  racial politics of, 25, 73, 106,
    145–146, 193*n80*
  and Reagan, xiv, xxii, 28, 41,
    100–101, 113, 122, 145–146,
    148, 149–150, 152–153
  Social Darwinism of, xvi, 134
  in southern California, xii, xiii, xix,
    xxi, 38, 48, 159*nn29, 30. See
    also* Orange County, politics of
  and George Wallace, xvii, 151,
    195*n20*
  Warren's views on, 9–10
  and "welfare state," xvi, 15, 27, 85,
    88, 148–149, 152, 155–156*n3*
Conspiracy theories, xi-xii, 50–51,
    52–53, 55–56, 85, 96, 129,
    174*n54*

Constructive Action, 193*n77*
Coolidge, Calvin, 152
Cordiner, Ralph, 37
Council on Foreign Relations (CFR),
    51–52, 53
Crail, Joseph, 177*n37*
Cranston, Alan, 103, 130, 147
Cristina, Vernon, 111, 158*n15*,
    166–167*n19*, 191*n45*
Crosby, Joseph, 118, 131
Cross-filing, 3
Cuban missile crisis, 50, 74–75, 78,
    173*n44*

Darling, Dick, 92
Dart, Justin, 134, 177*n34*, 191*n45*
Davis, Mike, 45
Democratic Party, 6, 9, 78, 147,
    186*n27*
  and Brown, 114, 135
  and civil rights, 104, 105
  divisions within, 16, 114, 153
  Eisenhower on, 35
  and liberalism, 8, 16, 153
Diaz Ordaz, Gustavo, 141
DeToledano, Ralph, 69
Dewey, Thomas, 6, 10–11, 18
Dirksen, Everett, 88, 130
Disney, Walt, 103, 184*n5*
Doolittle, James, 99
Douglas, Helen Gahagan, xiv, 14–15,
    60, 69, 102
Downey, Sheridan, 14
Drown, Jack, 177*n34*
Dulles, John Foster, 63
Dutton, Frederick G., 117, 119, 167*n32*
Dymally, Mervyn, 140

Edsall, Thomas Byrne, 152, 158*n19*
Edsall, Mary D., 152, 158*n19*
Ehrlichman, John, 72
Eisenhower, Dwight D. 16, 46, 48
  Buckley on, xviii, 25, 158*n22*
  on civil rights movement, 25
  conservative opposition to, xviii, 27,
    134, 148, 171*n23*
  and Goldwater, 27, 93
  on Knowland, 29

About the Author

A native of Wisconsin, Kurt Schuparra received his Ph.D. in history from the University of Arizona in 1995. He is the author of two award-winning articles on California political history and has presented a number of papers on conservatism and American politics. He is currently a labor and political analyst in Sacramento, California.